MW01031542

ENDORSEMENTS

Reading *any* Ken Mansfield book is an eye-opening experience. As an innovative producer and record company executive during the heat and heart of the sixties through the nineties music scene, his recollections of *the way things were* bring back not only the sights and sounds of the era but reveal the bigger picture of the Creator's purpose for all our lives. Joined by respected biographer/author Marshall Terrill, Ken takes us on a mesmerizing journey traveling alongside some of the greatest musical icons of our time. Within these pages are real life stories of famous men and women who have tasted struggle, fame, fortune, and loss, yet speak today of restoration and renewal.

Phil Keaggy

Gospel Music Association Hall of Fame

Seven-time Dove Award recipient and two-time Grammy® Award nominee

Where do rock stars go when they've tried everything the world has to offer and yet have continued to come up empty? In *Rock and a Heart Place*, Ken Mansfield provides engaging and perhaps surprising answers. This fascinating and fun-to-read book is loaded with inside stories of some of our favorite music makers. It is a classic reminder that regardless what messes our family or friends might encounter, the Creator is greater; nobody is beyond hope, and there is no need to give up on anyone!

Ken Abraham

New York Times best-selling author

Rock and a Heart Place is a compelling, fascinating read. Ken Mansfield's relationships throughout his impressive career include many famous artists, who, along with Ken, came to the conclusion that personal fulfillment cannot be satisfied with money, sex, and drugs, the trifecta of a rock and roller and that life ultimately holds little purpose without a relationship with their Creator.

Michael Omartian

Multiple Grammy® Award-winning producer, arranger, and musician
The Recording Academy (NARAS) Keyboard Musician of the Year

In *Rock and a Heart Place* Ken Mansfield and Marshall Terrill present a brave and masterfully written opus of faith that explores the unexpected spiritual rewards of music legends as they share their journey from rock to redemption and who've traded their quest for music charts to winning hearts.

David Pack

Former Ambrosia cofounder
Grammy®-winning recording artist and producer

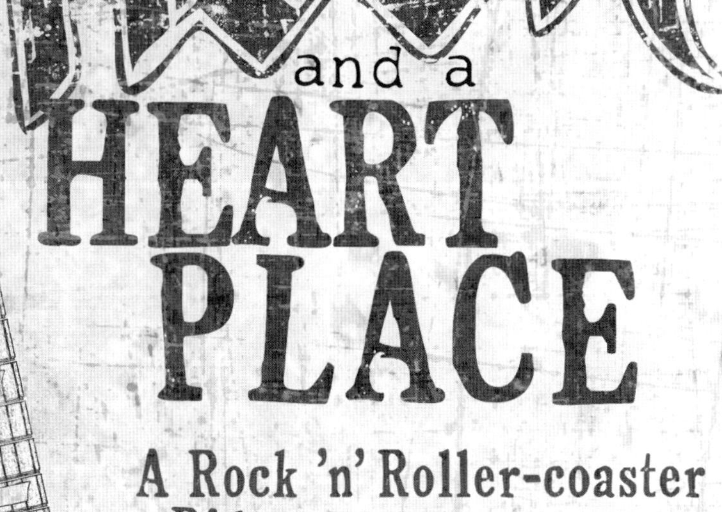

A Rock 'n' Roller-coaster Ride from Rebellion to Sweet Salvation

KEN MANSFIELD

AND Marshall Terrill

Rock and a Heart Place
A Rock 'n' Roller-coaster Ride from Rebellion to Sweet Salvation

ISBN: 978-1-4245-4999-3 (hardcover)
ISBN: 978-1-4245-5020-3 (e-book) – *Four additional artist chapters are included exclusively in the ebook for Jerry Naylor, Rick Cua, Chuck Girard, and Ken Hensley.*

Published by BroadStreet Publishing Group
Racine, Wisconsin, USA
www.broadstreetpublishing.com

Published in association with the literary agency, WTA Services LLC, Franklin, TN

Cover design by Chris Garborg at www.garborgdesign.com
Typesetting and interior design by Katherine Lloyd at www.TheDESKonline.com

The following artist pictures from their past are used by permission of PHOTOFEST (212-633-6330): Chris Hillman/The Byrds; Mark Farner/Grand Funk Railroad; Mark Volman/The Turtles; Nedra Ross/The Ronettes; Shane Evans/Collective Soul; Richie Furay/Buffalo Springfield.

All other images of artists used by permission.

Stock or custom editions of BroadStreet Publishing titles may be purchased in bulk for educational, business, ministry, fundraising, or sales promotional use. For information, please e-mail info@broadstreetpublishing.com.

Printed in China

15 16 17 18 19 20 7 6 5 4 3 2 1

SET LIST

OVERTURE

TAKIN' IT TO THE STREETS

To be blunt, the entertainment industry is built on induced fantasy and even less certainty. Long periods of being submerged within its abstraction does leave a person with the mind-bends when finally floating up from its depths. In some odd way, I feel those of us who survived this immersion find our salvation even more precious than some believers—because we paid for it so dearly. It's not because we are more saved or more loved; it just might be because once we emerge from that degenerate mire we are startled by the purity we experience through His unconditional love, mercy, and grace.

The contrast is rather extreme.

I didn't realize it at the time but in some obtuse way, I have been writing this book in the back of my heart for many years. I knew it wasn't going to be easy because I would have to ask some very famous people about very private matters—people who already have the feeling of being overexposed and intruded upon to the point of wanting to crawl inside their amps and pull the plug. Historically, these people tend to hold their cards close to the vest because of this. I feel as if I have circled unknowingly around this subject for a long time, but every time I would get close to it, I felt like I was approaching King Nebuchadnezzar's furnace.

The characters we will be climbing inside of are not normal, but after thirty-plus years of deep involvement with the most fascinating musicians and entertainers on the planet, I have gained an understanding of what makes them tick. They are people who are hard to read—like trying to tell time from oddly-shaped clocks with no numbers. They survived the highs of being a part of legendary music, the lows of bottoming out, and finally ended up in a much happier place after the fat lady finally ran out of songs, breath, and in most cases, drugs and booze.

One of the reasons it is hard for them to share their stories is because in order to tell the reader how blessed they are now, they have to deliver the contrast of their past in order to have it make any sense. They have to let it all out about what a mess they were back then … a time when we all thought we had found the answers through our success. We now discover, in reality, that for the most part we were more lost than Don Ho in Siberia.

Marshall Terrill sensed these stories behind my eyes long before I awakened to the value of gathering a bunch of fellow midnight marauders together to talk about redemption. He was persistent in his vision and finally with his promise to join me in the dance of syllables, sentences, and nuances. I reluctantly accepted the challenge to give it a go. So we sat down with a gang of incredible survivors to talk about the raucous years—me in reflection and Marshall in discovery.

Deep down we knew we needed to share and confess our mistaken quests. We definitely glorified our skewed way of life and, as hard as it is to admit, we did leave a sorry trail of misguided souls in our wake—folks who emulated the actions of the rich and famous and all the wrong things we represented.

But we have something much better than the typical feelings of being ashamed and sorry for what we did—we have forgiveness and restoration. We have a new song to sing, and the testimonies we now share are much better than the back-of-the-tour-bus tales of long ago. We have been given a platform larger than any concert stage we ever appeared on. Elvis left that empty building, and now God lives in our hearts and houses. Today the real Rock is what keeps our lives rolling, and we're taking it to the streets.

Yesterday seems so far away, but eternity is here to stay.

God bless us all,

Ken Mansfield

MARK VOLMAN

The Turtles / Flo & Eddie

The Turtles were a 1960s California pop-rock band and have sold more than forty million records. In 1999, BMI named their number-one hit, "Happy Together," one of the Top 50 songs of the twentieth century, with over five million radio plays. Cofounder Mark Volman was also a core member of Frank Zappa's The Mothers of Invention and the dynamic duo Flo & Eddie.

ONE

HAPPY FOREVER

MARK VOLMAN | The Turtles / Flo & Eddie

I thought Mark Volman and I had met before. I know we shared the same cramped, dark, funky space at one time—a place where we were chasing identical dreams. We wandered off the same crazy streets into a small Hollywood side-street recording studio in the mid-1960s. We were both making our bones in the exciting adventure of trying to make hit records.

Today as we examine one another across a table at a sidewalk coffee shop in Nashville, we can see nature's time deposits in each other's eyes—eyes that maybe have seen more things than they should have, but still sparkle with the memories of passing years. We said hello, and it only took thirty seconds into the midsummer day before we both knew that because of our similar journeys, we had kindred hearts. Hearts that had been broken, hearts that had been healed, hearts that had been worn on our sleeves, hearts that had danced and sung along with the same elusive tunes—aging hearts that had been filled with muted victories and dashed hopes more times than we both would ever try to remember.

Back in the 1960s, I was producing a band called The Deep Six for Liberty Records around the time The Turtles were recording their first batch of songs. Either Mark or his music partner, Howard Kaylan, dropped by my sessions one night and listened to the playback of our single, "Rising Sun." He said he wished their recordings were as good as ours or that they sang as good. Of course history puts a fine edge to that comment because, in time, our record never found a spot on *Billboard*'s Hot 100, while "Happy Together" is almost everybody's favorite song.

I was a street promotion man in Los Angeles along with The Turtle's managers, Lee Lassiff and Ted Feigin. Another local promo man was a guy named Sonny Bono. We were being paid to be promotion men for record companies, but we considered that our day job. We all had more exciting aspirations. While Lee and Ted were developing The Turtles and Sonny was working with a young girl named Cher, I was doing the same thing with my band. We all know how well Lee, Ted, and Sonny did with their projects. My band faded, and I began working with a more established band—a mop-topped foursome from Liverpool.

The point is there will never be a time like that again—the record business was a raw, no-holds-barred, no-dreams-considered-impossible, no-full-stomachs-guaranteed business. Everything was possible because we didn't know we were trying to accomplish the impossible. The British were coming, the south was rising, the surf was up, and a wall of sound was washing over everyone. Sometimes we had breakfast before we went to bed; there was so much going on in Hollywood. We hung out at Aldo's Coffee Shop on Hollywood Boulevard during the day and spent evenings at the bar at Martoni's Restaurant on North Cahuenga Boulevard. Promo guys, artists, managers, song pluggers, DJs, songwriters, music directors, booking agents, producers, and record company execs, all comingling and shooting for the stars. Martoni's had become the Hollywood rock and roll version of Manhattan's famous Algonquin Hotel, where journalists, authors, publicists, and actors hung out during the early decades of the 1900s. It was lyrical lunacy and a time that spawned a fresh creativity that in some ways fed the music industry from those days on, replenishing itself like the bread and oil in Elijah's story of the poor widow and her son. This was before logic, accountants, and attorneys took over the helm and made it boring and predictable. Okay, and yes, profitable, but they had to leave out a lot of soul and heart to do that. You put the guys from The Doors alongside the Backstreet Boys, and it is easy to tell that those animals would have never eaten from the same trough.

So here we are, Mark and I, almost a half-century later, in a meeting intended to break the ice before officially beginning this chapter in the book. The fact that we came out of the same incredible era, knew so many of the same people, and had experienced so many similar events and emotions created a flood of thoughts and remembrances. I looked at Mark, and he made me think of everything from Zappa to folk music to the mad professor to crazy rock star—and because of his learned, elder statesman demeanor—to flashbacks of my imagined grandfather. His trademark hair is still out there, his enthusiasm for the music is still smiling and unbridled, and his memory, like mine, shifts in and out. I admit we did share long pauses as we tried to remember things—old associates or current matters such as where we left our car keys. We had just met, but our bygone mutuality made it seem as if we had known each other forever.

While our musical paths were similar at that time, the roads traveled as we made our individual ways to those streets, studios, and fascinating experiences were very different.

Mark's childhood appears much happier and grounded than mine. He was born in 1947 and grew up in Westchester, California, an upper middle-class Los Angeles suburb. Mark describes himself as a happy-go-lucky kid from the 1950s. "Comedy was my first love, and it was a big influence on me and my music partner, Howard Kaylan," Mark says. "We were big fans of Stan Freberg, Louis Prima and Keely Smith, the Smothers Brothers, and their whole comedic style. They were funny and had this traditional approach with a straight man and the clown. I think The Turtles had that format as a live show, but we weren't as up-front about it. We were very subtle, and I think that subtlety came through in our songs and music. There was always some intentional kind of inference, satire, or tongue-in-cheek shtick going on. That all came from our parents, who bought a lot of fun records, and we tuned into them early in our lives."

Humor is probably what brought Mark's parents, Joe and Beatrice Volman, together in the first place. On paper they didn't seem to have much in common, given that Joe, a sheet metal worker, was the son of a Hungarian Jew and Beatrice's heritage was Spanish and Catholic. They were married close to sixty years and, according to Mark, brought a lot of fire to the union. However, they didn't allow their views on religion to affect Mark and his brother, Phillip. "I didn't recognize religion as being a strong part of my childhood by either my mother or father. The real push came from my maternal grandmother, who was a transplant from Mexico and spoke very little English. My grandmother raised me during the school week, and I rode the bus with her to Catholic church for mass on weekends. I also attended all the Jewish seders and celebrated the Jewish holidays even though my father didn't follow religion. You could even say he was a bit of an atheist. I didn't have a knee-jerk reaction to religion as a negative or positive. Once my grandmother died, I was floating in a sea of nondescriptness as far as my spiritual life."

Mark remembers their home was a hub of activity with colorful relatives, gregarious friends, and lots of laughter. "My mom was one of seven kids, and with all of the grandparents, kids, and grandkids, there could be twenty-five to thirty people at our house for a gathering. My mom used to describe our home as a racetrack. It was cool to hang out at our house. My friends loved it.

"I didn't surf growing up, but I hung out at the beach and became friendly with all of those kids too. I was a natural class clown and teachers liked me. I was like a spinning top. I enjoyed performing in the classroom and making them laugh. Teachers had a terrible time with me because I got more attention than they did."

Performing was in Mark's blood, and he gravitated to music in junior high. He took clarinet lessons and later joined the choir at Westchester

High School, where he met his lifetime pal and creative soul mate, the incomparable Howard Kaylan. The two tenors naturally gravitated to each other and spent most of their time clowning, much to the dismay of their choir teacher, Robert Wood, who often dismissed them from practice when they got out of hand. Howard was already in The Crossfires, a guitar-based band influenced by instrumental bands of the late '50s, such as Johnny and the Hurricanes, Duane Eddy, The Ventures, and The Viscounts. Mark thought it would be cool to be in Howard's band. The only problem was, the only instrument he could play—the clarinet—didn't exactly belong in a surf band. That didn't deter him from asking Howard if he could join.

"So I hear you're in a rock and roll band."

"Yep."

"Um, do you think I could join it?"

"Well, what do you do?"

"Nothing."

"Nothing?"

"Nope."

"Sounds good to me."

I love the humor in this exchange, but more than that I love their wonderful naïveté when putting this band together. If you have ever watched the professional Flo & Eddie (Mark and Howard) on stage, you can easily picture this scene going down between them as young lads. That meeting took place before real life entered the scene. There are so many stories in this book where famous bands were put together and the bass player couldn't play bass when he joined the band—but there is an uncanny sense of knowing that happens with artists. It is more often a study in chemistry than qualifications when the "get together" is decided. Technically Mark was going to bring nothing to The Crossfires, however, a towering presence and charisma like his can make or break a band. In the Mark and Howard case, it was something similar to the day the peanut butter man ran into the chocolate man.

The Crossfires were very resourceful. They knew Mark's gregarious nature, dynamic personality, and his popularity with classmates and the surf crowd would bring something to the band, mainly hordes of people showing up at their concerts. At first they put him to work as a roadie, hauling instruments and fetching sodas while they played. However, when Joe Volman discovered Mark wasn't being financially compensated, he demanded that his son be in the band. When it was pointed out to Joe that Mark didn't play an instrument, the situation was immediately remedied. Joe accompanied Mark and Howard to a local music store and purchased a new alto sax. Howard taught Mark how to play sax, and together they worked on choreography—The Crossfires now had a hip horn section. With the final pieces of the puzzle in place, The Crossfires (who eventually morphed into The Turtles) featured Mark on alto sax, Al Nichol on guitar, Chuck Portz on bass, Jim Tucker on rhythm guitar, Don Murray on drums, and Howard on tenor sax and vocals. They were in their teens, and stardom was only a couple of years away.

Armed with cool business cards featuring a burning Iron Cross motif, The Crossfires blazed the Southern California music scene playing at fraternities, teen dances, recreation centers, club houses, military bases, and anywhere there was a stage and screaming girls. At their high school, they developed a rabid fan base called the Chunky Club, based on an instrumental they wrote called "Chunky." Their imaginative followers showed up at concerts in droves with oversized soupspoons and ladles, dancing provocatively, making suggestive gestures toward each other's genitalia, laughing, and lapping up the great music. The Chunky Club grew exponentially, and The Crossfires drew almost five hundred people wherever they went. The band exploded when they answered an advertisement for a battle of the bands at Reb Foster's Revelaire Club in Redondo Beach. With their high-energy show and tremendous fan base, they handily won the contest. Foster, a powerful Los Angeles DJ, gave them a house gig at the Revelaire. "We were a really good band and playing cool songs, like The Righteous Brothers' 'Little Latin Lupe Lu,'

Don and Dewey's 'Justine,' Ray Charles's 'What I'd Say,' and Buddy Holly's 'That'll Be the Day.' Most of the songs that were coming out of bars at that time were traditional songs, but we played stuff that would start fights. In fact, that was always the most successful part of the show."

Can you imagine a band getting away with playing songs that started fights because that was the most successful part of their show? How about featuring that as a marketing tool to promote your concerts? Today no one would come out of the gig alive. A band would need a roadie, a medic, an arsenal manager, and a darn good lawyer. But music was more fun then because life was more fun. Shots at a party back then came from a vodka bottle, not an AK-47.

House gigs at the Revelaire Club and Rendezvous Ballroom in Orange County yielded great fruit and exposure. The Crossfires played three sets a night on Fridays and Saturdays and backed up visiting national artists. They learned these artists' repertoire and performed with several top soul groups and surf bands.

Without realizing it at the time, the band was grooming themselves for stardom by learning different musical styles that eventually led to becoming instinctual players. They learned the best riffs, structures, and textures created by other great musicians and catalogued this information inside their creative guts. When it was time to start expressing their own ideas, they would pull forth amalgamations of this stuff in an assembled form of fresh new arrangements. Many popular entertainers spent years in cover bands and later ended up being covered by other artists.

Stardom is a curious thing, and no two paths are alike, but certain important elements need to be present: preparedness, passion, perseverance, persistence, and opportunity. But the main thing that *must* be present is—you guessed it—luck. I left out another critical element—talent, but to be honest, I worked with more successful lucky bands with limited talent than I did extremely talented bands with no luck.

Back to Ted Feigin and Lee Lassiff, record executives with a new label, White Whale Records, and soon-to-be managers. Ted and Lee happened to catch The Crossfires' act at the Revelaire. The Crossfires had luck and talent. The two men liked the band, even though they felt surf music died once The Beatles arrived. Reb Foster suggested the band change their name to The Turtles. Mark and Howard almost laughed him out of his office. Turtles were slow, fat, ugly, stupid, and cold. Foster explained anything ending with *l-e-s* was trending, and like The Beatles, The Turtles were part of the animal kingdom.

"The public is going to think you're from England, and England is really hot!" Foster explained.

The intent and logic were clear, but it sucked the life out of The Crossfires. So did the lime-green velour shirts with matching caps that Reb picked out for them to wear on stage. "We were actually handing in our resignation to the Revelaire Club when we were introduced to Lassiff and Feigin, who wanted to sign us to White Whale Records. We immediately tore up that resignation and put together three songs. One of those songs was 'It Ain't Me Babe,' and it would forever change our lives."

After that song received major airplay, the group was picked up by Dick Clark's Caravan of Stars, which included Tom Jones, Peter and Gordon, The Shirelles, Billy Joe Royal, and others. In 1965 they performed almost 280 dates and experienced the seriousness of the music industry by having hit songs. "'Happy Together' is the record people talk about, but 'It Ain't Me Babe' was a million-seller and a top-five record and probably only missed making it to number one because it was distributed by an independent label. Acts like The Beatles, Bob Dylan, and The Beach Boys, who were on bigger labels, sold more records by default. Our people at the record company were hardworking and well meaning, but they were learning the business just like we were."

Mark is correct. It's a known fact in the music business that the major labels had more influence with the radio stations. They had the money to press more records, they controlled their own promotion team, and they had budgets set aside to throw money into advertising and tours when a record began to break. Ironically, the thing that could make an independent record label go under was having a hit record. It sounds crazy, but here's how it worked: when an independent record took off, the small label was forced to press a lot of records in order to fill orders from music stores and chains. With little time to respond, the company had to go all in and push all their chips onto the table, or watch the record die a fast death. If listener response was strong, then the outlay had to be humungous to match the demand.

Now let's have a reality check. Pressing records in the thousands was very expensive, and pressing plants were not typically gracious to the young scruffs who had just pulled off the impossible, so there were typically no credit terms and very limited financial breathing room for the independents. Also, just because there was a lot of enthusiasm from the public and record stores were clamoring for stock, there was no guarantee that sales would match that exuberance. So the upstart record company had to pony up the scratch by depleting their funds and assets, borrowing to the max, taking extra jobs, and signing away their next ten children. Once they did come up with the money, records were shipped to the distributors and music stores to insure they were covered with necessary stock.

Now we have two possibilities at this point. First, the record is a stiff and the inventory comes back. The records are then worthless, the band remains unknown, the label goes broke, and people jump off bridges. Second, the record is a hit and demand increases. Wow, they are rich, right? Maybe not—in fact, many times ... not! Distributors were famous for paying late, for poor accounting, or not paying at all. Now our heroes are desperately chasing down their money and hanging on to that illusive gold ring. If they didn't get paid, they were even broker, and not only were they jumping off bridges but their creditors and family members who chipped in were joining them.

So when White Whale hit pay dirt with The Turtles, it took a lot of savvy to ride that dragon, but as Mark said, they were unable to generate major label sales. This educational piece on the mechanics of the record business barely scratches the surface of the myriad of complexities involved in getting a hit record. Fortunately, The Turtles and the label's management team were imaginative and resourceful and pulled off the impossible. It would be hard to imagine what their real sales would have been with a major label, but The Turtles became a huge success and worked hard for every sale.

It was the mid-1960s and The Turtles, teens who had barely entered adulthood, were churning out the hits: "She'd Rather Be With Me," "You Showed Me," "You Know What I Mean," "Elenore," and their biggest hit and signature song, "Happy Together." To give you an idea of how big of a smash the latter was, in 1999, BMI named "Happy Together" one of the top fifty songs of the twentieth century, with more than five million radio plays. The Turtles have sold approximately 40 million records to date, and they are one of the few acts of the 1960s that still has a successful fan base.

The Turtles found an undiscovered niche that appealed to fans who lived just a little off the mark. They were a bit of everything, while there was nothing like them. They were quirky and they were smart. They were bubblegum with a joint hanging out of their mouths. The band had personality; their songs made you happy, and you could dance to them! They were on the money for the times, and it was great to be able to listen to creative, artful music while not being required to take it too seriously. That's why their hits have lasted down through the decades.

The Turtles not only dominated the radio airwaves but also became the darlings of '60s family television as the networks did their best to bring younger viewers to the shows that needed a shot in the arm. They appeared on *Hollywood a Go-Go, The Hollywood Palace, Shindig!* and *Kraft Music Hall*, and they made multiple appearances on *The Ed Sullivan Show*. Their life consisted of beats, babes, Buds, buds, and the road. There wasn't much time for spirituality, and these globe-trotting rock stars certainly didn't feel they were missing out on anything. The eternally sophomoric Turtles loved every minute of it. "We were smoking pot and doing more psychedelics than the deadly drugs. That's how we allowed ourselves to believe it was okay. We weren't doing as much damage to ourselves as we could have. At that point, there hadn't been a single rock and roll fatality, and everything the Establishment had warned us about hadn't happened. The drugs challenged me to experiment, read, and pursue many different outlooks."

Like millions of others in the Age of Aquarius, Mark was keen on learning more about yogis, New Age mystics, and Eastern philosophies. He found inspiration in Joseph Benner's *The Impersonal Life* and *The Way to the Kingdom* but was particularly impressed by Paramahansa Yogananda's *Autobiography of a Yogi*. "I enjoyed what that book did in terms of lighting the fire in my heart to seek and also to be a compassionate person. People were finding gurus everywhere. It's not like we were atheists or faithless people. We were spiritually inclined and not closed to the notion of a divine presence. I want to say that Eastern philosophy, even though it didn't stick, was the first form of enlightenment that got me to thinking that I wasn't as big as I thought I was."

Eastern philosophy was cool. So were long hair, bell-bottoms, neck scarves, skinny braless girlfriends, bongs, and saying "far out" and "groovy." The coolest part about being a New Ager was the lifestyle. It had more to do with changing the outside than the inside. You already liked being stoned, you had an excuse for being laid-back and noncommittal about things that required effort, and you definitely were okay with the free love. So you got to stay with all that and wear your chosen religion like a badge, while reveling in the perks of being spiritual. You changed from wearing a tie to tie-dying what you wore. You could say flowery nonsensical things and have the girls go "oooo" and the guys in suits go, "Hey, that's really sublime," pretending that they knew what you were talking about and that they also knew what it was like to feel sublime.

Identifying with The Beatles by saying you had a guru was always impressive, and when you were stoned or just stupid you could always say you were in a meditative state or blissed out from doing your special mantra—one that was brought down out of the ether by your yogi master. It was song and dance without melody or footwear. It was space walking without being able to spell NASA. It was truly turning on, tuning in, and dropping out so that you didn't have to be accountable for anything or to anyone. Reading *Autobiography of a Yogi* and quoting Ram Dass was much more interesting, and no one ever gave you a bad time by calling you a "Bhagavad Gita thumper." You could have a free pass into hipville simply by presenting a synthesis of the Brahmanical concept of dharma. You were cool as long as you didn't quote Scripture or bring up that guy Jesus.

I spent almost a full decade doing all of the above, and all I got out of it was to be ten years older and more confused than when I started. Oh wait … and a really cool bead collection.

Looking back, Mark blames the lack of spirituality for the demise of his first marriage to Patricia Hickey. They exchanged vows in January 1967 and eventually had two daughters, Sarina and Hallie. "Pat was just nineteen and I was twenty when we were married. We were high school sweethearts, but we had no spiritual connection in our life or relationship with the church, and that played a big part in causing our problems—divorce was imminent."

By the end of 1968, other problems began to emerge. White Whale Records demanded another hit ("Give us another 'Happy Together'"), which infuriated Mark and Howard. So off they went, and a half hour later they came back with "Elenore," a song dripping with sarcasm and cheesy venom. What was intended as an anti-love letter to White Whale execs had the opposite effect. The label didn't get the joke and loved "Elenore," which became the group's last top-ten song in the United States and the United Kingdom and went to number one in New Zealand.

Tired of living hand to mouth despite several hits, The Turtles decided to inspect White Whale's books. Mark recalls, "The record company put a lot of money aside because they felt like, 'Why don't we hold on to it for them so that they don't spend it wildly. They're a bunch of stupid kids.' By withholding our money, we challenged the record company and they fought back. So what started out as a plan to protect us ended up being the reason why we needed protection. Additionally, one of our managers absconded to Mexico with a large amount of our money."

After an inspection of the books, the group found $500,000 sitting idly in an account, which amounted to one year's royalties. They filed a $2.5 million lawsuit against White Whale in 1970 and had them fully audited for the five years they had been with the label. White Whale countersued by responding that they not only owned The Turtles' name, but also owned each band member's individual name. They further put the clamps down on the group by telling them they could no longer perform as The Turtles or professionally use their given birth names under any circumstance.

White Whale thought this legal procedure would force the band to back down, but the boys dug their heels in and waged a legal war that took four years to settle. The Turtles had been done in by the power of the pen and paper. Mark and Howard, both twenty-three at the time, had no future prospects and were wondering how they would put food on the table, feed their kids, and make their mortgage payments. About two weeks later, an offer came in from Frank Zappa, who wanted to revive the Mothers of Invention on an upcoming European tour. Were they interested? Yes!

Inspired once again, they billed themselves as Phlorescent Leech & Eddie, or Flo & Eddie for short. Mark remembers, "Frank came along at a very opportune time. He was very generous with his creativity, availability to us, and allowed us to improvise in our live performances as well as our performances on his records. This motivated us artistically and vocally. The musical content was much more challenging. It was 180 degrees from where The Turtles had been. It was really an exceptional time for us."

The "Mothers" had become the hippest traveling show on the rock circuit; their concerts were a mixture of irreverent playfulness and technical virtuosity. Those early Flo & Eddie shows with Zappa were always sold out and afterward featured a buffet of drugs, groupies, and unimaginable sex activities.

By late 1971, things began taking a darker turn. On December 4 at the Montreux Casino in Switzerland, a crazed fan shot a flare gun into the ceiling during the band's performance and caused the venue's heating system to explode. The fire forced the hotel's evacuation and burned the band's equipment to a crisp. The event inspired Deep Purple's classic song, "Smoke on the Water."

Six days later it became even more bizarre. During the band's encore at the Rainbow Theater, a raging twenty-four-year-old fan pushed Zappa into the venue's concrete orchestra pit, much to the horror of the panicked band and audience. Upon impact, Zappa's neck bent like it was broken; he had a gash in his chin, a hole in the back of his head, a broken rib, and a fractured leg.

While Zappa recovered, Flo & Eddie kept themselves busy by opening on Alice Cooper's Billion Dollar Babies tour and recording as Phlorescent Leech & Eddie on Reprise Records. They hosted a popular radio show on K-Rock in Los Angeles, dabbled in film (*200 Motels*), television, and even children's animation. But their real bread and butter was session work, lending their trademark harmonies to T. Rex, Roger McGuinn, Stephen Stills, Keith Moon, Alice Cooper, David Cassidy, Bruce Springsteen, and John Lennon, on his 1972 album *Sometime In New York City*.

"We did the live jam with Frank Zappa and the Mothers of Invention at the Fillmore East," Mark says. "John Lennon seemed to be overpowered by drugs at that time. It was a really negative time and he was very distant. We spent a few nights at his place going over the jam, which was the way it ended up on the album. I wish I'd thought more about the fact that John Lennon was not going to be here forever. We don't really consider mortality like that. We think we're all going to live a long time, and then suddenly someone's gone and it sure wakes you up."

More has been written in total about John Lennon since his death than about all The Beatles together, dead or alive. John was like the greased pig of rock and roll; no one could really get a handle on him outside of maybe Yoko. He was a moving nontarget—one you could never hit because he never settled into one place long enough to nail him down. I am often asked about my relationship and impressions of the four lads because of my time spent with them on both a business and personal level, and I get going real good until it comes to John. Then I have to be honest that I am at a loss for proper words. The problem in analyzing John's stamp on our time is that he never settled into one position long enough for anyone to understand him, beyond adoring the mystique of his persona. Then having him taken away so suddenly made it very hard to figure out where it would have ended up with him had he stayed with us.

The day John died, I was going over pictures from my Apple days to put on the walls of my new office in Hollywood. When I got the phone call telling me he had just been shot and killed, I was looking straight into his face on a picture he had sent to me years before. He was looking right at me; it was one of those pictures that no matter if you moved left or right, it looked like the eyes were following you. It was hard to look away and even harder to know exactly what I was feeling. I knew we all had suffered a great loss, not of a perfect man with perfect ways but a great man who would no longer do great things. I didn't react as an individual but took my place in the universal sadness.

A few years after their encounter with Lennon, The Turtles got new life when the White Whale lawsuit was settled in 1974. The judge ruled in the group's favor, giving them their name back and the masters for all of their albums. The $2.5 million they originally sought was squandered by White Whale defending themselves, but Mark and Howard were back in business. They signed with Sire Records and released the double album, *The Turtles Greatest Hits: Happy Together Again!*

Because Flo & Eddie had built their own following, they toured as Flo & Eddie with The Turtles during the 1970s. Later in 1984, when the '60s nostalgia boom struck, they flip-flopped the billing to read "The Turtles Featuring Flo & Eddie." That year, Mark and Howard crafted the "Happy Together Tour," featuring Spanky and Our Gang, Gary Puckett, and The Association. The Turtles closed out each show with an all-hands-on-deck encore. The formula was magical, with each act singing their greatest hits. The year 2014 marked the thirtieth anniversary of the tour.

By the early nineties, Mark needed a break from the road. His marriage to Pat had ended in divorce in 1991, and he was ready for a change. Never one for convention, he enrolled in a community college in 1992 at the age of forty-five. The move shocked the rock industry. He recalls, "I guess it was a little bit out of boredom. I'd been a touring musician since I was eighteen and accomplished a lot in the area of music. I felt there were so many other things I could do and contribute."

Mark graduated magna cum laude from Loyola Marymount University in Los Angeles as the valedictorian speaker of his class in 1999, earning a master's degree in fine arts with an emphasis on screenwriting. After his valedictorian speech, he led graduates in a chorus of "Happy Together."

Another benefit of Mark's higher education learning experience was meeting his current wife, Emily. "I was having a tough time meeting people because Loyola was mainly composed of young people. Emily and I became friends during our junior and senior years and graduated together in '97. We got married in 2000."

It was Emily, raised as a Methodist, who opened the door to Mark's once dormant spirituality. She suggested they seek out a church, and like a piece of fruit ready to fall from the tree, Mark was ripe. "It wasn't like I pulled over on the side of the road and saw a blinding flash of light. I had always been somebody who believed in God, and I always felt Jesus

Christ was a part of my life. I didn't put it into some sort of prophetic new finding. I remember The Turtles had two very close incidents in planes where we spun out of control upon landing and another where we had to land next to a freeway because our landing gear was stuck. I felt the presence of God with me both of those times. I've never felt like I was not born again."

Not content with just sitting on the wooden pews every week, Mark and Emily rolled up their sleeves and became involved with the church. Mark was baptized and became a lay minister, learning how to write and deliver sermons and lead worship services. "I began feeding on Scripture, attending services, understanding more about the Word of God, and finding things out about the religion that I hadn't really opened the door to before. I wanted to demonstrate my love for Jesus Christ and show people He was a true part of my life. Everybody has a different way of saying 'I'm a Christian' and what makes them a Christian. If you do make that commitment, you need to be with Christian people. And you need to learn the Word of God by reading the Bible and talking about it with other Christians."

God rewarded Mark for his faithfulness with an opportunity in the new millennium when he and Emily moved to Cleveland, Tennessee, where he did a stint at Lee University as an "artist in residence," teaching seminars and helping lay foundations for a music business program. He also worked as a substitute teacher at Belmont University in Nashville, Tennessee, for a semester, where he was later offered a job as an adjunct professor, which he accepted.

He is currently an associate professor and coordinator of the Entertainment Industry Studies Program at Belmont University in the Mike Curb College of Entertainment and Music Business. He conducts seminars about the music industry for various academic institutions, from junior high to university level. In addition, he offers consulting on music business and entertainment through the website www.professorflo.com. Mark explained his passion for his new career: "The music business has changed dramatically since that first contract was signed in 1965 as a member of The Turtles, but many things still remain the same. The incredible amount of stories I have personally heard, telling of lost careers and lost human beings, could fill a very large book. For every successful story, there are many more reflecting the outcomes of battered lives left to fade away in the wake of misguided choices and decisions. Many artists have no idea of a long-range plan for survival, and the idea of having a plan for a career is so far away from their reality that most will find themselves signing one bad deal after another … over and over again."

In addition to teaching at Belmont, Mark and Emily serve as youth advisers at Harpeth Presbyterian Church in Brentwood, Tennessee. Mark has a connection with youth, and that's where he wants to focus his energy. "It's very important. That's why my wife and I are working with high school kids at our church every Sunday night, going on mission trips, and being a part of their day-to-day life. I can picture them looking back when they're married and having kids—and although they might not have known who I was—they'll go, 'We had this guy there, and he was in The Turtles, and yet there he was every Sunday night at youth group, teaching the Bible, talking about the parables in Matthew, Mark, and so forth.' We sometimes talk about stuff I know they've never talked to their parents about. My relationship with music is a door opener."

Mark considers his involvement with the youth group a second chance at parenting, even though he remains on great terms with his two grown daughters, now in their forties. "There's a healing thing, of being able to be there and talk to them about things I didn't get to do before because I was touring all the time. My kids were young; I was young. I now feel like I have developed a lot of moral character that I may not have had during my youth—during my halcyon days, but that was in the past. The fishermen weren't perfect Christians, but God offered them a chance to walk in His shadow. And now, just like those ragtag guys, He's offered me a second life."

It did take Mark more than a "second" to finally get it right, but fortunately the only time clock that God watches is the one that tells eternity. So He had all the time in the world and would have given Mark not only a second chance but also a seven thousandth chance, if necessary. The Father knew His child was worth waiting for. Let's face it—He was dealing with a Turtle here, you know, so there was a good possibility it might go a little slow! But God knew all along how it was going to end because *it was Mark He was looking for (babe)*, and now Mark's life is complete—his church, his family, and God are all *happy together* … happy forever.

RUTH POINTER
The Pointer Sisters

The legendary Pointer Sisters scored dozens of hits in the 1970s, 1980s, and 1990s, and they sold close to forty million records, making them one of the most successful female groups of all time. For almost four decades, their brilliant recordings and fascinating shows kept them in the forefront of pop culture's newest trends, and they did it with great style and ease.

TWO

THE SONG OF RUTH

RUTH POINTER | The Pointer Sisters

Ruth Pointer may well be the poster child for the old adage, "What doesn't kill you only makes you stronger." Drugs didn't kill her, although she walked a fine line. Racism didn't kill her or her spirit, although ignorance and stupidity always hovered nearby. Motherhood didn't kill her; her instinct kicked in and her tenacity and love won out. Faith didn't kill her—it made her free. But it did take a lifetime of rebellion and pain for her to figure that out.

Ruth was born March 19, 1946, in Oakland, California, the daughter of the Reverend Elton and Sarah Pointer. Her father was a sweet-natured man with an obscure criminal past that he didn't talk about. Her mother, the disciplinarian, grew up sheltered in a small family. Ruth had two brothers—Aaron Elton and Fritz Herman. Ruth was the third child but the first girl in the family, a role she never enjoyed. Her sister Anita was a good combination of both parents, while Bonnie was a rebel much like Ruth. Then there was feisty June, who was moody with a kind heart like her mother; but, like Ruth, she fell to the darker side of the entertainment business—drug addiction. Talking about her youngest sister, who died in 2006 from cancer, still brings her to tears. "She was very misunderstood," Ruth says. You get the idea that maybe Ruth is also talking about herself.

The Pointer household was enigmatic, straitlaced, and controlled by religious values that allowed for little freedom. Ruth instinctually rebelled—a trait that seemed to follow her through adult life. "There comes a huge responsibility with being the oldest girl in the family. You're expected to set a good example, to be the moral leader, to be the go-to person when the other girls have a problem, since you've supposedly gone through it first." But Ruth wanted no part of the sibling leadership role. She highly resented the implication that solely due to birth order and not merit she was to be a guiding force with higher expectations forced on her than the others. The only thing she wanted to follow in her footsteps was her own shadow. Maybe it was a control thing. Maybe it was just wanting to be different, to find adventure. But with adventure often comes danger.

The early years were rife with church-related meetings and services. The week would begin Saturday night getting ready for Sunday morning. Bath, hair, getting out the white Mary Janes and polishing them with Shinola shoe polish, making sure Sunday school lessons were learned, which Ruth admits she never studied, always showing up unprepared. Church was Ruth's life as her father headed the local Church of God with her mom by his side. You did what you were told, participating in church activities and contributing to the ministry as much as you could. Even though Ruth wanted desperately to break free of the constraints brought on by church precepts, she genuinely feared the fire and brimstone preached for those who sinned.

"I had a real desire to be adventurous and do the things I saw my friends doing that were not at our church," says Ruth from her beautiful home just outside of Boston. "It seemed like the kids that were not in church were having much more fun than we were." Ruth's rebellion wasn't so much against church itself or its dogma, but against its rules of order.

"Organized religion never seemed to click with me. I was hearing things like the Golden Rule, turn the other cheek, heaven and hell, stuff like that. I had nightmares about angels, horses, chariots, and colossal figures coming out of the clouds, and judgment day with the earth on fire. That was hell. I couldn't sleep because there was so much preaching about fire and brimstone. That's where I'd end up because I just couldn't seem to get it right."

Ruth recalls listening to her father and mother's church services, thinking she would commit her life to the teaching that her father espoused. "The next day I would get in a fight with my sister or with somebody else, and my mind would go to a place that I was taught was sinful. 'I've blown it. That's it. I'm done. I am hell bound now. There is no hope for me.' Most of my childhood I felt that way because there was so much perfection expected with no room for error. If you said a bad word or if you thought something wrong about another person, that was it, you were going to hell."

It doesn't matter that Ruth and I grew up in two diametrically opposed worlds, because there are certain coming-of-age experiences that make us alike. Here I am, the kid who grew up in the country, about as far away from Ruth's city life and culture as you could get. Our paths never crossed, but they started out from a similar place. A path that was steeped in fire and brimstone, a teaching that insisted we attempt perfection through Christianity. I can see Ruth coming home from church along Oakland's city streets, eyes down, with that same fear in her heart that I had. When I would leave our little community church—where we lived in the "Orchards," up a long hill and a few miles from the small sawmill town where my father worked—I had been fed so much of that scary teaching that I was sure I was going straight to hell either before I made it home or at least before Sunday dinner.

My folks took my brother and me to that church (we were so rural that there were not enough people to have a denominational church, so we all attended a "community church"). Every time the doors were open. I sang in the church choir and attended Sunday school, vacation Bible school, Sunday morning and Sunday evening regular services, as well as all the picnics, special events, and workdays. I never felt any joy when I was on that property and had no concept of who Jesus was. I memorized some things so I would get my free Bible and gold stars on my Sunday school work sheets. The preacher scared me, and I never saw him smile one time in all those years. I find it interesting that he had two sons around my age and they were the most messed up kids in three surrounding counties.

One of the problems of that environment was being forced to try to reach perfection through Christianity—an unattainable goal that was set by the church, knowing it could never be reached. Only Jesus was perfect, and being held up to that standard meant guaranteed failure. The collateral damage to one's youth is negativity and insecurity that carries into adulthood. Instead of learning righteousness and the beauty of God's mercy, love, and grace, we learned failure and inadequacy. Then we grew up, walked out of the house, and tried to work through things in life, knowing that we'd never measure up. I didn't have a sense of God's unconditional love and how much more workable His way is than those rigid agitations. Of course, the way I handled this was, the day I left home to go out on my own, I not only left my toys behind but I also left God and all that mean stuff behind. As I am learning the song of Ruth, the tune is starting to become all too familiar.

Her church world seemed distant and contrived. Ruth tried to comply with the tenets her parents preached, to become what she describes as "a real Christian," professing salvation to others, but nothing jelled. The predominantly black church body itself was a small one, less than one hundred members. It was an offshoot of a larger church run by white people in another state. Some of the members wanted to project a middle-class image even though a majority of the congregation was dirt poor. There was no real fellowship, just loads of time spent in church-related duties and activities because it had to be done. Ruth felt very stifled even though her father was driven to serve others.

"I remember we lived across the street from a park, and my father kept his binoculars near the window. He'd watch people and if they got into a fight, he'd grab his Bible and head out the door to smooth things out. I remember my mother telling him, 'Somebody's going to hit you on the head if you don't stay out of people's business.' We also had a public phone number that was listed because my dad said, 'We're going to keep an open line in case someone is in trouble and needs prayer.' It didn't matter who or when, my dad would help people at all times of the day and night."

Sarah was the polar opposite of Elton. She was the disciplinarian of the household and church—rigid, blunt, and to the point. The congregation looked forward to her taking the pulpit since they knew they would get out of church on time that Sunday. "I vividly remember my mother sitting in the choir stand, or in the pulpit when she was speaking, looking down into the audience at me and giving me an eye like, 'You better straighten up and start listening!' That look just terrified me." But Sarah Pointer had a big heart and worked very hard to help provide for her family before herself.

Ruth recalls, "I know she struggled, and she didn't really ask for much. We shopped at secondhand and thrift stores. One particular holiday season I remember there was a suggestion that the congregation purchase a new outfit for my mother. They had to literally vote on that, and it was a big deal. It must have been big for me to remember it because there were some people who didn't want it to happen."

Taking care that her mother had beautiful clothes was one of the first things Ruth and her siblings did when The Pointer Sisters finally made it big. Sarah loved getting the boxes of clothes and other gifts in the mail over the years.

Despite the family's tight finances, Ruth's father bought an upright piano for her thirteenth birthday, wanting her to take piano lessons. The excitement wore off quickly as Ruth's "intensely wandering mind" prevented her from getting into practice mode. This mindset followed her most of her adult life. Still, she and her sisters managed to sing in her dad's church choirs from the time they could walk. "The first church choir we were in was called Little Soldiers. I remember wearing little poncho-looking things with red edging and big red bows on the front as we marched around the church singing, 'We are little soldiers, marching off to war.' We were only six or seven years old. There was a junior choir in my dad's church for the young people, and my sisters and I were a part of that. We were expected, as pastor's kids, to participate in most, if not all, church activities."

When singing the Lord's praises, the Pointer sisters weren't always solemn or averse to "shaking it" from time to time, much to their grandfather's chagrin. As soon as their parents were out of the house, "My sisters and I would tuck our dresses up in our panties, make little bustles out of them, and grab one of my brothers. They were athletes and had trophies sitting up on that upright piano. We would grab them and pretend they were microphones. Then we'd stand on the piano stool and dance and sing, and give little shows. For the longest time we didn't have a television, so we did whatever we had to do to entertain ourselves."

Singing eventually became a way for Ruth to find a way into the social limelight and the freedom she craved. The family moved to another section of Oakland—a predominantly white section—and became friends with an African American family whose daughters sang in their own father's church. They called themselves The Watson Sisters, and their signature song was "The Blood." *Why couldn't the Pointer sisters sing too?* they asked themselves. Ruth says, "We took their song and made it our own. It united us as a singing unit."

As a teenager, Ruth's attention shifted from home and church to mainstream social life. Her father understood that longing, perhaps due to his past, but remained protective of Ruth, not tolerating swearing or fighting among those he cared about—and that extended to the general public as well as her friends.

"I became a teenager when Elvis, James Brown, Little Richard, and Motown were popular. I could listen to that music only at my girlfriends' homes. I didn't dare tell my parents because we weren't allowed to listen to it in our house. I remember the first house party I went to wearing this lower-cut red dress I found at the secondhand store. My father wanted to go with me, which horrified me to no end. I remember sneaking out of the house and getting on the bus to meet my girlfriend at the party. I had to get off and transfer to another bus—lo and behold my father pulls up. I was shocked. He said, 'I'm just trying to make sure you're not lost and that you are okay. You want to go to this party? Well, then I will take you the rest of the way.'" Ruth got in the car and her father drove her to the party, going in with her. "I was so embarrassed. He sat right there with the parent chaperone. Not once did I get asked to dance, not once! Everybody knew that my father was with me. So no one dared.

"My mother never was social. She never danced; she never did any of that stuff, being a Christian since age twelve. I had a hard time relating to her because I was more like my dad. He did a lot of living in Chicago during Prohibition and didn't talk about his past. I know he loved to dance, and he knew that I loved to dance. I think that's what led him to allowing me to do it when my mother was out of town on missionary work. He could relate to my desire and my passion."

Ruth often wondered what led her father to become a minister, although family stories would circulate from time to time about his past. "I remember him telling us that he dipped and dabbed in some things other than alcohol. My brothers also talked about the possibility that my father was into gambling. We later found out that my aunt's husband had been shot to death wearing my father's coat. We think my father believed that bullet was meant for him, maybe because of gambling. That incident was a turning point in his life."

Soon house parties gave way to serious dating, with Ruth falling head over heels for her first boyfriend in her high school senior year. Her parents made her keep the door open when he came to the house—the door to any room—and no keeping company in the bedroom.

Ruth graduated in 1963 and from the innocence of youth. She began looking for work, anxious to get out on her own terms. The counterculture of the sixties had just kicked in, and the Haight-Ashbury section of San Francisco beckoned. "I didn't want anything to do with Oakland. I thought Oakland was *the country* and San Francisco was *the city*, and I wanted to be in *the city*. The people in the city across the bay had a whole different attitude, flavor, way of dressing, and that's what I wanted. I fantasized about moving to New York City. That's what I really wanted, but since that didn't happen, San Francisco was the next best thing. I started working at the Folgers Coffee Company and then got blindsided by a bad decision. I was eighteen years old, got pregnant, and that turned everything around in my life."

Her high school boyfriend became the father to Ruth's first children, Faun, born in January 1965, and Malik, born in December 1965. Like most eighteen-year-old unmarried pregnant girls at the time, Ruth thought she knew what she was doing and what love was. Although quite the bane to her parents' no-nonsense ministry, the fire and brimstone fell by the wayside and forgiveness welcomed her. She was always welcome in their home, but by the time she was nineteen, she was married with two kids. The marriage didn't last, but the repercussions did. Soon she was living alone, on welfare, trying to raise her children. She got major help from Sarah, who practically raised Ruth's kids.

Ruth also struggled with her father's public ouster from the Church of God. He was suddenly forced to resign without a pension—in part because he was getting older and also because some suggested he couldn't keep his four high-spirited daughters in check. Many in the church complained they were loud, laughed too much, and enjoyed themselves a little too much at parties. Ruth also got pregnant before a ring was on her finger. She says the remembrance of her father's ouster, almost five decades later, makes her cry. "My parents moved from Arkansas to start that church and dedicated more than twenty-five years of their lives to the place. My dad suffered an emotional breakdown and never held a decent job after that. It broke his heart and wrecked my faith for a very long time."

All the gospel teaching, church picnics, prayer circles, singing, and studying the Word for years were wiped out in a single moment by one godless act. This is especially true if all the lessons learned in church seem to be untrue—love, grace, mercy, kindness, etc. This treatment of their father was unkind, unloving, unfair, and cruel, and that's not how it is supposed to work. Who wants a God like that—who wants to live seeking that way of life? If people who would do that to their pastor, an aging man who had served them for years, were supposed to be Ruth's *role* models—then she decided she was going to *roll* on out of that place and find a better world. Actions like this can drive a person so far away from the Lord that they may never find their way back.

The timing of Elton Pointer's ouster coincided with the height of the civil rights, Black Power, and Black Arts movements in the United States. The childhood rebellion Ruth felt with her stringent church upbringing was tame compared to what was next. She immersed herself in the infamous Haight-Ashbury hippie/drug/free love scene and sampled all it had to offer.

"I began wearing an Afro. There was just so much going on. I was doing everything that I wasn't supposed to be doing—just trying to fit in. I hated being different, and once I got out of the house and considered myself an adult, which I know now was far from the truth, I experimented … it was crazy. I married everybody. I married five people. I often considered myself the black Liz Taylor because I grew up during a time when if you even considered having sex with someone you married them. The 'if it feels good do it' era was a crazy time. I feel blessed that I even lived through it."

I love Ruth's story because it is like watching a black-and-white movie rerun of my life. So here we go again: Ruth, a black city girl, and me, the white country boy, ending up in the same place both physically and emotionally. Ruth went across the bay to break free and rebel. She could almost hear the music coming from the Haight-Ashbury scene because it was so close—just a bridge away. I was drawn to the incense and uplifting herbs from a much farther distance, but it was country roads and crossing state lines that got me there. I also did the hair (long, not Afro), the drugs, the seamy relationships, the multiple marriages, and all the stuff that would separate me from my youth and rigid upbringing.

From the moment I heard Ruth Pointer was going to share her story, I knew without knowing where the story was going to end. I knew in my heart that it would become one story, our story. There is no way I could even come close to describing what it was like to grow up black in a white world and deal with prejudices, mean streets, and all the downsides that her culture and those times could bring. I also know she could never relate to what it felt like for me growing up hard country and the obstacles I had to overcome to break free from an environment that was very daunting to someone who dreamed of a better life. In fact, maybe people would have considered me "white trash."

There are many similarities concerning our lives, but our ethnic difference is so dynamic that we can only sympathize and not totally comprehend each other's pain. What I am getting to here is that all these differences fall by the wayside when we become Christians. Color, wealth, poverty, age, gender, location, fears, hopes, families, scars, categorizations, doubts, successes, backgrounds, tears, and memories good and bad all fade away into a simple, common, loving place. When we sit across the table from each other, we see one thing: a brother and sister in Christ who have become one because of a cross and a promise.

So it was both our similarities and our differences that led us to places like "the Haight." We didn't visit the place—we inhaled it, we soaked in it, and we wallowed in it. But like all things of that nature, it turned into vapor—something that doesn't exist after you have used it. In a way, we were running away from the very thing that we needed to run to. Unfortunately the bread of life had been served up and crammed down our throats in such a way that it didn't taste good. Free love replaced real love … for a while.

The San Francisco Bay Area music scene provided the backdrop for

The Pointer Sisters' early days. June and Bonnie played small clubs, calling themselves "Pointers, A Pair." Ruth continued to struggle to make ends meet. Four hundred dollars a month didn't go very far in an expensive and cosmopolitan city.

During that time, Ruth began to find her voice. Her sisters called her to do some studio work—backup singing for Bay Area–based artists such as Dr. Hook, Grace Slick, Taj Mahal, Elvin Bishop, Dave Mason, Sylvester, and Tower of Power. "I would go to the studio because June couldn't do the session. I believe she was bipolar. At that time, no one diagnosed those things. I know she had psychological issues from her past, things she never talked about to anybody. She couldn't deal with life, sometimes to the point where she would be physically sick. I remember making one hundred dollars in one night for singing and thinking, *this is better than being a keypunch operator*. I had two kids to support and no husband. I *had* one, but he decided he didn't want to be a husband anymore, so he just left. I was struggling, living in a housing project on welfare. Singing is something I loved, and it came naturally to me."

I love how God weaves incredible tapestries by using everything in our lives so that nothing is wasted. It is amazing how He turns coal into diamonds, grapes into fine wine, and trials into treasure. The result of our experiences becomes a beautiful offering to the world using the fabric He has woven out of discarded dreams, hard years, and separate ways. It is magical the way He combines all these elements into a work of art. With The Pointer Sisters, He merged all that went before into tight-knit vocal harmonies that only a sister act could provide. He took their hippie years, their sense of psychedelia, the feeling heartbeats from the church choir years, and clothes designed from a sense of fashion that grew out of their combined desire to show up and show off. Mix in their youth, hunger, and passion, and wham! You got the spicy hot Pointer Sisters who, along with musical soul mate Patti Labelle, became one of the first in-your-face black acts to break through in the early 1970s.

Comedian Bill Cosby once proclaimed on national television that in the event of his death, he wanted The Pointer Sisters to sing at his funeral. It's obvious he wanted to go out big, with style, soul, and a beat you could smile and dance to. With that in mind, it naturally all pointed to The Pointer Sisters.

Sarah, who always believed rock and roll was "the devil's music," unexpectedly came around after Ruth brought home a copy of Elvis's "All Shook Up" with "Crying in the Chapel" on the flip side. That song won her over, and she finally supported the girls in their musical aspirations.

Bonnie, June, and later Anita, now known as The Pointer Sisters, sought fame and fortune in Houston, Texas, in 1969. They were promised recording sessions, club dates, and a rosy future, but nothing ever materialized. They met total disaster, stranded and alone, and no help was in sight. Bonnie did the only thing she could. She called home. There was only enough money for their mother to bring one of them back, and that had to be her baby June. Then Bonnie had an idea that irrevocably changed their lives.

She called record producer David Rubinson, rock promoter Bill Graham's business partner at the Fillmore Corporation. Rubinson got his start at CBS in the mid-60s and moved from New York to San Francisco to take advantage of the burgeoning music scene. Even though Bonnie didn't know Rubinson personally, she called and asked for help.

Rubinson was aware of the girls' talent, and help he did. He not only paid for their passage back to the Bay Area but got The Pointer Sisters studio work and later, invested about $100,000 into the sister act. Bill Graham signed the trio to a management contract, and things moved quickly after that. Atlantic Records vice president, Jerry Wexler, offered them a record deal in 1971 after hearing them sing backup for Elvin Bishop at the Whisky a Go Go in Los Angeles.

Pop music gave way to the sisters' unique blend of jazz, scat, and bebop—basically the music of the 1930s and 1940s. But it was the era of pop, folk, and rock. The world wasn't ready for records like "Don't Try to Take the Fifth," which bombed. A second Atlantic single also failed to chart, falling short of Wexler's expectations. The label wanted a more traditional "soul" sound from the ladies, and neither the group nor the label were pleased with the results. Atlantic dropped the group.

In early 1972, Graham and Rubinson parted ways, and the three sisters followed Rubinson to his new production company, David Rubinson & Friends. He signed them to Blue Thumb Records, a label founded by Bob Krasnow, Tommy LiPuma, and Don Graham.

In The Pointer Sisters, Rubinson found a way to successfully bridge the white and black music worlds just as Berry Gordy had so beautifully executed with Motown a decade earlier.

When twenty-six-year-old Ruth was asked to make the trio a quartet, she couldn't resist. She quit her job as a keypunch operator in December 1972, but the move left Ruth with some reservations. "I had a conversation with my sisters about how my voice and presence made the group different. Historically, girl groups came in threes, like The Supremes and Martha Reeves and the Vandellas. They said, 'If we add you, that will make us different, we'll be four instead of three,' and that was it. But I stayed in the background on purpose because I knew my place. I didn't want them to feel like I was coming in and 'I am going to blast you out.' I didn't want to sing lead. I felt my time would come. I knew if I hung in there long enough I'd get my turn. They'd been doing this longer than me and deserved to be up front."

The first months weren't without their bumps. Money was extremely tight. "We were naïve. We didn't know any better. We thought we could clean out the hotel mini bars and someone else was going to pay for it. We would come home with no money, none, because we would spend it all on the road. It was a real learning experience."

That learning experience became the impetus for The Pointer Sisters' style. They revisited their frugal upbringing by raiding thrift shops and coming up with their signature look: 1940s secondhand chic couture, which would soon set trends. They didn't look back, practicing hours every day, honing their timing until they became "finger lickin' good."

In May 1973, five months after Ruth joined the group, they got their big break singing at the Troubadour in Los Angeles. Rubinson, who also managed Herbie Hancock at the time, found that Hancock's opening act, Ronnie Dyson, had cancelled. He wasted no time penciling in The Pointer Sisters as Dyson's replacement. They didn't allow their lack of experience to daunt them. Ruth, June, Bonnie, and Anita decided to strut their stuff and do what came naturally. Ruth called it their "judgment day." Big band–era thrift shop clothes, feather boas, and furs combined with hot scat, rock, jazz, and bebop for two solid hours of foot-stomping sexy fun, complete with several encores.

It was breakout time.

Gone were the demure girls of the Church of God. Hello, charismatic sexual beings that would leave their mark on the '70s and '80s. Ruth was in heaven, especially after meeting celebrities like Diana Ross, Linda Ronstadt, and Helen Reddy. She was precariously freeing herself from the constraints of the past. *"This is my stage, and I can wiggle and shake it the way I want to. I can raise my dress up over my head if I feel like it. I can put lipstick on as red as a firecracker and wear as much jewelry as I feel like, right here, right now, today,"* Ruth recalls thinking.

The Pointer Sisters' skin may have been sweetly chocolate, but the African American enthusiasts didn't find them anything like Aretha Franklin or Otis Redding. It seems they may have not been black enough. But that was okay with Ruth. She didn't want to be like anyone else. She was tired of being pigeonholed. Although The Pointer Sisters were unapologetically black, their audience was predominantly white. They began crossing color barriers within weeks after their Troubadour show. Critics raved about their unique look, versatility, and range of music, calling them "the most exciting thing to hit show business in years." That performance set the music industry abuzz, and fame beckoned.

They hit the ground running when it came to their studio work. "Yes, We Can Can," the single off their first eponymous album, *The Pointer Sisters*, crept up the *Billboard* pop singles chart, reaching a respectable number eleven. The Allen Toussaint–penned song was perfect for their intricate harmonies, big-band sound, and upbeat attitude. A second single, Willie Dixon's "Wang Dang Doodle," reached the Top 40 and pushed the album to gold status. Bonnie wisecracked that they became "the biggest thing to come out of Oakland since the Black Panthers." It wasn't that far from the truth.

After cutting loose at the Troubadour, the ladies made their first appearance on *The Helen Reddy Show*, coming a long way from their first television foray onto *Sesame Street*, singing "Pinball Number Count," a feature on the show for many years. Like a pinball machine, they began lighting up the room and making a lot of noise.

When fame hit the fan, it seemed to come out of nowhere at a speed no one expected, even though The Pointer Sisters had worked and planned for it for years. At first it feels like everything is taking forever and it's hard to tell if you are getting anywhere. There is so much downtime and feeling low. But when that pivotal moment occurs, you find you have created something much bigger than you realized, and then it feels like you can't keep up when it starts building momentum. You become redefined, and the new you doesn't always fit like a glove. You have to switch overnight from being filled with doubt and insecurity to being the king of the mountain. The point is, very few are ready for the hair-raising ride, and holding on becomes the only way to survive … at first.

Ruth began losing herself in a world of drugs, alcohol, and partying. "Everything was happening so fast. There were so many people around us, so many different influences, and we were on the road so much, there was hardly any time to think. I was being shoved along, going with the flow, and getting deeper and deeper into hard partying, child! Everybody was doing it. It was like you were the strange one if you weren't involved. I had been the strange one being a pastor's daughter for so many years, that I didn't want to be the strange one anymore. So I did what everybody else did to fit in. Stupid! The good part is that I survived it. A lot of our friends didn't make it out of that time."

Despite fast city living, The Pointer Sisters ended up in the one place they thought they had escaped—their early upbringing tinged with country flair. Nashville came calling. There was no pretense with country folk. Nashville wanted the girls to sing their brand-new single "Fairytale" from their second album at the Grand Ole Opry. Anita and Bonnie penned the Top 40 crossover hit, which was later covered by Elvis Presley. The Pointer Sisters became the first-ever black group to play the Opry, which garnered them their first Grammy in 1975 for Best Country Performance by a Group or Duo. Bonnie and Anita also earned Songwriter of the Year nominations that year.

The Pointers may have been the toast of Nashville, but before their appearance at the Opry, Ruth recalled the plane ride to Music City. "We were the only African Americans on the plane. When we walked off the plane, there were cameras waiting for us. A woman turned around and said, 'Who are y'all anyway?' We told her who we were and she said, 'Well if I'd-a known y'all were somebody I'd-a talked to ya!'"

An audience member at the Opry felt the same way, jumping out of his seat and shouting his surprise that The Pointer Sisters were black. Later at a private party in their honor, the staff took one look at them when they went to the door and assumed they were hired help and ushered them to the back door. Score another one for racism, but a victory for the Pointers as they worked hard to rise above what might have brought lesser hearts down. They went on to become the first pop act to perform at the San Francisco Opera House. Their performance was taped, and *Live at the Opera House* was released in the fall of 1974. Their parents cheered from the audience, truly appreciating their girls' talents, possibly for the first time. The hits just kept coming—for a while.

Bonnie and Anita penned another hit song featured on *Steppin'*, their fourth album. "How Long (Betcha Got a Chick on the Side)" hit the *Billboard* Top 20 and made number one on the R&B charts, solidifying their success. They continued singing background vocals for other artists and regularly appeared on *Carol Burnett and Friends*, singing "Salt Peanuts" or playing Cinderella's wicked stepsisters in a sketch entitled "Cinderella Gets It On."

The fast lane kept getting faster. Ruth lived in Los Angeles and got wind about a Richard Pryor movie script called *Carwash*. Bonnie had dated movie executive Gary Stromberg, who had a hand in casting the show, and he wrote a part for them as The Wilson Sisters, four glamorous proselytizers who accompanied smooth talking "Daddy Rich" (Pryor). Soon they hit the big screen, and the disco flick became an instant cult classic. Their song from the movie, "You Gotta Believe," (written by Norman Whitfield) was another R&B Top 20, continuing their amazing run of hits.

Like Pryor, Ruth got swallowed up by cocaine and alcohol. A misguided reward for her newfound independence and stardom became a bowl of coke passed around at parties. Ruth wasn't the only Pointer sister to succumb to drug use. June's drug addiction was also spiraling out of control. June had been a user since her teens, leading to a nervous breakdown in the mid-1970s. Ruth recalls, "Around this time we received an invitation to play Caesars Palace in Las Vegas with Paul Anka. It was our first offer to perform at a big upscale place like that. We showed up, and June refused to go on stage because she was so intimidated. My mother came to Vegas and tried to change her mind, but they flew back to Oakland together. We opened without her. The critics slaughtered us, and it was a long time before we were invited back."

The wheels were slowly coming off, and Bonnie wanted to get off the ride to see where a solo career would take her. She married Motown executive Jeffrey Bowen, leaving the group in 1977. Ruth makes no bones about how this move ticked them off, because each sister brought a distinct personality to the table.

June's addiction was causing her to miss concerts, so she temporarily bowed out of the group for "health-related issues." The Pointer Sisters went on hiatus after 1977's *Having a Party*, their last album under Blue Thumb. The record hadn't produced any hits or garnered strong sales. "Anita and I were having meetings with different managers, producers, and songwriters trying to get something going with just us. We even went as far as to incorporate a couple of young women that weren't our sisters in an attempt to pull the group back together."

That didn't work. Then they met Planet Records producer Richard Perry in 1978, and life began looking up. He wanted the group to have a new style and sound—a commercial mixture of pop, rock, and R&B—so the public wouldn't miss Bonnie. He asked them if they could get June back. "We told Richard we'd talk to her and see if she would agree to come back. With a little coaxing and some special stipulations in the contract, she agreed. Thus began our relationship with Richard Perry and the second coming of The Pointer Sisters. It never dawned on us that it would turn out the way it did, but praise be to God that it did."

The group, now reimagined as a trio, ditched nostalgic clothes and sound, as well as their manager David Rubinson. "We fired everybody! David was brokenhearted and upset with us. Let's just say some furniture got rearranged when we gave him the news. But we were so naïve and ignorant that we didn't know what else to do. We needed to stop and figure it all out. We were trying to crawl back into business at that time."

With a new lineup, look, and sound, The Pointer Sisters tore up the charts with a string of Top 10 hits, stylish videos, and gold- and platinum-selling albums. During this seven-year span (1978 to 1985) Perry helped them become the second most successful female act of all time, just behind The Supremes. The hits were plentiful and started with Bruce Springsteen's "Fire" in late 1978. From there it was like a faucet: "He's So Shy," "Slow Hand," "Happiness," "Should I Do It," "I'm So Excited," "American Music," "Jump (For My Love)," "Baby Come and Get It," "Automatic," and "Neutron Dance." They also participated in USA for Africa's *We Are The World.*

The Pointer Sisters were a major musical force again, this time bigger than ever. Their 1983 triple-platinum album, *Break Out*, produced five hit singles and kept The Pointer Sisters on the charts for another two years. The industry showered their talents with three American Music Awards, two Grammys, and several "Moonman" trophies from MTV.

Life was riding high once again—in more ways than one. Tours, studio work, video shoots, promotional appearances, and award shows coupled with drugs and alcohol eventually played havoc with Ruth's health. "We'd go to a restaurant or a club, and a bowl of cocaine would come around, just like they pass bread around as an appetizer. We got totally wound up in it, never realizing that it was addictive. We were told, 'This is not addictive. This is better than alcohol. Don't drink. Do *this*.' Plus, it was good for keeping the weight down, so that was my new diet. It was a crazy time."

Crazy indeed. Ruth's immune system finally gave in from all the substance abuse and not enough sleep. Soon, she was carrying extra weight as a result of an unhealthy diet—it didn't matter what she snorted up her nose, the weight just kept piling on. Hospitalized for viral meningitis in 1984, Ruth's body finally shut down. "I was on the road in Atlantic City and got sick. We had to cancel the show, which was unusual for us. We'd have to be near death's door for us to cancel … and I *was*. I woke up in a Chicago hospital and discovered my room was darkened. Meningitis is a very painful brain disease, and it's the worst headache you could ever imagine. It was bad enough that they had me on a continual IV drip of Demerol and morphine. I would wake up and see my brother or my mother and my six-year-old daughter, Issa, around my bed." Ruth's family flew in from California sporting sunglasses. They didn't want her to see their tears. The doctor's words were also a wake-up call: "Whatever your lifestyle is, you need to make some changes, or you're not going to be around very long."

But it was an ad in *Billboard* magazine wishing Ruth a speedy recovery that really got her attention. "It was a whole page. I thought, 'They think I'm going to check out.' I don't know what happened, but God somehow turned things around and gave me a desire to live." Ruth decided to get sober. She recovered through God's mercy and diligence to a twelve-step program.

Not only did Ruth have to face her own demons but also the habits of her two eldest children, who mimicked their mother when it came to substance abuse. "I would come off the road and my kids would be in my condominium and it was a mess. Drawers were rummaged, my jewelry stolen and pawned. They did whatever they had to do to get drugs."

Ruth felt it was time to get in touch with her Christian roots. "I decided it was time to give my life back to God and become a Christian again."

Sometimes God speaks in a soft warm voice. Sometimes He uses the people around us who may have a clearer shot at getting through to us. Sometimes He has to give a strong nudge along with an increase in His verbal admonitions to get our attention. But when He starts getting concerned that we may never respond to His softer touch, that's when He yells real loud. That's when He decides, no more Mr. Nice Guy, and slaps us "up 'long side the head" by dishing out a hefty trial or two that we can no longer ignore. That's what was happening here. I am not saying God was "fed up" with Ruth, but I am saying He knew if she kept going the way she was going that it was headed to the point where "time's up." God *is* love, and He loved her way too much to let that happen. It could have been that the very outer toughness Ruth had counted on in the world to keep her alive was killing her inner spirit and road to redemption.

Something she had shied away from her entire life was now coming full circle. She dove into her sobriety just as hard as she did her addiction. "My sisters still mention how annoying I was at that stage. I'd hang up signs in the dressing room, 'No Smoking,' or 'No Liquor.' No this, no that … and if they didn't adhere to my requests, I wouldn't go in that room or asked them not to come into mine. That's what I needed at the time. It's one reason why I finally moved to the East Coast."

Another reason for the move was Mike Sayles, whom Ruth met at a gym in Malibu in 1988. Today he is a successful real estate developer in Massachusetts. "When I met Mike, he was different from anyone I had ever known. I was into doing everything different than what I did in the past. First of all, he was white. He was not fashion conscious, or sly and slick, which was the kind of guy I used to go for. He was down-to-earth, a very solid, responsible person; and I thought, 'Okay, this is good. This is different from what I usually like, so I'm going to give this a chance.' We'd sit up and talk all night, and one night he proposed to me."

Ruth said yes, they married on September 8, 1990, and moved to Massachusetts where Mike had family, but not before she shared concerns and experiences with him about her addictions and things she'd gone through with her family. There were certain areas Ruth wanted to move on from, mainly her old lifestyle. Mike didn't have any children. In vitro fertilization was just being realized as a viable option for women, so they gave it a try. They gave birth to twins, a boy, Conor, and a girl, Ali.

Ruth's life continued to change and evolve, and The Pointer Sisters bravely marched onward into the '90s. In 1994, the group was inducted into the Soul Train Hall of Fame and received a star on the Hollywood Walk of Fame on Hollywood Boulevard. The latter event commenced a worldwide tour of *Ain't Misbehavin'*, and once again The Pointer Sisters donned stylish hats, boas, and high heels in the Fats Waller musical. In 1996, they were one of the legendary acts that performed at the closing ceremony of the Olympics in Atlanta, Georgia, and were honored by RCA Records with *Fire – The Very Best of the Pointer Sisters*, a thirty-six-song anthology chronicling the sisters' three-decade career.

Sadly, the new millennium ended an era. The untimely passing of Anita's daughter, Jada, in 2003 due to pancreatic cancer, was the first of three tragedies the family was forced to endure. June relapsed in 2004 after experiencing a period of sobriety. Ruth's daughter, Issa, born in 1978, permanently took June's place in the group in 2004. That same year their mother Sarah passed. "As we got older, my mother and I grew closer and we were like girlfriends. She was so naïve when it came to things of the world. I took great pleasure in sharing my experiences with her, and she took great pleasure in listening to them," Ruth laughs. "I even shared with her some of the things that I did as a kid that I probably shouldn't have done. She was just a special, special woman … so special."

In February 2006, June suffered a stroke and a heart attack. While in the hospital, doctors ran a battery of tests and discovered she had lung cancer. She died on April 11, 2006. Ruth often tears up when she talks about her. "June died in my arms. We knew it was coming. My brothers called us on the road and said, 'We think you need to come back home.' June was in hospice. Anita and I were basically taking care of her. We would visit UC Medical Center and bathe her. She couldn't talk anymore. We played music in her room and made sure she was surrounded by the people and things that she loved. She loved incense and things that smelled good, so we'd bathe her and lotion her down. Her body was still flawless. She'd mouth the words, 'I love you.' She was such a sweetie. I loved my baby sister so much, and I never will forget her last moments. I asked the hospice nurse if I could climb in bed with her and hold her. I held June in my arms as she took her last breath. As she was leaving us, Anita and I sang 'Fire' in her ears. That is a memory that I hold dear in my heart, and every so often her spirit comes to me and just reassures me that it's okay.

"We put June and Jada's ashes together in the grave with my mom and said, 'Okay mom, you get them back.'"

Although Ruth's life has been much more spiritual in the years after she married Mike, she's only recently learned to accept Christ and be comfortable in her contentment. Her testimony brings full circle a lifetime of searching. "I am happy. I prefer to be happy, and I do things on a daily basis to reassure myself that I have Christ's love in my life. I roll out of bed literally onto my knees, and I pray for my family. I pray for my girlfriends. I pray for my president, people in government offices that are running our country. Prayer is one of the most precious things in my life today, and I don't feel like I have to understand every element of my salvation in order to retain it or want it in my life, like I used to. No one has to explain it to me. I just know that I believe it and I love it, and I don't want to ever lose it.

"It goes back to all those restrictions that people used to put on us as requirements for being born again or for being saved. As time has passed, I've seen that those restrictions, a lot of them were manmade things, in my opinion. There's nowhere in the Bible that says you can't wear lipstick. There's nowhere in the Bible that says you can't sing rock and roll music. I choose to believe that my salvation is free. It was already paid for on the cross, and I don't need other people's opinions about my salvation or my relationship with my Savior. That's personal for me. I know that I'm loved and that I am going to heaven one day.

"I've taken a different approach, no longer thinking we all have to march to the same drum. I believe that God is much bigger than people make Him out to be. It's not that narrow. It's more love than I can ever really imagine."

Jesus was a carpenter two thousand years ago and so is Ruth today; I say that because she just nailed it. If you read the Bible and look deep into its teachings, it appears to be more about what she described than some of today's preacher's teachings. It's really about freedom, peace, joy, mercy, grace, fellowship, wisdom, caring, sharing, and yes, bearing up under the trials that go along with it by including Him in every thing, every day, and every step of the way. Jesus came to be the light of the world, and Ruth found the best way to get in step with Him was to "lighten up!"

Ruth's no longer the poster child for pain and tragedy. She's found peace of mind, peace of heart, and a wonderful life she wouldn't trade for anything. Her choices didn't kill her and in the end showed her how to set herself free.

Life may be calmer now, but *she's so excited… she just can't hide it…*

BRIAN "HEAD" WELCH

Korn

Korn's alternative rock-metal-industrial-rap-hip-hop sound is beyond categorization. In addition to chart-topping, million-selling records and two Grammy awards, their shows fill up arenas and stadiums worldwide. In 2005, Brian stunned music fans when he put away his guitar, quit Korn, and announced his newfound faith. But in 2013 he came back, and Korn is rockin' again!

THREE

BRIAN'S SONG

BRIAN "HEAD" WELCH | Korn

When Brian "Head" Welch announced to the world that the Lord Jesus Christ was his Savior and was baptized in Israel's Jordan River in early 2005, his conversion stunned millions of fans and Christians alike.

Hearing Brian's personal testimony, his addiction issues, the megalomania and teetering on the brink of suicide while on top of the world, frankly makes my time with The Beatles or Waylon and the outlaw gang sound like cookies and milk. The lead guitarist for Korn has literally been to hell and back, and if you listen to the group's lyrics, you'd know why. With songs like "Freak On A Leash," "Make Me Bad," and "A.D.I.D.A.S." ("All Day I Dream About Sex"), the group's lyrics and imagery are dark, sexually explicit, and profoundly disturbing in some instances. (Front man Jonathan Davis worked at the Bakersfield coroner's office in his twenties and sometimes wrote songs about his experiences). Clearly, these Bakersfield boys had their issues.

Korn's alternative-rock-metal-industrial-hip-hop sound is beyond categorization, but they clearly found mainstream success with eight top-five albums, forty-one singles, and two Grammy awards. They were a staple on MTV in the late '90s, selling an astounding 35 million records while filling up arenas and stadiums worldwide.

Brian's participation in this literary endeavor not only thrills but intrigues me, because he doesn't exactly fit the mold of most of the people chronicled in this book. He isn't older, facing mortality, or, for that matter, mellowed with age. But he has made a good living not fitting the mold, and so I was quite curious to hear how he ended up going from Korn to Christ.

We are two seemingly opposite people on the outside. His wrists, arms, torso, neck, face, and eyelids are covered with tattoos; his ears and the skin near his eye is pierced, and his dreaded hair is long, falling down to his back while, although I remain relatively unscathed on the outside, I must admit my insides have been spiked and tattered over the years. Even though we *are* different in many ways, we are very alike in one way—and that likeness is *the* One that brings us together, unites us, and sets us at ease as we sit down for lunch at the catering tables during the sound check and warm up for Korn's November 24, 2013 concert in Nashville's Bridgestone Arena. It is such an everyday environment for him and a "seems like old times" flashback for me. I can tell that he is getting a kick out of watching the old-timer relive these moments. As we break bread (and bar-b-que), I am reminded and drawn back into that smell, bustle, tension, and immediacy that precedes each performance. This very private time (only about a hundred crew, stage hands, roadies, promoters, hangers on, tech guys, producers, managers, label execs, friends, and family occupy this sacred zone) has an anticipatory narcotic effect on entertainers. It is a somewhat serious time because it is devoted to the professionalism of the performer's craft, and the core activity is shared with the select few who are responsible for and intent on pulling off a spectacular event in just a few frantic hours.

A support network has been trained and specifically placed in the lives of this band with the clearly defined purpose and vision of making sure they are okay once they hit the stage. They know that the minute Korn walks out in front of the crowd, that though there are thousands of faces staring up at them, there is something very lonely about being there.

In my experience, it is something you never get used to. I remember Andy Williams telling me when he was at the peak of his superstardom that just before he went on stage, no matter how many times he did it, he always felt like he was going to throw up. Of course, it wasn't exactly Andy Williams I was looking at on this day, but hopefully you get the point.

Brian reminds me of a modern-day messiah adorned in skate rat attire: a black T-shirt, khakis, a chained wallet and iPhone (he once lost one at an airport and vowed never again) give him a distinctive look. If I were to wear my most outrageous duds from the '60s—those long-haired, flower-child hippie days—or show up scraggly and bearded in my scruffy cowboy clothes from the Outlaw days, or in my spiffy Carnaby Street suits from the Apple days in London, or even, horror upon horrors, join him in what I wore when emulating John Travolta during the disco era, I would still undoubtedly go unnoticed. At best, people would be wondering, *who's the old conservative dude next to Brian?*

But on the inside, that's where we'll find some middle ground—although *middle ground* is not often a term used when considering Brian Welch. I get the feeling, as we sit across from each other on an unseasonably cold Nashville day, that he is an all-or-nothing kind of guy. I am chatting with a mild-mannered, focused wild man who tells it like it is. He reminds me of someone in my reckless youth—me. The difference is that he is in Technicolor!

For some reason, I feel both paternal and brotherly toward Brian because as I look into his eyes I can sense his past hurts, pain, and the inner turmoil that he has gone through leading up to this point. But I have heard his zeal for the Lord is real, and I want to go deeper so that we can savor that man in the middle ground together. Before there can be a middle we can understand, we have to know about a beginning. We have read enough about each other that we know where we are going to end up. It's a foregone conclusion that everything that transpires in our lives actually has to do with now. After a few minutes of getting-to-know-you chitchat, he leans back, crosses his arms, and off we go...

Brian Phillip Welch was born on June 19, 1970, and moved from Los Angeles to East Bakersfield when he was in the fourth grade. From the outside of his family's middle-class ranch-style home in a quaint cul-de-sac, life was seemingly normal. Brian's folks ran a Chevron truck stop with another couple, managing a staff of full-time mechanics, gas pumpers, and support staff, in order to provide a good life for him and his older brother, Geoff. However, Brian says, life was much different inside the Welch household. While his mother was cool and laid-back, his father was an alcoholic given to wild mood swings. According to Brian, there was an undercurrent of anger and rage that was never very far from the surface, and it kept the two boys on edge. "I don't want to sound like I grew up with some abusive father or anything, because he wasn't; when he was nice, he was really nice. But when he got angry, he got scary," Brian says.

My father was a good man too. He was honest, a hard worker, faithful to his family, and never abusive, or overbearing, or, *unfortunately*, interested in what I was about. While Brian was probably walking on eggshells at times in order not to rile his dad up, I was virtually banging on pots and pans, just trying to get my dad's attention. In a nutshell, we both came rocking out of our front doors with something to prove to our dads. This feeling hovers overhead like a dark cloud, and unlike God's daytime cloud that led the Israelites to the Promised Land, the ire that lies within this cloud, like polluted rain, can lead to addictions and other odd ways of coping with the world outside.

Brian says his father's anger placed fear inside him at times, and eventually he dreaded any sort of confrontation when faced with a situation. He constantly felt weak, and his male peers picked up on it by bullying him with shoves, slaps, and pink bellies. Many times they made him cry. "Because of that fear, I'd cower at school when kids would mess with me. When any of the bigger kids wanted to pick on me, I'd just let them. That fear of confrontation would kick in, and I wouldn't even defend myself. I was a wimp."

These bullies also gave Brian the nickname "Head," because they said his head looked too big for his body. It stuck. "It seems funny now, but at the time it really made me sad. I walked around feeling like I looked like a big-headed freak."

Not surprisingly, Brian's anger manifested itself at home when he was alone. Unfortunately, he took it out on April, the family dog, luring her into his room and beating her with his fists. This scenario made Brian the tough guy and someone else the wimp. It's a tale that Brian isn't proud of, but not uncommon among those who have been bullied. He also fantasized about getting even with his tormenters with a twisted game of hide-and-seek, where he would stab his victims with a knife, forcing them to cry like they made him do so many times before. Brian believes his love of slasher flicks fueled his evil fantasies, and I believe him.

As Brian's story began to unfold before me, I could see why my initial reaction was one that immediately wanted to empathize with him. I could sense that the inner child in him had been hurt and damaged. That's the reason I felt protective about him—the difference in our ages highlighted that. Whether you have been cut by a sharp knife or a butter knife, with some people the wound goes deeper than the physical incision, and the underlying areas may never completely heal. In comparison, while his were still raw, my wounds, after so many years, had become hard scar tissue. When dealing with past traumas, because we don't understand what is bubbling beneath the surface, the Band-Aids we apply only allow the feelings to fester to extremes over the years. This is where God's Word offers the healing balm needed to deal with these painful issues. The apostle Paul advises us not to dwell on the things from the past but to move on to the prize that lies ahead and to focus on what is good and true. Jesus died so we could be made brand new and have a fresh start.

Escapism is a common trait among children of alcoholics, and Brian's was an interesting combination of shoplifting, slasher films (*Halloween*, *Friday the 13th,* and *Nightmare on Elm Street*), and heavy metal music (AC/DC, Van Halen, Judas Priest, Iron Maiden, and Ozzy Osbourne).

Brian originally wanted to play drums, but his dad cleverly dissuaded the youth, telling him he didn't want to haul a drum kit around to gigs. Brian secretly believes his father didn't want to hear that racket in his house, and a guitar was preferable to the drums. Brian's godfather was a guitar player and heavily influenced his decision to pick up a Peavey Mystic, the preferred ax for metal heads. Brian says he had a good ear for music and was self-taught. After about a year of strumming, picking, and learning chords, he was coming into his own. He quickly learned the songs of Ted Nugent, Queen, and Journey, but was wired for something harder. In 1980, he discovered music that became his obsession. AC/DC's monster album *Back in Black* dominated the FM airwaves, and Brian clearly established his rock idol: the incomparable Angus Young.

Brian also adopted the metal look and lifestyle. He sported a huge collection of pins from his favorite bands and wore them on shirts, hats, and his favorite jean jacket. He had his mother sew his favorite jeans to make them skin-tight, tucking them into his white-top tennis shoes. He had both the look and attitude, and he spent hours listening to metal music in his bedroom or at a friend's house, smoking cigarettes and parsley joints. In ninth grade he traded the parsley for the real thing but was terrified by the experience. He didn't know where he was and felt as if his arms were melting off his body. After four hours of terrifying immobilization, he mostly swore off pot throughout his high school years.

While Brian was clearly hanging with the wrong crowd, he ditched them and bonded with an old friend named Kevin who lived down the street. In no time they became best buds, rode motorcycles in the desert, jumped on Kevin's trampoline, and spent nights at each other's houses. While in Kevin's home, Brian felt a certain peace and joy he couldn't find in his tense abode. Kevin's family ate all their meals together, faithfully attended church on Sundays, and genuinely enjoyed each other's company. They spoke often and openly about following Jesus and proudly called themselves Christians. They were a happy family, and Brian basked in their loving glow.

Brian's experience with church was limited. There was a brief introduction to an Episcopalian church by his mother when he was younger, but it didn't stick. It didn't help that his father simply didn't want to attend and made that fact obvious. Soon, the Welch family's participation petered out and church became a distant memory. Those summer months when Brian and Kevin first met were the most peaceful time of Brian's thirteen-year-old life. One afternoon while hanging out at Kevin's home, his mother must have sensed Brian was ready for a change. She told him in a sweet but convicting manner that Jesus Christ was the Savior of the world, and if Brian was open to it, He could come and live inside Brian's heart—all he had to do was ask Him. Brian listened intently, let it register, and went home that night and pondered her suggestion.

While at home, Brian couldn't shake what he had heard earlier in the day. Even while watching one of his beloved horror movies, his thoughts kept drifting back to Jesus. He felt drawn to the idea of accepting Christ, and it brought him a peace and love he'd never felt inside before. As instructed, he knelt on the tile of his basement floor and prayed, asking Jesus to come into his heart. As Brian simply says, "I felt something."

It's important to savor the importance of this moment. Natural tendency would be to say nothing really happened and it didn't count. I honestly believe because God made us uniquely "alike" that He also made our paths to Jesus unique. This way we can find our way to being "like" Jesus in a manner specifically fashioned for the special person God made us to be in the first place. Yes, Jesus is the one and only way to heaven, but where does it say there is only one way to His heart? No matter how many times I rejected him and lived my life in my own way, He was steadily and patiently coming at me in little pieces at a time until some of those pieces eventually glommed on to me where I couldn't ignore His wondrous truth anymore. I personally didn't have a "Damascus Road" experience … I had a "long and winding road" trip. The point is, I eventually got there, and what you just read about Brian is all about him "gittin' there."

The seed had been planted, but it had not been watered. About a month after Brian's born-again experience, high school started and he gravitated to his old ways. Eventually he stopped hanging out at Kevin's house and they drifted apart. He thrust himself into his music once again, doing his own thing and hanging out with a majority of the members who comprised Korn—Jonathan Davis, James "Munky" Shaffer, Reginald "Fieldy" Arvizu, and David Silveria. "I first met Jonathan in elementary school when we were nine or ten, and he was this nerdy little kid. Not that I was all that cool, but he was always carrying his books and was real nerdy like that kid Paul Pfeiffer (actor Josh Saviano) in *The Wonder Years*. It's crazy that he grew up to be this big icon rock singer."

He didn't see Davis again until several years after elementary school, but he says they all went through their routine of playing in "cheesy little bands." Brian tried the Los Angeles route, eventually migrating to Huntington Beach, where he found most of the other band members of Korn had also settled. They officially formed Korn in the summer of 1993. When thinking of a band name, someone suggested "Corn." Band member James "Munky" Shaffer decided to spell the name with a *K* instead of a *C* and a backward *R*. It stuck, and it made the band stand out.

By then, Brian was sexually active, dabbling in drugs, a master drinker, angry, insecure, and deeply depressed. But while gigging at a Huntington Beach bar, Korn was spotted by Paul Pontius, an A&R employee at Epic Records. Pontius saw several shows and obtained a copy of their first demo album, *Neidermayer's Mind*. The self-produced seventeen-minute album sparked what many critics called the "nu metal sound." Pontius described Korn's sound as "the new genre of rock."

They were pioneers when it came to building a fan base. "Korn stickers were all over Huntington Beach, and everybody kept asking, 'What's this Korn thing with the backward *R*?' We'd rent the 'Korn Party Bus'—load in our fans, invade these clubs, buy all their alcohol. We developed a really good reputation. Record companies started coming to see us because the word was out." Several record companies approached Korn, but Pontius guaranteed that Immortal/Epic Records would put 100 percent of its energy behind the band. They also gave Korn a $250,000 advance to sign on the dotted line. "It was crazy, because we were all working at Pizza Hut for tips. They could have just given me Top Ramen noodles and said, 'Here's some food,' and I would have been fine with that. I felt like I had just won the lottery. From there, things started clicking real fast."

By "fast," we are talking about *the* fast lane, and it was mostly fueled by crystal meth (also known as "speed" and "crank") that Brian says was reintroduced to him by an early manager of the group, a guy named Ball Tongue. Ball Tongue astounded the band with his boundless energy, passing out flyers, setting up shows, and printing T-shirts and stickers to promote Korn. One night after band practice, Brian did a line of meth so he could shake off his drunkenness and drive home. "I had done speed a couple of times with some friends back in Bako (Bakersfield), so I knew when you snorted it, it instantly took away your drunkenness. It also takes away your sleepiness. Then it takes your mind ... and your body ... and your soul. After that night, I started doing speed about three days a week." It turns out that Brian spent so much time tweaking on speed, he called his weekends "tweakends."

Brian wasn't the only tweaker in the band. Jonathan and Munky joined in the shenanigans, and the group began writing songs on the stuff. Brian says in the beginning the drug was fun, until it turned on him. He began experiencing out-of-control rage, confusion, paranoia, and weight loss. It was also right around this time he met his first wife, Rebekah, who was even wilder than Brian. A few months after they met, she was pregnant, and the timing wasn't ideal for either one of them. Korn had major touring obligations with their record deal, and Rebekah wasn't exactly the steadiest person. She had drug and alcohol issues of her own and was homeless. The two had discussed abortion but instead opted to put the baby up for adoption. Rebekah, who was twenty at the time, wasn't ready for the responsibility, and Brian was about to hit the road again. They gave their child away to another couple at the hospital. The move, Brian says, haunted him and Rebekah and was perhaps the most traumatic event of their lives. A part of him died that day and left him and Rebekah in total shock.

Korn's self-titled debut album spawned four singles when it was released in October 1994, and it eventually sold two million copies. Not bad for a rookie effort. It was followed by *Life Is Peachy* in 1996, which debuted at number three on *Billboard* and racked up another two million copies.

Predictably, the road was a crazy place for a sensitive soul like Brian. He was exposed to all the crazy trappings of the rock-star life—booze, drugs, women, and what he describes as some "dark, dark things." Much of what he saw on tour was not part of the rock-star dream he had as a kid. He envisioned himself carefree and happy, but it's not what he experienced. "I got everything I wanted, so I told myself, 'Stop whining like a baby. Just be happy.' So I just drank more, and it became this cycle of trying to be happy, but whatever I did, I just couldn't be happy."

Part of Brian's unhappiness was that Rebekah had been partying at home just as he had on the road. She began using meth again, and on the rare occasion she visited on the road, they fought both verbally and physically. One time she punched him hard in the face, causing his nose to spurt blood. At the heart of most of their arguments was the adoption.

"How could you let me give my baby away?" she cried.

As topsy-turvy as their relationship was, Brian and Rebekah had their good moments as well. They decided to get married and were given another shot at parenthood. Their daughter Jennea Marie was born on July 6, 1998, and it changed Brian's life and outlook—for the time being. "When Jennea was born, she came out and it was like the breath of life just hit the room. She was this little miracle. I thought, 'This is crazy! How did I create this little angel?' I was such a proud dad. I stayed at home, started going to the gym; I was going to get sober. I wanted to be a good dad. Started eating vegetables. My body's like, 'What's this?' And then a few weeks later Korn hit the road."

Korn's next release, *Follow the Leader*, finally pushed the band from cult to mainstream status thanks to two of their biggest hit singles, "Got the Life" and "Freak on a Leash." "Freak on a Leash" won a Grammy for Best Music Video and nine MTV Video Music Awards. *Follow the Leader* shot straight to number one on the *Billboard* charts in August 1998 and eventually sold 10 million copies, making it the band's most commercially successful album. Korn exploded, and Brian says the sudden and mass adulation definitely messed with his head. "I was tripping out ... we all were tripping out. We're on MTV every day; we've got private jets, security guards, doing in-store appearances with five thousand people showing up. Girls are crying when they look at me—I mean, I was driving a beat-up Toyota Celica barely two years before, and now they were crying about being around me? Who am I?

"We were winning awards, sitting next to people like Dr. Dre, Eminem, Jennifer Lopez, Christina Aguilera, and Tommy Lee from Motley Crue, who gave us our MTV Moonman trophy. Then after the show I went to a party, walked in, saw Paul McCartney and Madonna talking at this little bar, and I'm like, 'Am I in the Twilight Zone?' It never clicked that I was this famous dude. So we were in the bar that night, and I remember Rebekah was spending time in the bathroom doing coke. We got into a big fight that night and I remember thinking, 'Man, this is not what I thought this was going to be.' It's so empty here at the top."

There is something very uncomfortable about being "on top." In some odd way it can prove to be a perilous place, an insecure place, a lonely place with no place to go. "The top" is like Mt. Everest that can be seen in the distance—it sparkles in its magnificence when the sun (or spotlight) hits it just right. Only a few get to perch on its peak and look down on the rest of the world. The problem is that by the time you get there, the trials of the trek can rob you of the joys of the conquest. The wear and tear on your body, the things of importance that you have to cast aside to lighten your load (moral values, family, friends, mates etc.), and the fuel (drugs and alcohol) needed to make it there leave a person empty—plus the air is so rare you become light-headed, and breathing in the sweetness is almost impossible. Like the top of the mountain, you find it is very cold there, you discover you can only stay there for a minute, and, worst of all, you realize the only way from there is down. What you can see looking back down the mountain is a trail of climbers coming up to occupy the spot you are occupying, and you freeze. You've given it all for that teeny moment, and you can't jump to a higher "top." You have to go to the only place available… someplace lower.

Brian wasn't the only one in the group who felt empty. He says lead singer Jonathan Davis's demons had finally caught up with him and turned him into a raging alcoholic, with Jack Daniels and Jagermeister fueling the ride. "Jonathan was drinking the stuff until he got sick, sometimes four times a night. He would come, find us, and punch us in the head because he was so wasted. We eventually hid from him when he got into these moods. I remember one night he was in the bathroom throwing up. We went into check on him and asked, 'You okay, man? You've been throwing up a long time.' He looked back at us, scoops his vomit out of the toilet, and eats it. It was just party, party, party … same thing every night."

So this sounds like pretty gross stuff, but if you live, breath, drink, eat, and wallow in poison, you are eventually going to become poisoned. Sadly, what Brian described with Jonathan doesn't appear that abnormal after a while—the darkness in the hole that has been dug is so deep that it covers the slime and dulls the stench. Of course, the typical way to deal with it is to get more stoned and kinkier—a good example of how the devil works. He is patient and also has no limits to his depravity; in fact, he doesn't really start having a good time until you are eating puke and becoming hopeless. Satan was just getting started. With each new incarnation of bad-boy behavior, he introduced another level of madness and depravity to the mix in such small doses that no one knew how gross each new normal had become. In the 1960s and '70s, the eventual outcome of sex, drugs, and rock and roll was a dark and dirty place that many were not able to crawl out of in time to save their lives. But the era Brian walked into offered even more challenging trials. Regardless of the level attained in these emotional and physical self-mutilations, it is true that the scars on your body can heal in time. It's the ones on your soul that leave a lasting mark.

Brian might not have been as bad off as Jonathan at the time, but he knew something had to change. He vowed that he would get sober for Jennea when he came off the road, but his attempts were futile. "We toured so much, and when I'd get home I'd go, 'Hey, it's Dad!' and she'd just run to her mom like, 'Who's that guy?' It broke my heart. We wanted to be good parents, but kept doing meth. It was just a party rock-star life. We would promise just to do it one night, but when I went back on the road, she kept doing the drugs."

Like most addicts, Brian and Rebekah thought changing their playgrounds might slow down their fast-lane lifestyle, and moved. "I wanted Rebekah and Jennea to be happy and comfortable when I was on tour, so I bought this huge house with an awesome pool and waterfalls. I even bought Rebekah a white horse just because she'd always wanted one. The neighborhood had no sidewalks, and we lived five minutes from the beach. It was the perfect June Cleaver neighborhood. I was trying to buy her happiness and did what I could. But she took up again with some of her old friends and started doing meth again. When I went back out on the road, she fell in with these Nazi skinhead low-riders, gnarly dudes, who were in and out of jail like crazy. They'd come to my house, jump in my pool, have eight balls of meth fall out of their pockets, and be swimming around looking for it. I'd hear these crazy stories and think, 'Dang, my daughter's there.' I was tripping out."

On one particular leg of the tour, Brian hadn't heard from Rebekah in days. He caught wind that she had left Jennea with a babysitter while she partied for days with a new boyfriend, a skinhead and second-strike felon. When he finally did get in touch with Rebekah, she told him she was going to divorce him and take all of his money. Brian almost cracked.

"I bailed home, got Jennea, and took her on the road with me. I didn't think I would ever want to kill someone, but I wanted to kill the skinheads. I wanted to kill them so bad. Korn had our own security guards, and I remember having late-night conversations with a few who used to be in that underworld. I would be like, 'What would it take?' One of them looked at me and said, 'Head, if you go down that road there ain't no turning back.' He was looking at me right in the eye just as if he'd been through it a lot of times, and I said, 'Okay.' His eyes scared me and got that idea right out of my head."

Brian did, however, eventually get custody of Jennea. Rebekah didn't show up in court and eventually got pregnant by her skinhead boyfriend, which left Jennea feeling as if she'd been abandoned. Brian found himself in an unfamiliar dark place. "I felt bad for Jennea. Her mom bailed and was pregnant by this jerk, who started abusing her. Rebekah started calling me for help. So it was this big whole drama, and then 9/11 happened ... the planes hit the towers. I woke up that day and said, 'What is going on in this world?'

"Everything was shaky and I was getting anxious and depressed, so me and a friend decided to get sober at the same time. He said, 'Man, if it goes to World War III, are you going to be sober?' I was scared. At the time there was talk of anthrax going through the mail, talk of World War III, and so I started drinking again. Then I got a wisdom tooth pulled and they gave me Vicodin, and so I got a Vicodin habit. I was taking like five a day, then ten, then I got close to twenty a day toward the end, and that scared me. I put myself in a personal rehab—I checked into a hotel and went through withdrawals on my own. I got off that, went on the road, and began drinking, snorting coke, and doing the whole rock-star thing again. It just left me empty, man. I was a shell. I would look at my daughter, who brought me great joy. What was I supposed to teach this kid? You know, 'Do good in school, grow up, go for your dreams. When they come true, you'll be happy.' But I was totally miserable, and all of my dreams had come true."

By this time I believe Brian realized he was having "bad" dreams because he wasn't living the life God "dreamed" up for him. Things weren't adding up—if he had accomplished all the things he had fantasized, how come his life was a nightmare? We are beginning to circle around back to that seed that was planted so many years ago. But as we are getting to know Brian better, we can see the Master Gardener was having trouble harvesting his crop.

Wanting to put as much distance between his marriage and party lifestyle as possible, Brian and Jennea moved to Bakersfield for a fresh start. Brian's parents were still there and helped with Jennea as much as possible, a godsend when he was out on the road. Unfortunately for Brian, Bakersfield was a hotbed of meth activity, and he soon hooked up with local drug dealers. "I was a spun-out, functioning drug addict, scoring eight balls left and right. I'd come home and make dinner for my daughter on meth. I remember on a European tour my dealer would send me eight balls hidden in candles. I would watch for the package, track it online, and be paranoid the cops were going to come busting through the doors. I was mixing Xanax and speed every day, and I didn't know if my heart was going to hold out. I'd go to bed some nights feeling the Xanax work—my heart would go slower and slower so I could finally fall asleep. But you hear stories about people's hearts popping. So I was hoping that maybe my heart would explode and I could get some rest. I would be totally free and never wake up. After two years of doing that, I was at my end. I was like, 'Man, this sucks. I hate my life.' I was hoping I would die. I was sick of being a shell and walking around and feeling nothing inside like a zombie. That's exactly how I felt ... like a zombie."

Despite the fact that his personal life was in shambles, Brian was doing quite well financially. Besides his royalties and tour money from Korn, he'd hooked up with a friend named Doug, who was a real estate agent, and cleaned up on real estate deals. He was close to being set for life. Doug was not typical of Brian's friends—straitlaced, a family man, and a church-going Christian. Doug's broker was a gentleman named Eric, who was also a Christian, and surprisingly, Brian liked hanging with these guys. He enjoyed their upbeat personalities and respected their business acumen.

"These guys were cool. Their marriages were together, they were happy, their kids were doing good, and they were making good money. Maybe I could get out of the rock-star life and do real estate with them. I put money in and got more back. I was a functioning businessman who happened to be a speed addict. I thought that maybe this could be my out. So I decided to go to church with them and I was like, 'Here comes a bunch of Ned Flanders people. They're going to be, 'Hey brother … praise the Lord … glad to see ya … come on in … Jesus loves you so much.' But it wasn't like that at all. It was just common people. People tatted up. Whites, Mexicans … former gang members and prostitutes. I was more scared at church than I was at a Korn concert!"

If these two business associates had taken Brian to a straitlaced, old-lady-sitting-at-an-organ, polyester-preacher place, he would probably have been unreceptive. But he was able to see that everyone is invited to God's party and it is always a BYOL affair (Bring Your Old Life). He could see the tattered outsides and sense the sweet insides of a bunch of people like him. It is my guess that the main thing he saw was the victory in their eyes, the love in their hearts, and the restoration of their souls. Brian began attending church in between Korn tours, but despite this, the old temptations came roaring back with a vengeance.

A friend suggested he rid his house of drugs. While the suggestion was practical, the application was not and it backfired. "I went looking through all my stuff and opened up a first aid kit and an eight ball fell out. I found it, broke it open, and snorted it. I felt horrible inside, yet I kept on doing it for five days. But I couldn't get the same high because I remember what the pastor said. 'Jesus comes in, and you become one spirit with Him. He lives inside of you.' So every time I snorted a line, I was like, 'Oh, I don't want to get Jesus high.' I felt so bad. I was depressed.

Felt sorry for myself. 'I'm gonna die. I'm a horrible father.' I put my Bible away and stopped going to church."

But Brian did go find a clinic in Los Angeles that specialized in getting actors and musicians clean through a discreet outpatient program. They gave him meds that got him through the initial withdrawal, but he found he couldn't sleep. He'd lay awake at night, depressed and away from his family. His insomnia plagued him with thoughts of meth. If he didn't have a line soon, he'd go nuts. He left, went home, and plowed through his stash, giving up on the idea of quitting. But what disturbed him most was that the experiment confirmed all his worst fears: meth controlled his life, and there wasn't a damn thing he could do about it.

Temporarily lifting Brian out of his depression was the 2003 recording of *Take a Look in the Mirror*, the group's sixth album. However, the sessions quickly took a nosedive because Brian couldn't curb his addictions. He says it was all a blur because he was strung out during the entire album project and its subsequent tour.

By mid-2004, Brian says he was "saturated with evil and depression." He sniffed more crystal meth than he'd ever done in his life and became obsessed with Internet porn. But he really hit rock bottom when he watched his five-year-old daughter sing the lyrics to "A.D.I.D.A.S." He knew it was time to pull the plug, but he didn't know how. Out of the blue, he received an e-mail from his real estate partner Eric, who had stumbled across Matthew 11:28–30 and felt obligated to share it with Brian. It read: "Come to me, all you who are weary and burdened, and I will give you rest. Take my yoke upon you and learn from me, for I am gentle and humble in heart, and you will find rest for your souls. For my yoke is easy and my burden is light."

At this point, God was dropping hints to Brian that were not so subtle. As Brian recalled, there was a battle going on in his brain and soul. It seemed everywhere he turned someone or something was making reference to Jesus. He'd bump into old party friends who claimed they were clean and observant Christians; neighbors would ask if he wanted to go to church; Jennea started asking pertinent questions about God. The questions made Brian feel both guilty and infuriated with himself, for he did not have the answers or know how to respond.

Two things were happening here, and although Brian was too stoned to see it on the outside, the Holy Spirit was clearly working on the inside, and God was in on the program—an inside job. First, Eric was the good and faithful servant by responding to God's call to plant another seed in some very parched and hard ground. Then God sent a whole landscaping crew to surround our hero and fence the garden in to keep the "wildlife" away that was always on the prowl.

In November 2004, Brian hit the road again with Korn, hoping to escape these mounting questions and coincidences. Thoughts of suicide emerged, and Brian began to embrace the idea that it would be a peaceful ending. However, on one of the flights, he believes he had a vision (induced by drugs)—he was on another plane and fully awake, preparing for takeoff. As the plane began making its ascent, a wing dipped and the entire plane tilted. It was going down, and Brian knew he was going to die. He then heard a huge explosion and saw a cloud of orange fire envelope him in slow motion, but he felt no pain.

His body was still in motion, but moving upward. As he inched higher and higher, he felt a peace unlike he'd ever felt before. He hadn't felt the burn or explosion, just heard it. He finally realized he had died and gone to heaven. The vision was so strong that he shook violently and screamed when he awoke. Almost every passenger on the plane turned to look at Brian, who was convinced the plane was going to crash. His plane landed just fine, but he couldn't stop thinking about what he had just experienced. He wrote it off as a weird dream brought on by substance abuse and tried as much as he could to put the vision out of his head. He says at the time it was too much for him to comprehend but he has a much better understanding today. "Now that I have examined my dreams and visions for almost a decade, I know which ones are real and which ones aren't. That was definitely real because it left an impression on my mind and soul. It wasn't a fearful thing for me, it was more like, 'Wow, God is real and if I did die, I would be with Him.'

Soon enough, God would supply all the answers.

The tour ended in December, and Brian used meth throughout the holiday season. He spent time with family, opened Christmas gifts, and at the suggestion of his daughter Jennea, bought Jesus a birthday cake. He says the suggestion "freaked him out," and no doubt the Lord was calling him out. Despite this, Brian used meth and was taken to the hospital when he thought he was having a heart attack.

The next day he called his friend Eric, who met him at a coffee shop and tried to lead him in the Lord's Prayer. Brian was resistant because he knew what Eric didn't know—that he was still high on speed. He thought if he said the Lord's Prayer while he was under the influence, he would go to hell for sure. When he got home, he walked straight into the bedroom, located his Bible, and started talking to God like he never had before. When he was finished, he snorted more lines and stayed high for the next week.

Tired of being a slave to his routine, Brian decided to attend church one Sunday at Valley Bible Fellowship with Eric and his family. There was something soothing about the music and prayer, and he felt a strong sense of peace. The pastor got up, and a projector flashed the Scripture he was going to teach that day—Matthew 11:28–30—the very same Scripture Eric had e-mailed him a few weeks prior. Brian instantly became paranoid that Eric had told the preacher he was coming to church that day and asked him to flash the Scripture on the screens to set Brian up. But it was no setup. It was an awesome God who wanted to bring Brian into a living relationship that could replace all the die-hard scenes that were driving him crazy. God decided to stay simple with Brian by not making it too complicated to understand. He gave Brian something that he could look back on and see how God had been with him all along. That Scripture incident was no accident, and neither was the 9/11 terrorist act that moved Brian so deeply a while back.

Brian recalled: "The pastor started talking about how he used to be an alcoholic and threw his wife up against the wall when he was drunk, and she left him. He said he got down on his knees and asked Jesus to come into his life and take all that stuff away. The people there seemed so real, and I was drawn to it. He said, 'If you talk to Jesus, be real with Him, take all your junk to Him, and all the heavy things in your life will fall away.' It was as if he had been reading my mail. He's talking directly to my heart, and I've got eight balls at home that I'm getting ready to snort in like thirty minutes. So I said, 'Alright, I don't have to be perfect. I can take all my junk to Jesus and pray. If it doesn't work, then this guy is a quack and I will try something else.' So I decided to raise my hand, say the prayer, and accept Jesus into my life."

The date was January 9, 2005, which Brian says was the day he began his new relationship with Jesus Christ. The relationship was severely tested from the get-go. When he got home from church that day, Brian put on a movie for Jennea and headed to his master closet to open a safe containing his best bag of meth. He rolled up a dollar bill, snorted a line, and prayed God would take away his desire for drugs and rid his thoughts of suicide. He wanted to be there for his daughter, Jennea, and he also wanted to be a role model. Then he snorted another line. The behavior of flip-flopping between Christianity and meth continued for a few more weeks, but Brian was talking to God more and more. He felt his addiction beginning to fall away from him.

The timing for all of this was obviously God's big plan. Korn's contract with Sony had just ended, and the next record deal meant that Sony was going to give the band a $25 million payday. But Brian had had enough. All he wanted to do was be with his daughter and shield her from his rock and roll lifestyle. He told the band he wanted out altogether. Because they were negotiating a new record deal, the band countered with an offer—Brian would record *See You on the Other Side*, and they would find another guitarist to tour with them in Brian's spot. It was a sweet deal: Brian could continue making music with his friends, spend his days at home with Jennea, and continue his Christian life on weekends. It seemed too good to be true. Brian then prayed to God for guidance and wisdom. But he didn't count on getting such a strong message from his Creator:

Go home and write an e-mail to all of the Korn guys and managers and tell them you are quitting the band and there is nothing left to talk about!

I have never read a passage in Scripture where God had a vague idea, or where He suggested a vague approach to anything, or had vague feelings about how He feels we should live our lives. When a person becomes lost in the meth world, they find a way to carve out an obscure and mysterious hole to live in and operate from. As long as they can keep guidelines from being clear-cut, they have a lot of moral wiggle room to move around in. But God had waited long enough for Brian to start waking up to His presence, and He was not in a suggestive mood when He gave him this message. For a new believer, this is pretty startling stuff—only a true friend would be so forthright with such earth-shaking advice. Whether this really was what Brian wanted to hear or do, he knew he had been spoken to from a better place.

If Brian had any doubts about his actions, then what happened later that evening as he sat at his computer, flipping through his Bible, was confirmation from on high that he did the right thing in not taking their option of just recording with the band. "I felt this presence around me and it's like an eternity opened up and heaven touched me. I was frozen. I looked up and said, 'Father.' The only way to describe it is that I felt like I was home for the first time. I felt satisfied. My lights came on and I thought, *This is it ... this is it!* It was like God took a needle and just stuck it in my DNA and put Christ in me. It was the most euphoric feeling I had ever experienced."

Let me put this another way—Brian is a street guy, and in street terms, God stuck it to him! With some more saintly followers, God may be more pragmatic about revelation and conviction, but He needed something that felt more symbolic and more dramatic when it came to getting through to Brian Welch. Think about it: Brian felt lost, and God gave him a sense of home. Brian was trying to get away from drugs, and God gave him the feeling that he had just been injected.

Brian's conversion to Christianity was a major victory, and the devil wasn't about to let go so easily. Brian says shortly after his visitation from God, he received a few house calls from the devil or a demon. He says it caused him instant paralysis, and his voice sounded like one of the characters from the *Exorcist* when he spoke. It happened two nights in a row, but when Brian said, "Let me go, Satan," it never happened again.

It's hard for new Christians to understand phenomena like this and even harder yet to share it with people for fear it may sound too crazy. Brian was in a fight for his life at this point, and it wasn't his nature to sugarcoat the effect of the beating he was taking. Satan would strike crippling blows, but then the Holy Spirit would come to Brian's aid by giving him the tools to defeat Satan's below-the-belt tactics. Isn't it interesting that this exchange sounds a little bit like a rock and roll version of the time Satan tried to tempt Jesus when he was at a weak point?

Even though this was a victory for Brian, his e-mail saying he was quitting caused hard feelings between him and his band mates for several years. Brian made the announcement of his departure before Korn could seal their new record deal, costing them potential millions. As Munky so aptly put it, Korn without Brian was like a "three-legged dog who could still get around, but couldn't run as fast as it wanted to and wasn't as strong." Brian still loved them, but he knew deep down he'd end up overdosing or committing suicide if he continued with the band. Though there was no way for his buddies to know it at the time, Brian's decision was an act of self-preservation. Live or die … he chose to live.

With the final decision behind him, it was time to tell Jennea that he was going to be a full-time father. "I told Jennea I was going to be home all the time, and she looked at me and asked, 'Oh, you quit Korn?' I said, 'Yes, because I love you and want to be home with you.' And for the first time ever, I felt like a good dad."

A few weeks after he got saved, Brian says he felt the Lord wanted him to make a public statement. Brian's personality dictated that he do this in a big way, and he gave his testimony in front of a church—approximately thirteen thousand congregants. MTV, FOX, CNN, and millions of newspapers around the world picked up the story. This was followed by a trip to Israel, where he was baptized in the Jordan River with an MTV camera crew filming the entire expedition. Brian said he cried while waiting to be baptized, and when he went under, he put his old self to death.

Think about it—Brian had been trying to kill himself for years with killer drugs. He was doing this because he thought it would make him happy. Now he was having tears of joy because he was going to finally kill that old self. He knew in his heart that a new life was waiting for him—a forever life of purpose. Before he was crying out in pain, but when he came up out of the water that day, he was crying tears of joy.

That said, Brian's problems didn't simply dry up and blow away. In 2009, he lost a bundle on the real estate market thanks to the Great Recession. "All the money I made with Korn grew wings and flew away. Bye, bye. I lost everything. The house and my BMW—hey, it had 22-inch rims. I started having second thoughts. 'Oh man, what if these people are right that I was a brainwashed Jesus freak?' But I knew God was real, and I'd look for things in the Bible to speak to me. One passage read that if you have food and clothing, be content with that. The Korn managers were after me to come back, but it didn't feel right at all. In the end, it turned out to be the best thing for me. God had to clear out all the junk in my soul. The negative reactions had to rise to the top. He wants to strengthen us so that we can walk through life and face any trial."

Brian kick-started his own solo career and in 2011 formed a group called Love and Death. In May 2012, his path and Korn's crossed when the two bands played at the Carolina Rebellion Festival. He visited backstage with his former band mates—the first time in seven years—and they picked up where they left off. They asked him to play "Blind" onstage, and the crowd went ballistic. A month later, Munky called and said, "The door's open if you ever want to come back." It opened up lots of possibilities, but Brian, now wiser and smarter, said he would have to pray about it. "For years, the guys in Korn were raging partiers, so I couldn't be around that and my daughter needed me at home, so there is a purpose for everything. I felt like the Lord never said 'No,' it was just, 'No, not yet.' There's a time and place for everything."

In May 2013, it was official. Brian was back with Korn, and the reason was much more than just for money. He also pulled double duty on tour, opening with Love and Death. Brian explained, "Everyone is broken in this world. There's so much divorce, hate, and unforgiveness. For people to see this, I think it's just really uplifting. I never thought this would happen, and I'm not sure they did either. The fans love it, because a lot of them were like, suicidal, from broken homes and abuse. They looked up to us like their family and to see their family split up was hard on them." Five months after Brian rejoined Korn, their eleventh album, *The Paradigm Shift*, shot straight to the Top 10 on the *Billboard* album charts.

I saw Brian after the first leg of the tour. And while he was doing well, he revealed that problems threatened to derail Korn's reunion when he rejoined the group. Brian's new maturity and Christian-based wisdom not only helped him see things more clearly, but in many ways he helped to right the Korn ship, which was sinking because of Jonathan Davis's Xanax addiction. For years, Davis suffered from acute anxiety and was suffering from serious withdrawal symptoms. After years of prolonged use, doctors were worried that he might suffer a deadly seizure, so he checked into a Bakersfield hospital for ten days to kick it under medical supervision. Brian said for years the band had been asking him back, but the timing never felt right. Even though Davis was heading into another rough patch, Brian prayed about it with his pastor and trusted friends. "I knew what Jonathan was going through—all messed up on pills. I had this word from God that at least Jonathan was trying to do something to get sober, and it was very clear that I was supposed to go back. God sees the beginning and end, and He knew this was all going to happen, so I walked in there by faith. It was a little scary because I thought, 'What if I have to come back and deal with all of this again? How is this all going to work? It was nerve wracking, but I knew I was supposed to go, and when I went it all made sense later on."

Compounding the problem was the fact that Davis's six-year-old son, Zeppelin, developed Type I diabetes during this time. His blood sugar level was off the charts—almost three times the normal rate. Jonathan freaked, thinking his son was going to die, but eventually doctors got it under control. Overwhelmed by these twin problems, Jonathan failed to show up at Korn's Bakersfield studio when the band began recording *The Paradigm Shift*. It would have been easy and understandable if Brian had bolted for the door, but his compassion for the situation took over. "We wanted the best for Jonathan and for him to be with his family and just soul search. He loves his kids so much, and they helped him heal probably more than anything. So the four of us—Munky, Fieldy, Ray, and me—looked at each other and went for it. We started writing and hoped for the best. We ended up having a great time."

Brian brought in six new songs and played them for the remaining band members. They bounced ideas and riffs off each other, experiencing a spark they hadn't felt in ages. The chemistry was instant, the groove was natural, and the material came organically. Brian's presence forced the band to fall back into place, and Korn became *Korn* again.

When Davis finally came back at the tail end of the recording session, he didn't like the band's new direction. His head was into electronic music, while Brian wanted to make a metal record and rock out like the Korn of old. Unlike the Korn of old, the band was able to find room to agree and incorporated the best elements of the old and new. The results were stunning according to Brian. "I mean, 95 percent of the album sounds like old Korn. It's just mixed with some newer sounds."

Korn gathered together and overcame a common situation that takes many bands down. When members do not agree on the direction their band should be going, it creates a dilemma that hits the very hearts of their individual creativity and goals. The guys had two options—everyone could hold tight to the way they wanted to go, which meant the band could end up in an emotionally destructive slug fest that would create nothing of value, or they could work it out and find a middle ground that would meld the best of their ideas together. They chose to work together as a team, and the outcome was, as Brian stated ... stunning.

Korn's cooperative attitude and final result showed that the band had tuned in to each other on many levels—maturity, creativity, and the special sauce of godly wisdom. A sense of unity, working for the common good, and circling back around to what made them great in the first place yielded multiple levels of great rewards.

Korn is a family, albeit a dysfunctional one, but if you look honestly and carefully inside any family you will discover many dysfunctional aspects. Families do stick together, and no matter how much conflict there is behind the scenes, they, just like bands, work around the idiosyncrasies of their teammates. "Playing with Korn again is so much fun. None of us are doing drugs now, but we're still crazy. We're bagging on each other, cracking jokes, getting onstage and going wild. I've whipped Fieldy in the back with my dreads and spat water at the guys. We're all brothers playing and having fun again. I feel like God humbled me through the years, and then He prepared me and sent me back out. God will use anything, even the shallow fame that we've all gathered throughout our life. He'll use it for His glory, and it's just amazing."

It would seem that one of the most oft-covered subjects in the Bible is how to be patient with trials and tribulations. We are told in time God will reward us for our faith, perseverance, and trust. Like Job, it would seem Korn's and Brian's fortunes have been restored many times over for hanging in there with and for each other and not dissing God. In Brian's case it was a matter of life and death, or more poetically, Love and Death. As he explains it, the name Love and Death was chosen for his new band because he feels love and death are the two most significant things you can go through in life.

Their kinship has been restored, and Korn's popularity has provided Brian with an incredible, massive, and worldwide platform to bring truth into so many young people's lives. You have to see Brian and the band live to believe how incredible it is now—and believing is what it is all about for Brian. Today when Brian steps out on the stage before a crowd, he rocks out for *the* Rock!

CHRIS HILLMAN

The Byrds

A key figure in country rock, Chris Hillman helped define the genre by his work with The Byrds, The Flying Burrito Brothers, Manassas, Desert Rose Band, and Gram Parsons. Historic concerts and record sales in the millions, with classic recordings such as "Eight Miles High," "Turn! Turn! Turn!" and "Mr. Tambourine Man," have cemented his place in popular music history.

FOUR

FOLK SCORE AND HEAVEN YEARS AGO

CHRIS HILLMAN | The Byrds

There are two artists in this book that embody the heart of my personal musical experience and career essence: Richie Furay and Chris Hillman. I wish Gene Clark were still with us to help round out our story. I didn't know anything about Richie or Chris as they grew up, but as I look back on our history, I feel in an odd, ethereal way that we are related. We came out of small towns and landed in the same big towns—each carrying a guitar and a dream that we didn't understand or plan on having. It just happened. One day ... there we were.

We all seem to share country music as our root cause, folk music as our siren call, and rock music as our ragged edge. We heard these strains take over our lives, each one fighting for a piece of our creativity, each one being an incredible art form of its own. However, we needed to assemble them all in one place, and even though each musical force was monumental, none of them totally satisfied what our fingers wanted to do, what our ears wanted to hear, or what our souls wanted to share. Forgive the repetition on this one point as we bounce from story to story; but almost without exception, none of us thought it through to a logical conclusion as we plunged into our lifetime obsession. It is a good thing no one had the money attraction as the prime mover, or we may have had second thoughts.

Everyone thought about the music, but no one dreamed that one day they could be sleeping in a van with five other guys. They all heard this faraway sound and then, in time, God gifted them with the ability to create it. And no matter how they tried to go about it, they couldn't help but be drawn to parallel souls with similar abilities and matching visions. As I observe how their music developed and look at the groups they migrated into and out of, it was as if they were truly in search of the same magical lost chord. The magic lies in the results, and they were among the few who actually struck that chord, if only for various moments. The original bands are no longer together, but the echoes of their achievements go on forever.

This chapter is about Chris Hillman, and if you were to look at his life along with the others from a high perch and were asked to draw what you see as a symbol or graphic, it could look like lines coming onto the page from different angles into a big circle. Within the circle, you would see these lines dancing and moving about in rhythmic ways, blending together and ultimately filling that circle with harmonious creations never imagined. Then, in time, when the circle got all squiggly, you would see these same lines going off in different directions with their piece of the circle wrapped around their necks like favorite guitar straps. It's not unexpected when you listen to and examine the intricacies of each group Chris was in over the years, that no matter who was in the group, or how many players were in the band, you could always hear Chris—your eyes and imagination would be drawn to him. It wasn't just the parts where he sang the lead or picked the solo, but by his nature he brought a part of that special circle into each new gathering, and the fans experienced new rings that spread out from that fresh vinyl center. The country-folk-rock music that was birthed in the sixties, flourished in the seventies, and then became a sonically iconic forever thing was the product of a handful of the same people at its core. I am not suggesting that Chris, Richie, and the late Gene Clark were the only major dudes in this wondrous happening, but I am saying they typify the heart of the phenomenon.

I wanted to lead into Chris's story talking about the special contribution that he made to a genre. I needed to describe the magnitude of that special music form and its import to the general music scene so that we can see how he uniquely assembled his pieces from that core circle and took a rural beginning into an incredible story of raucous redemption and sweet salvation.

Take it, Chris…

"I was born in 1944, and I'm a third generation Californian. I had a wonderful family upbringing. The first twelve years of a child's life are some of the most important, and I feel later on I survived some very hard times because my parents brought me up with such good values," Chris said. "We were brought up with a sense of civility toward one another regarding respect. Families stuck together. People stayed together and rarely got divorced. You took a vow and you stuck to it. It was a different world then. One of the greatest times to ever be alive was the 1950s. Not to get too political, but things are not quite the same today, and I'm not happy about it."

If I were a college English Lit professor and my students were reading this chapter, I would make them go back and read that paragraph a hundred times. It is an era so few people today can identify with. When Chris described life in those days, I immediately went back in my mind to the riverbanks and dirt roads of my youth, when life was simple—simple because we had rules of morality and homespun teachings based on God's Word. True, we weren't given much wiggle room, but that way we didn't bounce around so much. There was an order about the way we were brought up, and we were given a structure that became an irreplaceable part of our being. Because of this, we had something to fall back on, no matter how we messed things up in later life.

We may have felt we were held back from growing up as fast as we would have liked by our family dynamics, but this restriction actually left us with a little more energy stored up for when it came time to tackle the course before us. We were completely aware that there was something different about us as we rolled out of those simple beginnings. We also knew that we did not have to explain it to other people. There were smells and sensations out of those loving homes we had inhaled and harbored in our growing years that became a part of our being. To this day, I can drive by the house where I grew up, pull over, and smell memories, soft and sweet, sad and bitter, pure and true, all a part of growing up in a godly home. Because of this common upbringing, when I had my initial conversation with Chris, we could have gone on about these simple things forever. In time we left our homes and came to the same place, and a time where we shared the same music, towns, friends, and truck stops as part of our lives. Most importantly, as we moved about these places, we had the same point of godly reference buried deep inside.

Of course, we talked about religion, and I found it interesting that his mother's cousin was a minister whose church was about seven miles from the Hillman home. Somehow, someway, Chris says he came to love hymns, which mysteriously seeped into his subconscious. "I don't know how to explain it other than it was waiting to get out of me. When I started listening to bluegrass and folk music in high school, it just grabbed me. I later wrote lots of songs with Christian subtleties in them, just following my heart."

Once again I see a certain intrinsic pattern that keeps repeating itself in a person who didn't grow up religious but heard hymns as a child. It's easy to see how those songs grabbed them and eventually helped shaped the future musical landscape of their lives.

Music constantly played inside the Hillman household, and Chris adds that his parents had great taste. Chris remembers hearing Count Basie, Duke Ellington, Benny Goodman, Artie Shaw, Frank Sinatra, Billie Holiday, Dean Martin, Peggy Lee, and lots of big band records. Chris also remembers his mother playing the piano when they were young.

In 1955, when Chris was in the sixth grade, rock and roll exploded and out of nowhere, he like millions of others got swept up in it. Elvis Presley took the best of blues, gospel, rhythm and blues, and country music, and the effect was like a bolt of lightning. Then came the folk movement, which was life changing for Chris and millions of others. "Rock and roll sort of went to sleep around 1958 to 1959 and all of a sudden folk music started to come along, and that's what got me … Woody Guthrie, The New Lost City Ramblers, Peter Seeger, The Weavers, Lead Belly, Cisco Houston, and The Kingston Trio. I didn't want to learn guitar when I was listening to rock and roll and the Elvis years. But when folk music came along, that all changed. I wanted a guitar."

A lyric shift had taken place in the creative minds of songwriters and musicians of this era. For the first time, young people were finding they had a voice as well as a political and societal instrument in their hands. The music, melodies, instrumentation, chord progressions, and general tone of the songs of the past no longer reflected what was going on in their lives. Moon, June, and spoon were not cutting it anymore. The traditionalists, folk singers, and ethnic artists had been telling their stories of real-life experiences for a long time, and the poetic pictures they painted weren't always musical Maxfield Parrish renditions. Once The Kingston Trio sang a folk tale about a blood-and-guts love story and caught the attention of the masses, then rock and roll came in and gave the messages some gaudier guts, racier rebellion, and juicier excitement. Now the cat was out of the house and papa got a brand-new bag!

"I learned my first chords on a ten-dollar guitar from Mexico. I was totally involved, playing, listening to records, and then I started listening to bluegrass. Something about that sound clicked with me."

Part of Chris's musical education was not only in the doing, but witnessing how the masters performed. Chris and a carload of friends would often make the 140-mile trek on weekends to the Ash Grove, a legendary club in Los Angeles that was the nexus of the West Coast folk movement. “We'd be five feet from the stage, and it was fantastic! I saw everybody—Doc Watson, The Stanley Brothers, Flatt and Scruggs, and the Kentucky Colonels. I practiced until I became proficient. I just took to it and continued listening to records because our learning tools at the time were records. We didn't have DVDs or YouTube, or anything like that, which can be useful tools.”

What is the cause of this driving force to learn everything you can about an instrument? What makes someone want something so badly that they are willing to face personal, physical, emotional, and financial starvation in order to feed a part of their soul they have yet to define and discover? What pulls them into those struggling years involved in seeking the Eden of the flawless song, the perfect chord, the impeccable tag ending that pulls them out and away from a simple life into an existence defined by sonic composition? If I had to summarize what this is all about into a simple phrase, I would have to say … *it just happens.*

It's as if in that moment when their ears hear a completely formed musical chord that their hand has created by pressing down real hard on the strings of an old guitar, they immediately want more. They credit themselves with accomplishing something magical, and they want more—more notes, more tones, more volume, more intricacy, more music, more recognition, more fellowship with kindred souls. So they have to go find the rest of the orchestra to play out the score of their lives. Five hundred miles? I think Chris would have gone five thousand miles if that is where he thought he could find what he was looking for—the holy modal grail, you might say.

People like this want to acquire full ownership of the word *free* when they discover a life that encompasses all the offshoots of that word: freedom, free flowing, free form, free spirit, and yes, free beer! This awareness comes about when that something down inside that has to do with everything that has gone before in their life finds the magic carpet that allows them to escape into what they have always wanted. This sounds a little fluffy, but that's what happens when setting out to describe the mind of a master musician and what motivates them to make this their life's work. In summary ... *it just happens.*

Chris forged ahead with his musical aspirations and progressed on the mandolin (an old Gibson), developing a reputation as a serious musician. He met and played with the Scottsville Squirrel Barkers, a bluegrass band based out of San Diego. They asked him to join the group, who played the coffee house circuit. In addition to Chris, the lineup featured founding Eagles guitarist-songwriter Bernie Leadon, future Hearts and Flowers member Larry Murray on dobro, future Flying Burrito Brothers and Country Gazette member Kenny Wertz on banjo, Ed Douglas on stand-up bass, and Gary Carr on guitar.

The Barkers lasted barely two years, but they managed to record one album, *Blue Grass Favorites*. The album, now a much sought-after collector's item, was recorded in four hours and was later distributed in supermarkets. Chris and his band mates were paid the tidy sum of ten dollars apiece. It was all a part of the journey, says Chris. "When we were younger, we had no fear. You just played. I didn't even think I was going to get paid. I starved in the Squirrel Barkers ... I starved all the way up into The Byrds. I played underage in clubs, but that's where I learned about the music. Not many people get that sort of opportunity, but I made it. It was a great time. It was fantastic."

Let's pause for just a second and ponder this—Chris was fifteen when he learned how to play guitar, and within three years, he had his first number-one record.

It would be hard to not relate this to growing up with challenges, strict parenting, strong work ethic, and having to begin making your way at a very young age. This level of accomplishment is very unusual in the new millennium. It looks like it takes longer to "find yourself" these days and, of course, being able to crash at mom and pop's all-night hotel and eatery until you are in your late thirties does take the edge off of having to fend for yourself. Heaven forbid having to provide for basic utilities and not living in a comfy dwelling that took parents a lifetime to obtain.

Please hold all applause, but I was also brought up to be on my own. I worked for my clothes, spending money from twelve years on until I left home in northern Idaho at age seventeen to make my way in the world. (I like to tell people I heard a rumor that my folks had already rented out my room the Monday after graduation from high school.) I used volunteering for the military draft as my exit strategy. I overlapped my armed forces stint and college attendance while working outside jobs to pay for my education. By the time I was twenty-three, I had completed my six-year military obligation, graduated with honors and a BS degree from San Diego State University, married, had two children, toured with a mildly successful folk southern California folk group (Town Criers), and then built and owned San Diego's premier folk club, The Land of Oden, where I joined forces with Chris's band mate, Ed Douglas of the Scottsville Squirrel Barkers. My Land of Oden folk club and Ed's Blue Guitar shop became the folk music center in San Diego. Basically it was us in San Diego, The Troubadour (Doug Weston) and Ash Grove (Ed Pearl) in Los Angeles, plus the hungry i (Enrico Banducci) in San Francisco. I knew from early on that I had to "play in the cold if I wanted to drink at the harvest." There was a zest for life, a pull-yourself-up-by-the-bootstraps hunger, and a sense of adventure that seems to have somewhat dissipated in subsequent generations.

People like Chris, Richie, and Gene just went for all the marbles and threw caution to the wind. What is lost in the marvel of our superhuman strength in all this is another more mellifluous key element. We weren't coddled, but we were covered … by family, by love, by hard work, by a cuff behind the ear when we slacked off, and by giving, getting, and going for it. Now that this has become so poetic, there is one more thing—we didn't know any better; we didn't know we couldn't do it; in fact, we didn't even know what the word *naïveté* meant, and I believe that's what allowed us to pull it off.

When the Squirrel Barkers disbanded, Chris received an invitation to join the Golden State Boys in late 1963. These boys were no slouches.

They were regarded as one of the premier bluegrass bands in Southern California and were fronted by future country star Vern Gosdin, his brother Rex, and banjoist Don Parmley. The Golden State Boys made one album under their new moniker, The Hillmen, named after Chris. They were featured performers on the weekly television show *Cal's Corral*, a live country music show on LA Channel 13. They also worked in numerous hillbilly bars and juke joints in the Los Angeles area while Chris was still underage. He obtained a fake ID so he could play.

The Hillmen also ran its course, and Chris considered taking a break from music and enrolling in college. He had contemplated UCLA. "College had always been a passing thought because I was a starving artist and you get to a certain point where you have to get something going. It was a hand-to-mouth existence, and I was nineteen at that point. It was tough. But it seemed at that time there was always a door opening, I would go through it, and something would always work out musically. I think God had a plan for me, because as stubborn and as stupid as I was as a young man, somehow I made it through. There is a divine plan for everyone. It's opening your eyes to see what it is."

Another way to look at this is to say that you need to close your eyes and let God lead the way. God clearly had a plan for Chris, and it sounds like He kept heading him off at the proverbial pass every time Chris got sidetracked.

In February 1964, days after The Beatles had appeared on *The Ed Sullivan Show*, a friend named Jim Dickson, who had previously worked with The Hillmen, invited Chris to World Pacific Studios on Third Street in Los Angeles. He wanted Chris to hear a trio of musicians who sang Beatles tunes with acoustic guitars. The three musicians were Roger McGuinn, Gene Clark, and David Crosby. Along with drummer Michael Clarke, Chris was recruited to play electric bass, and when they joined forces, the world soon came to know them as The Byrds. "It was Roger, Gene, and David. Roger was playing a Gibson acoustic twelve-string, and Gene had an acoustic guitar, and they're all singing Beatles songs. I heard them and I knew they were going to be great. They wanted a four-piece band like The Beatles, and they needed a bass player. At the time I didn't know how to play bass, and when they asked if I could play I said, 'Yeah.' Yes, it was intimidating, but I felt it was the right thing to do. When I walked into that first rehearsal, I thought they were going to play rock and roll. They didn't. They were folk guys. We all literally and figuratively plugged our amplifiers in the wall. We had no blueprint and started from scratch. That's why The Byrds were a very unique band."

During my San Diego days, a jazz musician introduced me to something he called syntonics, which is based, I believe, on a psychology phrase describing being responsive to and in harmony with a given situation or environment. In music, syntonics, I was told, happens when you put one sound directly on another and it creates an entirely new sound. Sometimes vocalists will use this technique singing while exactly matching the notes they are playing on the piano or other instrument they are playing. The first time I heard this done, it blew my mind. One time in a recording session, I doubled a banjo playing single notes with a xylophone, and it was magical. That's how I would sum up The Byrds' unique sound: magical. It affected the world in the same way syntonics affected me when I first listened to it, and it was their special uniqueness that projected them so powerfully into the pantheon of all-time greats in rock and roll.

Yes, it was magical when these five musicians piled their sounds on top of one another and created a whole new sound that had never been heard before. It was too rocky to be folk, too folky to be rock, and how did they work that country stuff in there? An interesting thought here has to do with The Beatles. The Beatles influenced them, and in turn The Byrds influenced The Beatles. Think about it. The Beatles were influenced on the American side by everything from The Everly Brothers, Carl Perkins, Chuck Berry, Buddy Holly, Motown's Marvelettes, The Beach Boys, Little Richard, Roy Orbison, Bob Dylan, Duane Eddy, and Buck Owens. They then mixed that in with their British bent, which was originally inspired by the likes of Rory Storm and The Shadows. Now take this musical stew and send it back to America and the fresh potpourri of what the individual members of The Byrds were all about, and *bam!* you got masterpieces like "Eight Miles High" and "Turn! Turn! Turn!" Magic, creativity, and decades of the sounds of those who had gone before met at World Pacific Studios on Third Street in Los Angeles one day, and out came a flash pan explosion of something undeniable.

It's so fascinating that The Beatles and The Byrds are among the most unique and undeniably distinctive bands to ever come our way, and yet when you listen in depth to their body of work, and listen carefully, you will almost hear a small slice of every artist of note since music began in our time. For England, much of what happened next there came out of The Beatles' hard driving sound, while in California and the States, it was The Byrds flying high into our hearts and across our time. The blend of the guitars, the folk influence, the lyrics, the dynamic of the band, and their overall ingenuity pioneered folk rock and a whole new branch of musical freedom. Now you could look, play, and think however you wanted to, and you could do it with … a tambourine man!

The Byrds signed a contract with Columbia Records in November 1964, and the quintet bucked hard out of the chute. Their debut single was Bob Dylan's "Mr. Tambourine Man," which shot straight to number one in both the United States and the United Kingdom, making it the first folk-rock smash hit and creating an entirely new subgenre of music. With their Beatle-esque mop-top hair, trademark granny sunglasses, and unconventional duds, The Byrds became "America's answer to The Beatles." During a two-year stretch, they produced classic tunes such as "Turn! Turn! Turn!" "I'll Feel a Whole Lot Better," "So You Want to be a Rock 'n' Roll Star," and "Eight Miles High," becoming one of the most successful and influential bands of the '60s.

While David Crosby and Roger McGuinn seemed to get the lion's share of attention, in many ways it can be said that it was Gene Clark's genius that quietly fueled the band. "Gene was so talented as a songwriter.

When we lived together, he would write four or five songs a week. He'd then show them to Michael Clarke and me, two of them would be masterpieces. Gene was a good guy, and I really liked him, but Hollywood just ate him up and spit him out. It affected me, too, but somehow I kept it all together. But Gene, I'll be honest with you … It's amazing he lasted as long as he did."

My relationship with Gene was also special and deep—it had that rare element of when we first met we both knew immediately that there was a kindred flame burning inside. We loved the Mendocino coast in northern California, and we would gather around his fireplace in the private remoteness of a historic old stagecoach stop he bought on the Albion Ridge. Other times we would just chill at my quiet little hideaway a few miles from there, just north of the small town of Anchor Bay. Unlike his place that was tucked in the woods, mine was on the ocean, perched on the edge of a hundred-fifty-foot cliff … two entirely different vibes, two people very different in nature, similar in nurture, drawn to the same place. We didn't live there then, but this is where we went when we needed to escape from our Laurel Canyon digs and the craziness of the Hollywood scene. What was ironic about this was not only the fact that we had zeroed in on the same remote area that was more than a ten-hour drive from Los Angeles, but many times we would go there without telling each other and find when we got there that the other was there also.

Gene was a tough guy with a heart of gold, but when something inside would go awry with him, you never knew if he was going to slug you or hug you. What was odd about this was that both of these reactions had to do with the fact that he loved you. Although Chris spent so much more time—intense, creative, and dynamic times—with Gene, I am glad that my friendship with him started after that electrifying part was over. Ours was a more reflective time, and we both were in a confused but somewhat mellow survival mode. Maybe part of our closeness came about because we weren't clear on what we were trying to survive.

It became apparent to me that he paid dearly for his genius and creativity, especially when it would collide with the business end of the world he had chosen to live in. He was at his worst and most unlikeable when he would go crazy in reacting to certain situations. As trying as that could be, oddly enough, I loved him the most when he would come to me, remorseful and apologizing for whatever bad deed he had committed. After a while it was easy to understand why he would lose it in those moments of rage—you could see the confusion written all over his face. At the same time it was easy to see what a sweetheart he was, and you could feel the tenderness inside when he brought the repentant side of his nature to your doorstep.

This chapter isn't about Gene, but it is about that part of us that people like Chris and I shared in our navigation of the many years in our chosen professions. Some of us became real good at taking the beatings, backstabbings, and broken dreams by keeping them inside until the memories would go away. Gene was a bit hard to handle at times because he was very open and honest with his feelings. The point I am getting to here is that there were people like him that were part of this folk, rock, country, pop, musical story that came roaring through our lives and not only left a lasting impression but had a way of changing things inside our souls. Chris shared the fiery, blazing years with Gene while I joined him for the fading coals part. In short, I have discovered there was a common thread that ran through the hearts and dreams of most of the people who were a part of this incredible time in our musical history. Gene and Chris had their own special colors that were woven into the tapestry of the genre. Whether Gene was recognized as a leading force in The Byrds, there is no question he brought something special to their flight pattern, and his departure did affect their momentum.

Chris felt the same way and tried to dissuade him from leaving The Byrds. Chris remembers, "I told him, 'I don't think you should be doing this. I think it's a mistake.'"

Gene's departure allowed Chris to develop as a reliable

singer-songwriter in the band, and he came into his own on The Byrds' 1967 album, *Younger Than Yesterday*, cowriting and sharing lead vocals with Roger McGuinn on the hit, "So You Want to be a Rock 'n' Roll Star." He also wrote, "Have You Seen Her Face," "Thoughts and Words," "Time Between," and "The Girl with No Name." Chris's prominence with The Byrds' next album, *The Notorious Byrd Brothers*, allowed him to continue to develop as an artist and shared songwriting credit on seven of the album's eleven songs. Chris's creative streak helped paved the way for The Byrds' next musical adventure—the exploration of country music on the watershed *Sweetheart of the Rodeo*.

I should mention that by this time—February 1968—The Byrds were down to two original members: Chris and Roger McGuinn. Chris recruited his cousin Kevin Kelley on drums, and then they hired Gram Parsons to replace David Crosby. Gram was an incredibly talented and innovative force, but he eventually self-destructed at age twenty-six through substance abuse. In the beginning, Chris says he and Gram got on well and collaborated almost effortlessly. "Gram was a charismatic guy, very charming, bright, and for two years he really wanted it. He was ambitious and had such a love for country music. I first met him at a bank in Beverly Hills. He was a young kid, and I'd heard about him. I invited him to a rehearsal because we were looking for a keyboard player. Once I sang harmony with him, I said, 'Here's a guy who understands what harmony is.' I told Roger McGuinn that we should hire him and we did."

Sweetheart of the Rodeo, which was recorded in Nashville, is considered the first major country-rock album recorded by an established act. When it came out in 1968, I was a dyed-in-the-wool Byrds fan that grew up country, my favorite music was folk music, I was heavily immersed in the new rock and roll scene, and I loved it when established bands would make a sharp left-hand turn off the well-traveled highway of creative expectations (like when the Beatle's recorded *Sgt. Pepper*). So, ignoring more learned dissertations on this album, I have my own timeline of emotions about the recording.

The Byrds had it all for me: how they looked, how they sounded, the way they interpreted material, and they also represented a sense of cultural freedom. The record had all the aforementioned ingredients logically necessary to knock my socks off, but for some reason *Sweetheart of the Rodeo* lost me. The band made their hard left turn onto an untraveled country back road with this album. With their previous record, the slightly more successful *The Notorious Byrd Brothers,* it would appear the band had somewhat purposely evolved into a psychedelic rock band and because of this, to a number of their fans this new offering was sort of a sonic whiplash. I also think for some of us the reason we loved The Byrds was because they had delivered us out of our common beginnings, and now with *Sweetheart of the Rodeo*, they were trying to take us back home … and some of us didn't want to go.

The fact that so many critics labeled this collection as groundbreaking made me wonder at the time, because I honestly didn't grasp the effect it would have. *Sweetheart* was a fresh sound, a new sound, but I think it might have become a dividing sound when it came to their audience. It was a recording that changed many musicians' and fans' outlook at the time, while some fans just changed favorite bands. Looking back, it is easy to comprehend how it was important in the evolution of contemporary music, plus it did create a new subculture of sorts in its honesty and rawness. It would be hard to ignore the fact that in 2003, *Sweetheart of the Rodeo* was ranked #117 on *Rolling Stone* magazine's list of The 500 Greatest Albums of All Time.

Some critics and reviewers said this album was influential on the outlaw country movement, which I helped to pioneer as a producer. As a member of Waylon, Willie, and the boys, we never admitted to anyone that someone else could have had any effect on what we did. Maybe that album did make more of an impression on me than I realized. It is also very easy to understand why The Flying Burrito Brothers was Chris's next stop.

So despite the fact that *Sweetheart of the Rodeo* is considered by many music historians as a seminal moment in the country-rock genre and received mostly positive reviews, it was The Byrds' least commercial venture. The album reached number seventy-seven on the *Billboard* Top 200 and failed to chart in the United Kingdom, where The Byrds had a fervent following. With Parsons' genius also came trouble. He was still under contract to his previous record label, LHI, which threatened a lawsuit. McGuinn also feared that Parsons was taking too much creative control of the album for a newcomer and replaced three of his vocals. The final blow came when the group toured England a few months later. Parsons, who met the Rolling Stones, became enamored of Keith Richards and lost his focus and drive. Following their July 7, 1968 appearance at London's Royal Albert Hall, Parsons announced he wouldn't accompany the band to their imminent tour of South Africa, where apartheid was in full swing. "This was two hours before we boarded our flight. The bottom line was, it wasn't a moral dilemma over race. It was just an excuse to stay and hang out with Keith Richards. Gram was climbing that ladder, and we were just one of the rungs."

Following the South African tour, Parsons (who was only with The Byrds for five months) was out of the band and replaced by longtime Byrd-in-waiting Clarence White. Their drummer, Kevin Kelley, was also dismissed from the band soon after. Chris exited The Byrds in September to join Parsons, Sneaky Pete Kleinow, and Chris Ethridge in what soon became known as The Flying Burrito Brothers. Yes, you heard right—Gram Parsons. "Gram was very charismatic and I must confess, I forgave him. In hindsight I should have known better, as his behavior only became worse over the years. I loved the man, but our relationship was, at the end, like Cain and Abel."

Creative relationships often make for strange bedfellows. As in love, war, and bands, opposites do attract. It has been said that there is a fine line between love and hate. It has also been said these are two of mankind's most passionate emotions *and* the spark point of our most creative accomplishments. The only one of these scenarios that I feel comfortable in commenting on is how this plays out in terms of a gang of guys bouncing around the world in a band. Any writer, whether of prose or musical composition, will readily admit they do their best job when they are either madly in love or totally in the pits. Artists who bring their talent, their personal oddity, and their gifts of creation to a group of other artists often find they come up with their best ideas because of conflicted relationships with their brothers in arms. The attraction to the inherent creative genius is the fire that draws them to each other's flame, and it is usually the heat of their idiosyncrasies that makes things go crazy. I found over the years that it was the moments of joy that inspired me to write lovely things, and the painful interludes were the causation factor for my most insightful offerings.

It is the love-hate thing that comes about in bands so often. Rock stars are not normal people, but if they were, we would have never had *Sgt. Pepper*, "Light My Fire," "Paint It Black," "Good Vibrations," "MacArthur's Park," or "Great Balls of Fire!"

With their debut album, *The Gilded Palace of Sin*, The Burritos opened the door wider to those who wanted the legacy of *Sweetheart of the Rodeo* to carry on—in a more raucous way and in an even more freeform manner. And for me, I eventually understood the reason reviewers were using the word *seminal* with The Byrds' *groundbreaking* record! The fans now had a full-blown, broad-appeal genre that in time accounted for much of the success experienced by artists such as The Eagles, Emmylou Harris, Poco, Pure Prairie League, The Nitty Gritty Dirt Band, and Rick Nelson's Stone Canyon Band. Even the Stones tipped their hat to the Burritos with "Wild Horses" on their classic album *Sticky Fingers*. All the ingredients needed were now firmly laid out on the writing and performing table, and the artiste chefs of the day were able to blend these elements together and formulate these incredible groups.

One of the album's standouts, "Sin City," was cowritten by Chris and Gram. The 4:12 song, about Los Angeles at the end of the 1960s, became a lasting cynical anthem for the music industry. When Chris looks back and examines his writing at this time of his life, he believes God was starting to knock on the door. "Absolutely He was. We had already done 'Turn! Turn! Turn!' which sort of brilliantly wraps up all of King Solomon's verses—a time to be born, a time to die. We did The Louvin Brothers 'I Love The Christian Life.' The foundation of 'Sin City' is like a Baptist hymn with references to Satan. We wrote that song in about thirty minutes. Each little verse had to say something about our culture at that time, and it just sort of flowed out of us. I think evil is in the world all around us, especially in the entertainment business. The door swings open, and the devil is going to come in. Everybody loves you and you can have anything you want. Not many people can handle that."

So here we have this subconscious stream of lyrics pertaining to God flowing out of Chris, and it is easy to see how Christ was working in his life at that time. When you look at the lyrics in "Sin City," such as "On the thirty-first floor a gold-plated door won't keep out the Lord's burning rain," you can see Chris recognizing that there were places he should no longer be going. I am not sure what was behind that gold-plated door, but I know it was not a Monopoly game.

Like The Byrds, the Burritos' debut was promising, but the cracks started to show. Once again, Parsons' devil-may-care attitude and erratic behavior often fueled discord. "I loved Gram dearly. We wrote some really great songs together. But by the second year and the second album—1970's *Burrito Deluxe*—Gram began losing interest in the group. He began exploring other avenues, and his drug abuse overwhelmed him."

The Burritos after Parsons turned into a successful recording and live act, producing two well-received albums with the addition of Bernie Leadon and Rick Roberts. I did work briefly with a 1990s incarnation of the band, producing four songs and touring Europe with them. At that time two of the original members were in the band, Sneaky Pete Kleinow and Chris Ethridge, along with John Beland and Gib Guilbeau. Two decades from inception, the revolving door was swinging wildly with its membership and in a very short period of time, I probably encountered a total of eight people in the band.

Chris and the original members had created a sound that keeps echoing on through time and space. I was completely surprised by the giant following they had in Europe. The crowds would stand during their concerts and mouth the words to some of their songs I had never heard before. The thing that really blew me away was one day in Barcelona, Sneaky Pete (I called him "the Pete that sneaked") and I were walking down a narrow street looking for a mom-and-pop restaurant with some real authentic Catalonian food. The street was crowded and bustling, and a guy stopped us on the sidewalk and excitedly said to Pete, "You're Sneaky Pete Kleinow, aren't you?"

Sensing the Burritos were sputtering, Chris received a phone call from Stephen Stills that set him on a new musical journey. Along with drummer Dallas Taylor, they formed the eclectic band Manassas and produced two albums—*Manassas* (1972) and *Down the Road* (1973). The band toured around the world, and Chris and Stills wrote some memorable tunes together, fusing elements of American contemporary music with rock, country, bluegrass, salsa, and the blues.

A Byrds reunion with the five original members and the breakup of Manassas coincided with the 1973 deaths of close friends Clarence White (Kentucky Colonels and The Byrds) and Gram Parsons. These fateful events took a toll on Chris. Still, he forged ahead with John David Souther and Richie Furay to form the band Souther-Hillman-Furay, signing with Asylum Records and releasing two albums in 1974 and 1975. The band, Chris says, had great musicians and songs but never fused together in a believable form.

The most significant event to come out of this time was when band mate Al Perkins led Chris to Jesus. "Al brought a lot of people to the Lord, and he's an incredibly beautiful soul. I accepted Jesus in a moment of real doubt and fear: 'Dear God in heaven, please let me survive this. I will follow the tenants for the rest of my life.' And then of course, when things got level, I walked away from it. But in reality, I simply wasn't ready. I wasn't ready to make that commitment. I turned my back on Jesus, but He didn't turn his back on me."

Chris may feel like he walked away from the Lord but as time has proven out in his life, he just stepped outside for a minute. I love using the phrase "we are everyman," because what Chris just described is so common to many of us guys. We are like little boys most of our lives, and it is typical for us to want to run to Daddy when we get in trouble. He takes care of our pain, and then in time we start feeling rambunctious again and away we go. So, in the midst of our fears and remorse about getting caught up in our mistakes, or more accurately, when life catches up with us, we evolve into an adult version of this child. We crawl into a form of those arms by repenting and embracing the Father, Son, and Holy Spirit. We get in trouble with our lives, and then when someone presents an alternate situation, we jump into the waiting arms of the first big Daddy that comes along who will wipe away our tears and give us a fresh start.

So in a way we were making deals with God just to get us through, but because we were often dealing from desperation, our sincerity level was not always up to par. This sounds a little convoluted, but the messier it gets in trying to describe all these shades and aspects, it begins to get real simple. I can see Jesus sitting on a hill watching us, smiling lovingly, scratching His head in amazement as we make simple things so complicated. For instance, He keeps sending guys like Al Perkins into situations, and people keep coming to the Lord every time they get around him. If Chris walked away, Jesus wasn't worried, because He knew they were going to meet up again. He would reside within His true nature: patient, loving, and all knowing. He would stay the course because there would be a perfect time for Chris to welcome Him into his heart.

Chris was baptized in 1980 after what he calls his true conversion. "I was by myself and I just heard *The Voice*. I just broke down into tears. I don't know what triggered it, but something did something to me, and that was it. And I accepted Him, truly accepted Him this time. Accepting Christ in your life is very hard, and people will do everything they can to get away from you. They don't warm up to that at all. It scares the unenlightened. When you accept Jesus, your problems aren't over—they're tripled because you will be challenged by the devil. New converts to Christianity definitely have a heavy battle in front of them."

When we are new Christians, we have just had a world of sin removed from our being, and there are scars and sensitive spots that need to be handled tenderly until they are restored. A lot of healing needs to take place before we are ready to receive all the complicated stuff that well-meaning, misguided souls tend to pile on to the sore spots. We are still very susceptible to guilt trips and the condemnation that the world thrives on in its survival pattern of deceit and manipulation. So it is frustrating and confusing when some very insensitive brothers and sisters start piling on their personal demons in the form of judgmental advice.

Chris converted to the Greek Orthodox Christian faith in 1996. "My wife was already there, but it took me many more years into my marriage to where I made the decision and felt the calling. Suddenly, I got this strong feeling in my heart to go and find out what Orthodoxy was all about. I went to the priest at that time at our parish, St. Barbara's Greek Orthodox Church, and I said, 'I want to join the church.' I love the tradition. I love that it was the very first apostolic church. The apostles established the five patriarchates in Jerusalem, Antioch, Constantinople, Alexandria, and Rome, and carried on Christ's ministry. After three or four visits with this priest, I was Chrismated into the Orthodox Christian faith. I've never looked back. Everyday I learn something new about the faith. I've never, ever felt so fulfilled, yet I know nothing. It is my personal belief that as far as Christian denominations are concerned, if we all believe in the Holy Trinity of the Father, Son, and Holy Spirit, we're on the same ball team."

The untimely passing of Chris's father when Chris was a young man had left an empty place in his heart … and bewilderment. The father-son relationship was a core element in his life, but what happened next is where God brought great peace into his life. Like a skilled surgeon, He removed all confusion and replaced it by filling Chris's heart with love, forgiveness, and a memory of beautiful moments with his dad. God's not a halfway, half-good, half-in and half-out God. He is the great I AM and the one and all. That's what makes it so easy when He simply asks for our all in return.

The Lord was also there to help Chris with the grieving process when his mother died. "About two years before my mother passed, she wrote me this incredible card. It basically said, 'You have turned into this incredible man. I always knew you would and now you have. I can't tell you how proud I am of you.' One of *those* kinds of cards. She saw the change in me."

Chris has been happily married for more than three decades, and in addition to being active in his community and church (he's a member of the choir and sings the Byzantine Liturgy), professionally he remains busy and in demand, having recorded seven albums since 1995. In addition to being a member of the Rock and Roll Hall of Fame, he is a strong supporter of artists' recording rights and mentors many aspiring musicians. He has lectured at the Library of Congress in Washington DC and at UCLA, Point Loma Nazarene University, and the Grammy and Getty Museum in Los Angeles.

Chris also still writes, records, and tours. All the while he still remains hungry for music and spirituality and is not done fighting the good fight. "You have to stand firm and tough as Paul says in the Epistles. Life and spirituality are not something to be approached in a superficial way. I mean, I'm very leery of anybody who is always happy going, 'Praise the Lord!' Something's not connecting with me on that. We're human beings. We are all climbing out of something all the time. I don't care who you are; it's a constant struggle. I asked this of my wife the other day, 'How does a parent deal with the loss of a child without a Judeo-Christian foundation? How do they do that?' I don't understand. I don't know how

I could ever deal with something as heinous as that, God forbid, without having God in our lives. Somehow, someway we are just genetically predisposed to have God in our lives. I think we are.

"I love my family and I love my life. I wouldn't trade anything I have right now. I don't want anything. I have everything I need. I'm still going to try and do better. I know that God had a plan for me."

It may sound pompous, but it is so comforting to know that we have all the answers. They are not in our head, not in our songs, our words, or stories, but in a Book and in our hearts. It is a humbling thing to learn how beautifully insignificant we are compared to His wondrous glory. It is also relaxing to no longer be under the extreme pressure of running our world while telling Him how He should be going about taking care of the rest of it in order to suit our needs.

Turn, turn, turn! It's about a season and our purpose under heaven.

JOHN ELEFANTE

Kansas

John Elefante was the lead singer of the multiplatinum-selling Kansas from 1981 to 1985 and wrote "Play the Game Tonight" and "Fight Fire With Fire," two of their highest charting singles. After leaving Kansas, he became one of the most successful Christian producers of all time and has collaborated or performed on more than one hundred records.

FIVE

CHASING SHADOWS

JOHN ELEFANTE | Kansas

John Elefante's soulful brown eyes, Italian American, dark, smoldering good looks, and inviting smile make him eminently likeable. Despite all that, when I stepped into his stately Nashville home and studio, I found it hard not to be intimidated by his accomplishments as a contemporary singer, songwriter, multi-instrumentalist, and producer. As a singer he recorded with artists ranging from Pat Boone to Bono. He was Kansas's front man for four years, his golden tenor one of the best in the business. He's also produced approximately one hundred albums and collected multiple Grammy Awards. I wasn't sure what to expect during our three-hour meeting, but my uneasiness soon gave way to a relaxed openness. I was impressed not only with his musical background and business acumen, but with the man's spirit, his outlook on business and life, his faith, and his genuine modesty.

Such humility is only vested on a chosen few. Others have to go through repeated trials of the soul to glean an understanding of who God is. John's humility comes from a lifetime learning how he fits in with that understanding. He was born March 18, 1958, into a very loving, but not overtly religious, working-class Italian family in suburban Levittown, New York.

Levittown later became synonymous with the late baby-boom era, with mass-produced, budget-friendly, cookie-cutter tract housing, each with open floor plans, informal family rooms, and the same backyards. It was perfect for a late '50s nuclear family like John's, where work was factory consistent and the pay modest.

His upbringing reflected baby-boomer suburbia and all its working-class trappings. Dad Donato, or Danny, as he was known, worked on the assembly line at the aircraft factory, got off work, and had some beers and played cards with his friends to unwind. Mom Nora stayed home playing music all day and raising the kids. John didn't find his entertainment on the streets of New York; he found it at home banging on homemade drums made out of cardboard boxes, while his older brother, Dino, belted out classic riffs on his wooden guitar with rubber bands for strings.

"Mom and Dad always had a stack of records on the turntable. One would finish and the next one would drop. Once that stack was done, she would put on a whole new pile. There was always some Sinatra or bossa nova music playing around my house," recalled John.

Music was in the Elefante blood. Whatever musical influences John took from his family, tenacity helped him hang tight to it. He taught himself everything he knows, playing music by ear as he learned to play each new instrument.

It wasn't until the family moved out to California that the Elefante brothers got their first real instruments, although John has no idea how they managed to afford it. "My dad bought me a set of drums, and Dino was already serious about the guitar, and we started playing together."

Life was good. Dad was always around when needed, and Nora raised John, Dino, and Danny, or "Skip" as he was called, with the fierceness of a lioness guarding her cubs. It was the height of the Vietnam War, and those who lived through it understood that it was more than a conflict. The war inflamed the nation, and John's family was not immune. As America searched for a synthesis between war and peace, so did Family Elefante.

California was sprawling and laid back, with kids racing their Mustangs down the drag strip—a world away from New York's suburban cocoon. It was new and exciting, but fitting in wasn't easy. Skip soon joined the hippie movement and all that went with it: the drugs, demonstrations, and hanging out in San Francisco's notorious Haight-Ashbury neighborhood.

While Skip burned "rancid incense" and listened to Hendrix, Strawberry Alarm Clock, and the psychedelic flavor of the month in the garage, John tuned in, but never turned on. He took what he liked from the music, but Skip's lifestyle never tempted him to do drugs.

His mother encouraged church, wanting her children to be fed with God's word—what John calls the "real fine parts about being Christian"—but it felt too imposing and complicated, and John needed to proceed at his own pace. "Catholicism was never pushed on me because my dad had a bad experience. I did learn about spiritual matters, but I never heard about being born again."

Spinning records with the family quickly evolved into the real deal. It began with a fourth-grade talent show at Patrick Henry Elementary School. "I forget the name of the song, but it was an instrumental. It was a packed auditorium and right before we were to go on, Dino's amp blew out. We're thinking, 'What are we going to do?' Then Dino said, 'You're going to play a drum solo, bro.'"

"No way!"

Dino was insistent.

"Look, your drums are set up, we're up next, but we can't go up without the amp—so you go out there and do a drum solo, man!"

The curtains opened.

John recalled: "I did a smokin' five-minute Buddy Rich–type solo, and I not only got a standing ovation but won the contest."

Anyone who has entered the "business" knows what happened to John that day: he got a taste. Okay, it wasn't Madison Square Garden or Carnegie Hall, but it felt like the LA Forum to John. There is something potion-like about hearing that first applause, the first recognition, and the first time you move out of the garage onto a stage with real live people looking up at you. It's mesmerizing, and like drugs, you want more and you want it in stronger and larger amounts—it swallows up your senses in one fell swoop. Keeping with the drug analogy, it only takes one time and you are hooked forever. There is a deeper thing that happens at that moment, and it is only for those who have true talent. The applause and accolades are one thing, but there is a knowing for the elect that they have discovered their "place to be" in the limited universe they have been poured into. John felt a real sense of belonging when he hit that sweet spot of tasting the meal he wanted to serve up for the rest of his life.

The first paying gigs popped up when John was around twelve or thirteen years old. John and Dino enlisted their two cousins Jon and BaBa Elefante and formed The Brotherhood, their first official band. It was Top 40 all the way. "My cousin, Jon, was a fanatic about practice. We'd drive to Ontario three or four days a week, an hour from Long Beach, and my parents would visit relatives. They'd shoot the breeze in the house while we grinded it out in the garage, practicing, and practicing, and practicing. Then after practice, we'd work for hours on our harmonies. We'd go places without instruments, start singing Beach Boys songs, and blow people's minds. Of course it didn't hurt that the girls dug it too."

This is definitely one of those "you had to be there" eras that John is talking about. Sun tans, bleached hair, surfer girls, woodies, surf racks, and special days when "the word" would vibrate through school, almost as a spiritual calling among the special few, that "surf's up" at such-and-such beach. As with all special times and places, a new music was created to identify its core heartbeat. If you were in Southern California in the early '60s, you not only listened to this music, you breathed it, smelled it, and rubbed it on your chest. Dick Dale made you feel adventure, The Beach Boys hit your every nerve with unheard harmonies and adventurous suggestions, while The Rip Chords, The Bel-Airs, The Challengers,

The Chantays, The Surfaris, Jan & Dean, and other members of surf music nirvana grabbed you and dragged you away to something that had waves and bikinis in its makeup.

The Brotherhood's sound drifted all the way to the Capitol Records building in 1972. Capitol was about to sign the band to a singles deal for their cover version of The Beach Boys' "Darlin'." The record didn't come out as well as hoped, and the label lost interest. Despite the setback, The Brotherhood were "great copycats" and played all the radio hits from the era, according to John. They netted lots of Southern California gigs in the early '70s and were booked out two years in advance, including a dream gig at Orange County's Disneyland. "There was a stage that came up out of the ground in Tomorrowland and, by hook or crook, I was going to get on that stage, man. It was the coolest thing in the world. I wasn't thinking in terms of playing the LA Forum—performing on that Disneyland stage was my big vision.

"George Morales, a thirteen-year-old child prodigy singing sensation from Long Beach, was our lead singer, but he was climbing the show biz ladder on his own. George had a big-time manager, and when he sang on *The Lawrence Welk Show*, we knew he was a goner. One night his manager pulled him out of The Brotherhood just before a gig in Ontario, California."

John learned two important lessons that night. Keep your promises in business was the first. They pulled off the gig without George because John knew the material note for note and sang in public for the first time. The second lesson was confidence. That night he discovered that "Wow, man, I *can* sing!" The crowd loved his Jackson 5 high tenor—a lot. He had been hooked at the grade-school performance, and now he had been skewered. There would be no turning back for John Elefante.

With George gone and John on lead vocals, it was time to find a hot new drummer. The group lucked out and found Jim Ubernosky, an incredible drummer-singer. "Jim's voice reminded me of Terry Kath from Chicago. I was more like Peter Cetera. So, for half the set he'd come out and sing Eagles type stuff because that was lower range. Then I'd sing the higher stuff, Peter Cetera, Michael Jackson stuff. Jim would play drums 50 percent of the time, sing 50 percent of the time, and then we'd trade off. We covered all the bases by having two completely different types of singers."

Talent, versatility, and a supportive mother who hauled the band from gig to gig made The Brotherhood very popular around Southern California. "We started doing high school proms, weddings, bar mitzvahs, and Mormon stake dances, which catered to kids ages fourteen to eighteen. These gatherings were open dances for the entire community, not just LDS members. The individual stake dances were numbered to show their location … Stake 110 was in Newport Beach, and Van Nuys was Stake 95. The Newport Beach Stake was a good gig for us because they hired us constantly and had the best-looking girls."

Life was chugging along for John until what he calls a "supernatural experience" took place at age fourteen. "I was in the eighth or ninth grade, and my school was about a mile from our house. I walked home every day with a buddy who lived on my block, but on this particular day he was sick. I walked across Woodruff Avenue, a busy four-lane thoroughfare that ran through Long Beach. Being the knucklehead I was, I didn't use the designated crossing area and ran across the street. I noticed when I got halfway across that a big city bus was coming directly at me. I was a dead man, because this bus had to be going at least fifty miles per hour. I thought I could outrun the bus, but I looked over and it was twenty feet away from me, and my heart was going about three hundred beats a minute. The bus, somehow, went from being right in front of me to being behind me and I thought, *how did that just happen?* It was impossible by the laws of physics that bus didn't hit me. I didn't believe in anything supernatural at that time, so I found ways to justify what happened. I thought about that incident from time to time—the Holy Spirit never let me forget."

It is so fascinating how growing closer to the Lord works in incidences like John just described. At the time it is basically confusing, something that lodges in your mind and fiddles with your thinking. Because of your chronological immaturity or your decided distance from God's Word it can also be just a matter of pondering, a delayed reaction of sorts until eventually it simply becomes something that fades away … a "hmmm" and shrug of the shoulders kind of thing. When pressing into God's promises and His ways, the past starts popping up years later and demands another review. We begin seeing His hand on our shoulders, His eye on our moves, and the hedge of protection that He places around us. I can look back on God's continuous presence in my life and regardless of what my relationship was with Him or how bad I was, I can see how He loved me so much that He never left my side. It became more apparent over time that worthiness or being deserving of His grace and love are not prerequisites in how He deals with us.

But John was moving so fast at a young age, he didn't have much time to ponder. The Brotherhood broke up in the mid-70s, but John was so convinced that music was his life that he dropped out of high school a few weeks into his senior year. His parents converted the garage into an eight-track recording studio after John's mother received a $10,000 inheritance. It was here he and Dino learned the art of recording, all self-taught. It was a whole new world with endless possibilities. "I'd sit in that studio all night and not go to bed until nine o'clock in the morning. I'd sleep all day, then get up and do the same thing the next night. That's where I learned my craft."

But it was also during this time that John began to harvest the seeds of faith that his mom had planted when he was a kid, constantly reminding him that his grandmother was praying daily for him and his brothers. Those loving kernels would sprout and grow in unexpected ways. In John's case, it was a childhood friend who helped an abundant crop finally spring forth. "When I was about eighteen, I had a friend Mark Ambrose, who I had known since elementary school, come back into my life. Mark was noticeably different and told me about Jesus Christ.

He took me to the Calvary Chapel in Costa Mesa, where the Jesus Movement started. There were altar calls at the end of every service and I wanted to go up, but I never did it. I was either embarrassed or scared or whatever. Mark was going about this at a good pace, not forcing anything on me, but he kept asking me *the* question. *If you died tomorrow, do you think you would go to heaven?*

That is the million-dollar question. It is also the millions-of-years question. I am not a gambler, but the odds in this equation are hard to ignore. If anyone said to me that I have to pick between Plan A or B and explained the risk factors, to me the right choice is a no-brainer. Check it out. Plan A: assume there is no God and no heaven or hell. If you are right when you die, you just die and game over—no problem. Plan B: assume there is a God and there is a heaven and a hell and you choose to believe in God and His Word. If you're right, then you go to heaven when you die and do not spend eternity in a real bad place. Back to Plan A—if you are wrong, when you die you go straight to hell and suffer for eternity. If you are wrong in Plan B by deciding to go with Jesus and then you die, that's it—no problem. The point is, who in their right mind would make a choice where, if they guess wrong, they would have a 50/50 chance of suffering forever? So I like Plan B, the one where if I am wrong there is no disastrous outcome but because I'm right, I will have eternal life filled with good things and wonderful people. Thank you, Jesus!

John says he finally accepted Christ in his home studio with Mark, but had yet to make a public declaration of faith. He finally answered an altar call at Calvary Chapel, making it official, but becoming a Christian wasn't easy nor did it bring him much peace at the time. Things were going exceedingly well for John, and Atlantic Records was showing interest in a solo deal. A long-held dream was about to become reality, but John felt convicted and thought there was no way to navigate the rock and roll lifestyle with his newfound faith. "I began to think I had to get out of music; how could I serve God playing nightclubs? I can't be a Christian and play music. That's probably sinful, isn't it? I was totally confused, wondering what God was doing. I remember praying, 'Lord, is there a way I can play music and still serve you at the same time?' I asked my friends to pray for me. I was attending a Bible study, and they were praying for me. I was close to signing with Atlantic, and I was freaking out. What do I do? Do I call the guy and tell him to forget the whole deal? It was total chaos."

Sometimes God pulls us closer by letting us swim in shark-infested waters for a while, before He reels us back in with a simple word or prophesy. In John's case, he received the word through Mable John, an elderly black woman who was a pioneer on Motown's Tamla label and later had success with Stax Records. "Mable used to come to our home studio to record gospel, and she was someone I really adored. She told me, 'Honey, you can play for the Lord. Play your music loud and proud. Play it the way you play it, but use it for Him.' Great, but I knew I couldn't write songs about chicks anymore. That sort of thing wasn't going to fly."

As believers, we all have Mables in our lives. They are part-time everyday people and full-time angels. God scatters them about so when we are too choked up in our own small world and need a friend or a word from Him, He sends needed answers through clearer vessels. This is an example of a "perk" we receive when we give our lives over to Him. It is something He plants deep inside so we will know when He has sent a message and a messenger.

John went back into his home studio and applied Mable's down-home wisdom. He quit playing clubs and focused exclusively on writing with his brother Dino and recording demos in the garage. It was late 1980, the year that began the slow metamorphosis of change, and that change started in Kansas. Steve Walsh, the lead singer for the group Kansas, left the band, and they were looking for a replacement. Kansas had become a staple of '70s FM radio with songs like "Carry On Wayward Son," "Point of Know Return," and "Dust in the Wind." Their unique sound, heavy lyrics, and iconic album covers branded them a thinking man's rock band with a progressive twist.

When I think of the state of Kansas, I think of broad sweeping topography—expanses open to the senses that allow perception of the many subtle nuances within the terrain. I think of this band's music in much the same way. My mind wanders when I listen to their songs—not away to other places, but I find myself exploring the many intricacies in their playing, writing, arrangements, and production. It's as if in my mind Kansas (the state) becomes a giant auditorium for Kansas the music. Ask any producer what he strives for when taking on an artist or group, and one of the key goals is to create a fresh, unique sound. With Kansas you get sonic intimacy immersed in vastness.

"One day, as I was coming out of my studio, guitar player Chuck King, who was in a band with my friend Mark Ambrose, drove up all excited. 'John, have you heard, man?' 'No, heard what?' 'Steve Walsh left Kansas and they're looking for a replacement.' 'Okay...' Chuck looks at me and goes, 'You're the guy, man. You got that high tenor voice, you've been performing Kansas stuff for years, I mean, you're a perfect fit!' I thought, *never in a million years, man.* But that night I started thinking about it. I talked to my brother and mom, and they said, 'Go for it. What do you have to lose? Go for it!'"

John's interest was piqued. How could it not be? By 1980, Kansas was one of the top grossing acts in the world and creatively at the top of their game.

With Kansas, John wouldn't have to worry about compromising his integrity as a Christian. Kansas' guitarist, keyboard player, and primary songwriter, Kerry Livgren, had a born-again experience in July 1979. Their bass player, Dave Hope, was also a believer. Livgren's progressively Christian lyrics had driven lead singer Steve Walsh out of the band, which created an opening for John.

He was the perfect replacement for Walsh. While John cut his teeth on The Jackson 5 and The Beach Boys, his musical tastes progressed to Genesis, Kansas, Boston, Foreigner, and Styx. With so much encouragement from family and friends, it made sense to go for it, so he called his attorney, Jay Cooper, who was shopping his demo. He told Jay he needed to get it to the powers-that-be in the Kansas camp.

"Piece of cake," Jay said. "Chuck Hurwitz, in the next office, is Kansas' attorney."

"What? Really?"

"I'll give it to him today."

It was that quick. John received a call from Kansas Manager Bud Carr a week later. He said he wanted to meet John in person, and could he come up to the house? "I went and we spent probably an hour and a half, two hours, talking. I was very nervous—this was a big-time manager and I was a small-time kid."

According to John, the meeting went well, and Carr passed the demo to the musicians in Kansas. It was a long shot. There were approximately three hundred people applying for the gig, but he had nothing to lose, right? About a week later over Christmas break, Kerry Livgren, who was the main musical force in Kansas, called John at home. "I thought Dino was playing a trick on me, but it *was* Kerry Livgren. He said, 'I dig your stuff, man. I dig your voice, really dig it, man. I hope we get to play together.' It was unreal."

Carr called shortly thereafter saying he wanted John to fly to Atlanta after the first of the year. He was told they hadn't finished their album, *Vinyl Confessions*, and wanted to hear how his voice sounded on the record. When they discovered that Chateau Studios in Los Angeles, where they were recording, was only forty-five minutes from John's house, they moved up the meeting so John could join them there instead. "Dino and I got in the car and drove to Chateau Studios. We're sitting in the lobby listening to some other guy auditioning, and I could tell he wasn't going to get the gig. I'm up next. Bud comes out, shakes my hand, then shakes Dino's hand."

John got behind the microphone, skittish as a kitten, sitting in front of big-time manager Bud Carr and legendary English producer/engineer Ken Scott, whose work with The Beatles, The Rolling Stones, Elton John, and David Bowie was legendary. "I couldn't control my voice because I was so anxious and nervous. I'm singing 'Windows' and probably sang it three or four times. Maybe by the fourth time I sounded okay because I was starting to get over the jitters. But when I sounded nervous, Ken would stop after a verse and say, 'John, let's try it again. I know you're nervous but there's nothing to be nervous about, so just give me your best shot, and we'll try it again.' A total gentleman. I sang the song one more time and they said, 'Alright, that's good. Come on in, man.' I came in and they thanked me for coming out. On a scale of one to ten, I probably pulled off a five and a half or a six.

"It was a godsend that Dino was there, because he's a smart guy. He read their body language the entire time, especially the manager, and managers like to play their cards close to their chest. I thanked them for giving me a shot, thinking it would be the last time I'd ever see those guys. Dino drove home because I was too nervous to drive. I told him, 'You take the wheel, man. I need to just come down.' I never should have drank that coffee before I sang; it hyped me up even more."

On the drive home, John berated his performance. "I said to Dino, 'I sucked. I was horrible! I'll never hear from those guys again.' Dino looks at me and says, 'You got the gig.' I said, 'What? You're crazy! Are you smoking something?' He assured me, 'You got the gig. Start packing your bags.'"

John recalls how nonchalant his brother was, very matter of fact, insistent he had landed the gig.

"What do you mean? I stunk."

"Your voice fit that music like a glove. It was perfect. Yeah, you were quivery and a little out of tune in spots, but the tone of your voice and your range is perfect for that band, and they all knew it. At one point, they turned around to each other and smiled. I'm telling ya, you've got the gig."

A few weeks passed while John remained in limbo. Suddenly he was summoned to Atlanta, where the band was based, to rehearse and so they could hear his and Dino's new songs: "Right Away," "Chasing Shadows," and "Face It." They were impressed with the quality of his songwriting and vocal range. Later he got the call at his hotel from drummer Phil Ehart notifying him that he was officially a member of Kansas.

In late 1981, John joined the band in Los Angeles to complete the recording of *Vinyl Confessions*, Kansas' eighth studio album. All three of John and Dino's songs, plus one John cowrote with Kerry Livgren, called "Play On," made the album. They sounded good. Really good. From there it was all a blur.

John found himself busier than ever, learning his cues, perfecting the man they needed on stage. He was a workaholic, learning every angle of the business, hitting every note of every song, and giving his best as John Elefante, front man for Kansas. As far as he was concerned, he was not replacing Steve Walsh, but filling his shoes. But success began to affect John. Like many of John's contemporaries, he got cocky. Never in his wildest dreams did he think he'd have a Top 5 single. "My first single with Kansas, 'Play the Game Tonight,' reached number four, charting higher than 'Carry On Wayward Son.' Months before, I was this snot-nosed kid from Long Beach, California, who was begging and kicking the door down trying to get a record deal. Now I'm with Kansas, watching one climb the charts rapidly, *and* … I'm complaining because it didn't make number one. Having a hit single is cool, but in the world of rock stars, number one is the brass ring. That's how fast people change. That's how fast I changed."

"Fight Fire With Fire," which John cowrote with Dino, was the group's fastest and highest charting single, peaking at number three on *Billboard*'s Mainstream Rock chart in the summer of 1983. The song, and its memorable video, placed Kansas firmly back on top. There were also Grammy Awards, riding around in Learjets, playing outdoor mega-shows, and rubbing elbows with the rich and famous. The bands John admired—REO Speedwagon, Foreigner, Heart, Starship, The Outlaws, Molly Hatchet—were now colleagues as well as targets. He'd shoot the breeze with fellow musicians before the show and then try his hardest to blow them off the stage. "These were big-time bands and they were good, but I wanted to show them what a *great* band Kansas was. I really felt like a rock star at those times, and I'll be frank; there were times when I abused my power with people. I won't say I was backslidden, but it was like, 'Hey God, I'm busy right now, be with You in a second.'"

As success enveloped John, God took a backseat. This is an interesting phenomenon but a very common one when a person is thrown into his situation. It didn't take long for an innocent young man to get light headed and dark minded once he became immersed in the land of rock and roll superstardom. As I've said before, home and hearth tend to get farther away as the band bus travels on to bigger and bigger crowds and intoxicating backstage adulation. A big difference in how this plays out often has to do with the seeds planted growing up before this new reality sets in. For some odd reason, it is sometimes easy for a naïve young person to turn his or her back on God, knowing that His love is constant and never changing. The thought process in simple terms is, "I'll set Him aside for a while because I know He will be there when I decide to meander back in my own sweet time." Yes, He is waiting, and yes, He will welcome us home and love on us. Yes, He will forgive us and restore us to Him and make us brand new. And yes, we do suffer the consequences of our actions and decisions. Kansas was very big and John had become a bigger star than he had ever dreamed, but there were much bigger things going on in John's life. He had been ignoring God, and God waited as long as He could. But eventually He had to show John who the real Rock star was!

God could feel His child was drifting away, so He gave John a big wake-up call one night on the road. "We'd just finished one of those megashows with multiple acts on the bill. We're outside this stadium in Hershey, Pennsylvania, probably fifty thousand people or better, and we just killed it that night. Despite the fact we were playing in front of huge crowds, we were not staying in five-star hotels. Our road manager put us in roach motels. This night's place was a dump. So I walk into the room, shut the door, and I'm stripped down to my underwear. I walk past the dresser with a big mirror and I stop to look at myself. Inside I said, 'Wait a minute. This is quite a contrast here. Back there you walk on water in front of fifty thousand people, but you're still the same kid from Long Beach. What's really changed?' It hit me that I was the same exact person even though when I walked out of that hotel room door, I had to transform into somebody else. That hit me hard. It was God's way of humbling me, to show me I was really nothing. I was just a person He chose to take and put in a situation, a situation according to the world's standard was big time and important. But as I stood looking at myself in front of that mirror, man, that facade just crumbled."

Isn't it amazing how much clearer we can see things when we look through the right end of a telescope and find what we are focusing on becomes recognizable for what it really is? When we see ourselves through God's eyes, there are those moments when we have to look away, especially when we see what we have become. God may seem to be mean when He slaps this revelation on us, but the only thing mean about this is that He means well. He wants to bring us alongside His purpose so we can check out what is happening from His viewpoint of the way our walk with Him should be.

Not only did God work on John, but He had already done a good job on two of the other band members. Kerry Livgren and bassist Dave Hope had accepted Christ about a year before John's arrival. Kerry later told John their prayers were answered when John told them he was a Christian. According to John, this was not in the management's playbook. "Kerry's conversion turned things upside down. Kerry went to the management and said, 'Look, my heart has changed and I want to write about different things.' Everybody was freaking out, thinking this was it for Kansas, because Kansas was really a corporation, not just a band. When management found out I was also a believer, they were scared about what I might say in interviews. I was urged to talk about what it was like being the new singer, chosen from among three hundred people who auditioned for the band. That was the angle; they did not want me to discuss my faith."

Management didn't need to worry about John's faith splitting the band in two. That would take care of itself over time, and the enemy who eventually emerged totally blindsided everyone. "After Kerry and Dave got saved, Kansas built a Christian following. These followers would now claim Kerry, Dave, and myself as their own. But because I was from New York and had a little more street sense than the others, I could see through a lot of their motivations. They wanted into our inner circle and would use what I called the 'Hey brother' tactic. 'Hey brother, God told me we need to do this.' 'Hey brother, God told me that maybe I should manage you because you're starting this Christian career.' 'Hey brother, can we pray about this because I'm really concerned about you?' I'm all for prayer and I'm all about prayer, but these prayer sessions usually took place in the hotel room after the gigs. I went to a few, and some of it just sickened me because I saw through what was going on. I mean, all sorts of hangers-on and people with very weird motives."

What John is describing here is very real and can tear your heart out, especially when you want to be obedient to God's calling and follow Him in a pleasing way. Your relationship with Him, especially in the beginning, is so pure and personal that, like sweet spring water, you don't want it muddied up, so you can continue to drink from the deep of its precious well. Jesus warns us about those who use faith as a tool to further their own agenda and desires. How do you say to someone you don't want to pray with them? But what if you sense they have a suspicious objective and are falsely using religion as a gateway into your life, time, and pocketbook? I call them spiritual energy sappers. They set you up in such a way that if you don't respond as a "good Christian" should, then they criticize and debase you. Here's how this plays out. Being on the road for extended periods of time, dealing with the stress of travel and the psychological enormity of being in a successful group, is completely exhausting. You become very vulnerable and susceptible to every kind of satanic attack and sidewinder scheme. Your defenses are down, and your mind has become a study in phase shifting. You need time off to empty out, to regroup on an almost daily basis, and to keep in touch with the important people and situations in your life. It is a dilemma because as a Christian you never want to turn your back on a godly need or turn away anyone who looks to you as a brother in Christ. It is a tightrope—it takes a long stretch of road experience and time in the Word to know how to walk that line.

John recorded two albums with Livgren and Hope in the group—1982's *Vinyl Confessions* and 1983's *Drastic Measures*, as well as "Perfect Lover," the lead single for 1984's *The Best of Kansas*. However, tension was growing in the band as Livgren and Hope were starting to drift, focusing their efforts on forming AD, a Christian rock band. John said Livgren's new faith and the never-ending pressure of having to write hits pushed him right out the door. "It was becoming a singles world because of MTV and, despite the fact that Kansas had hits, the label wanted us to focus more on churning out Top 40 material. The record business changed and MTV introduced bands in a whole different way, which I thought was cool at first, but I liked the faceless era better. You know, when you used to see an album cover, the pictures on the back, and wonder what these people would be like? The only way to see them was in concert. The mystique was humongous, and a lot of that was lost with music videos. There was a lot of pressure on record companies and management for hits. For some bands, like Styx and Foreigner, it wasn't a problem. They wrote songs that were hits, and that sustained them. But for Kansas, it was a big change."

John says today he wishes Livgren would have taken a sabbatical to do his AD side project and remained in Kansas as a full-time member. "The AD thing was sort of a musical relief for Kerry and although I thought it was great, it didn't warrant him leaving the band. There were so many people tugging at him to leave, and I think it was a mistake. I believe it was mistake that Dave Hope left too. They left a platform they never regained. It was a tremendous platform for Christianity and if it were up to me, I would have kept Kansas going with Kerry and Dave.

"There was a lot of ear tickling and posturing going on. I watched it happen and didn't like it. I was bummed because the major reason I enjoyed being in Kansas was because of Kerry and what he brought to the band. Kerry and Dave started taking a lesser role on *Drastic Measures*, and I was taking a bigger role. I didn't care about more John Elefante on that record. I wanted more Kerry Livgren and to cowrite with him because he's so talented and had his finger on the signature songwriting style of Kansas. I began thinking, *this isn't fun anymore, it's getting strange and turning into a thing that's not really Kansas*."

John stuck around, but the low moment came when he had to face which path he would continue on. John calls it his "Peter moment," and it brought him to his knees.

"We did a USO tour in the Philippines with a couple of acts … the Doobie Brothers, Cheap Trick, Pablo Cruz, and a member of AC/DC. It was so much fun playing for the military. Those guys ate it up."

One night on that tour, John was walking toward his guest quarters at Clark Air Base in Luzon, Philippines, arm in arm with a nice-looking lady. As he was jiggling the key of his hotel room door, Rick Nielsen, the zany and talented guitarist from Cheap Trick, squinted at John from down the hall, looking at him sideways. "Hey aren't you one of them born-again guys, man? Isn't Kansas a Christian band now?" he asked with a suspicious tone.

"Uh, uh, uh … I gotta go."

The rhetorical question hit John square between the eyes, making him realize that the path he was taking wasn't the path he wanted after all. It left him both flustered and troubled. "Rick Nielsen was a very smart guy, and he caught what was going on. And I gotta tell you, it was a good question … a fair question. No, it was a great question. He had every right to ask it. I don't know if Rick was intentionally trying to call me out, but I know God was. God definitely used him to call me out. Most definitely."

Yes, God created everything in the universe and everything is within His domain, under has care, and available to use as He so pleases. Because He is the Creator, He can be very creative. Using Rick Nielsen was a very creative way to bring John up short on what he was doing and to reveal the kind of witness he was projecting. It was worse than having a brother in the Lord busting him. Deep down, John knew there was a possibility that by his actions that night he could have caused someone, who might have been considering becoming a believer, to now decide they weren't interested in a belief system with that kind of duplicity. The good news is that John did have a tender heart for the Lord, and he got the message loud and clear.

John says the incident left him emotionally reeling and wracked with guilt. Around midnight, he picked up the phone and called his brother Dino in the States. "I don't know what time it was in California, but I was crying hard. Dino said, 'Calm down, calm down, what's going on?' And I told him. When we hung up the phone, I got down on my knees and I said aloud and confessed, 'Lord I'm not living right. I want to come back.' He certainly was right there with open arms."

What John just described is one of the most beautiful aspects of being a Christian. To go from being a stench in the nostrils of heaven one minute and then in a sparkling instance later to experiencing a God who loves you so much that He can't wait to make you brand new. All He needed was for His wandering child to confess his error and bring all the sensory road kill and bawdry backroom stuff to Him in repentance and obedience. Forgiveness between the Father and His child is one of the most incredible feelings in the world. It is so beautiful that if every nonbeliever in the world could experience this feeling just once, there would be no more nonbelievers in the world!

It was then that John decided to give up life in the fast lane, leave Kansas, and strike out on his own. However, Kansas' management put up a fight and threatened litigation. "I remember having lunch at the Ivy restaurant in West Hollywood, California, with Kansas' management and attorney. They were working me over, giving me a real brow beating, and threatening to sue if I left the band. I finally said, 'Guys, I'm gone. This isn't the place for me anymore.' And that was it."

That bold decision to strike out solo gave way to big changes and surprising opportunities, including an offer to join Toto, one of the biggest acts in music at the time. "I had an interesting conversation with Steve Lukather and Jeff Porcaro, but I got off that phone call thinking, *No way, uh-uh. I don't want to be known as 'The Replacement Guy.'* I had to go out and try my own wings. It was time."

It is easy to see when someone has been listening to God for a change. John went on to marry, have a family, and become a megasuccessful producer with his own Nashville-area studio called Sound Kitchen, which later became the largest recording studio in the southeastern United States.

Today he is focused on his family, his music, producing Christian rock, and growing his ministry. In fact, Petra, one of his most successful Christian bands, was the first to attain mainstream status in the 1980s. Their music has spanned over forty years. Mastedon, the band he formed with brother Dino, is considered a titan of the Christian rock genre and still performs from time to time.

John's life wasn't full of harsh realities or tragedies like some of our stories, but he sweated the small stuff. It was everyday challenges building up over a lot of dramatic years that brought him to the realization that God was bigger than anything he could do on stage or in life.

John's life has not slowed down, and neither has his faith. His spectacular album, *On My Way to the Sun*, features "This Time," a song about his adopted daughter's birth after a near abortion. The song and provocative video received national attention in 2013 and has become the new anthem for the pro-life movement. John continues to thrive musically and continually astounds me with his talent and his servitude to God. "If

I can write my own epitaph, it would probably say, 'John Elefante, used by the Lord to minister to people through his music.' Actually I would like to say *many* people. I could say that without boasting. 'John Elefante, used by the Lord to minister to many people.'"

Unaffected by success—affected by the Lord. What a great feeling to know the day he dies, that when his eyes open, he won't be in Kansas. He will see that the Holy Spirit, along with those ah-ha moments, were his tour guides to eternity.

Toto, I think we're in heaven!

RUDY SARZO

Ozzy Osbourne / Quiet Riot

Rudy Sarzo has been a professional recording artist for more than thirty years and a member of Ozzy Osbourne's band, Quiet Riot, Whitesnake, Blue Oyster Cult, Yngwie Malmsteen, and DIO. His recordings with all of these artists combined have sold more than thirty million copies worldwide, making him one of the most in-demand bassists of the rock era.

SIX

ROCK AND ROLL FANTASY

RUDY SARZO | Ozzy Osbourne / Quiet Riot

Loss. Denial. Anger. Bargaining. Depression. Acceptance. Grief is a disparaging set of emotions; its footprint carried a lifetime.

Rudy Sarzo experienced his first loss a few months shy of eleven years old, when his family sought political asylum in the United States in September 1961. Fidel Castro's communism had taken hold of Cuba's mainly Catholic population and was weaving itself into the fabric of every citizen. "When Castro came in and the revolution was over, he followed the blueprint of Marx, Lenin, and Stalin when it came to indoctrinating children," says Rudy from his Los Angeles area home. "I remember being kept after school and the teacher would ask us certain questions, very calculated questions like, 'How does your father and mother feel about "Papa Fidel"?', which is what we used to call him. Or the teacher would say, 'Now pray to God for ice cream.' Of course, we'd get none. Then they'd say, 'Now pray to Papa Fidel for ice cream.' Of course, we'd get ice cream. I was old enough to know the difference at the time, because my parents made it very clear what the reality of the situation was. But all the other kids, they bought into it."

Rudy's father, a printing technician, saw no future in Castroland, and gathered his family to leave it all behind, taking with them only a few pieces of luggage. They left the furniture, the appliances, and personal belongings in order not to raise suspicion with the Castro government. Rudy's family flew to Miami long before it was coined the "Exile Capital" or "Cuban Capital" of the United States. Once granted refugee status, the family settled in.

Industry had yet to take root, leaving coastal Miami mostly a tourist town. Many Cubans fled Castro's emerging regime, and as long as they had a passport, a visa, and someone to sponsor them, they could claim refugee status. Rudy and his family were among thousands of displaced countrymen coming into Miami by the droves. Except for occasional jobs in the tourist industry, finding work in a primarily retirement community was tough, so Rudy's father, Rodolpho, relocated everyone to New Jersey in the summer of 1963. It was culture shock followed by teenage angst. Where do many angst-ridden teens go when they feel lost? Music. But it wasn't Cuban music that attracted Rudy. It was good old American rock and roll, folk music, and yes, even country. Music became a social network and a great way to meet girls. What more could a slightly hormone-driven teenager new to town want?

Kids are resilient like that. Rudy was no exception, quickly maneuvering through the canyons of peer pressure by losing his Cuban identity; he began to assimilate into the American way of life, embracing its culture and attitudes. At thirteen, he had already mastered the art of adapting and survival in a new jungle.

Born November 18, 1950, and baptized Rodolfo Maximiliano Sarzo Lavieille Grande Ruiz Payret y Chaumont, Rodolfo's American persona became Rudy Sarzo when, on his first day of school in New Jersey, his teacher "renamed" him. Once Rudy began to answer to his new moniker, it fit—and it would be much easier to get on the back of a baseball jersey in Jersey.

"I love baseball," Rudy says. "I've always been a team player. I love teamwork, team effort. Camaraderie." Because of this attitude he eventually began to fit in.

"In the old days, we didn't have Facebook or any of the social networks, so music was our social network. It's tribal. It's just like the Internet nowadays. The tribe got bigger and bigger because you know you're part of a global tribe, rather than just a neighborhood tribe like it was when I was a kid in the '60s. You had the kids on your block. It was a way for us to hang out, play music, and have something in common, so we put a rock and roll band together."

Rudy referred to his musical gatherings as "tribal," and when you follow the synonym and definition trail for that word, the most common description revolves around the word "family." Family suggests a kinship and a bond, but instead of the bonding of blood and old traditions, many young people desire something of their own selection and creation. The pulse and heartbeat of music runs so deep in a person's soul that it is a natural leap, especially when in essence he was escaping one identity into another that had fewer obstacles. I am not analyzing this as anything remotely negative, because we all make this move in some way when we want to break free—it's the stuff that was a part of our identity that we had nothing to say about and in becoming our "own man" we felt the need to run from.

Think how wonderful it would be if all the neighborhood gangs, where young people often go to bond together in order to become something other than what their family suggests they are, would have decided to do it with music, bands, or choral groups! Instead of banging, they would be "sanging." Instead of breaking into buildings, they would be breaking out in song! Instead of doing hard-time sentences, they would be playing in 2/4 time signatures! I made my "break" when I was seventeen years old by moving to California from Idaho. I didn't want to be known as a "potato head"—I wanted to be known as being vichyssoise bred.

Rudy's musical background consisted of an uncle who was an opera singer/classical pianist and an aunt who was a lounge singer in Cuba, but something in Rudy drove him to the heavier side of rock. He got a guitar, later switching to bass, and he's never looked back.

I've met many gifted people in my three decades in the music industry, and Rudy stands out for being rock solid. As bassist for some of the most prominent rock/metal artists of their time—Ozzy Osbourne, Quiet Riot, Whitesnake, Blue Oyster Cult, DIO, and Yngwie Malmsteen—Rudy reigns prolific as a musician, author, graphic artist, and music teacher. He's come a long way from Miami, Jersey, and Cuba. He had parents who cared. He had a supportive family and admirable work ethic from the beginning. Society often judges a man by the company he keeps. Rudy was never a drinker, doper, or womanizer and has been faithful to his wife of nearly thirty years. He keeps his ego in check, is kind to fans and strangers, has a warm personality, and makes one immediately feel at ease with his engaging demeanor and invigorating smile. There's no dirt swept under his rug—just lessons in humanity, friendship, judgment, and dealing with loss. Lessons all of us at times need to be reminded of.

So what is this squeaky clean guy doing in a book about sex, drugs, rock and roll, decadent success, devastating failures, and righteous redemption? His life doesn't appear to be very interesting, does it? It sounds like he skipped the middle part the others endured, without much emotional adventure, doesn't it? Read on…

These are lessons learned while growing up in Cuba, long before Ozzy or guitar legend Randy Rhoads came into his life. They're lessons that parents try to instill in their children—handed-down values concerning family, tradition, and religion. Rudy and his family never became members of a particular church, although he does have a vague recollection of being introduced to Christianity. He does remember being raised Catholic, feeling intimidated and daunted by the life-sized statues so prevalent in Cuban Catholic households.

"When I'd visit my grandmother's house, she'd open the door and behind her would be a life-size statue of Jesus on the cross. It was overwhelming. I'm closer to God today as a Christian than I was following Catholicism with all its icons."

Rudy embraced the personal side of Christianity more than the rituals of Catholicism and the Mass. "To me it's more about having Christ inside of you, having God become a part of you rather than going into a certain building where there are statues and a daunting atmosphere where you worship surrounded by stuff."

I like following Rudy's spiritual path as it evolves. It says a couple of things to me. First, I sense that God imparted His truth into Rudy's spirit early on so that he wouldn't get sidetracked and set off onto a wrong course of action in life. God had a purpose for giving him natural talents and then moving events around in his life to where in time he would become a light shining in the darkness. Think about it—Rudy was already put off by the rituals and statues; then when family pressures to be a good, religious, Catholic lad were added into the equation, he found himself facing all the typical things that can send a young man in the opposite direction. Like many of us, rebelling is exactly what we do when we leave home and are able to spread our wings. This isn't a knock on Catholicism, because you will see others in this book who go the opposite direction for the same reasons. We are talking about Rudy right now, who in spite of his solid upbringing quietly evolved and formed a relationship with his Creator in a way uniquely fitted to his understanding.

Music created balance in Rudy's life. From the moment he watched The Beatles perform on the *The Ed Sullivan Show* to watching Elvis in *Viva Las Vegas*, he knew that rock and roll was going to change the music world in the '60s with a vengeance. With The Beatles came The Rolling Stones, The Who, The Kinks, The Yardbirds, The Animals, and so many others who channeled a brand-new energy that suddenly broke the US music scene out of its stone-cold music mold. The days of The Platters and the beachy bubble-gum pop of Frankie Avalon and Fabian were over.

Folk music from Peter, Paul, and Mary and country artists like Jimmy Dean inspired Rudy to pick up his first guitar. At first, it was acoustic guitar and singing simple stuff. But then the electric guitar charged the planet, and rock changed the tune he was going to dance to for good. Yet it wasn't enough. Rudy Sarzo wanted more.

"I listened to all types of music on the radio—Jimi Hendrix, Johnny Cash, Janis Joplin, The Beatles, Johnny Mathis, Santana, and The Ventures. I loved The Ventures. It was something about the guitar playing melody that really caught my attention. One of the first bands I joined needed a bass player. They convinced me that playing a bass was like playing a solo through the whole song. I was already playing melodies when I played along with The Ventures' records, and they said that by playing the bass with their band I could essentially be doing the same thing. So I said I'd give it a shot, and they were right. Through the years I actually got to know what the real role of the bass player is all about."

The year he switched instruments was 1967, a year after his family moved back to Miami and settled in once and for all. Rudy spent hours on his Fender Jazz Bass, playing any rock record he could get his hands on and jamming with local musicians. Rudy likened being a bassist to being the link between rhythm and melody. "Bass players listen more to everything that's going on than any other musician within the group. They have to listen to what the drummer is playing, lock in with the drums, listen to the flow, and stay tight with the rhythm guitar player. I like to make everybody aware that we absolutely must lock in with the drums. The drummer, to me, is the conductor. The most important factor is to be able to hear the singer, because that's the story. If you're not listening to the story, the dynamics of the lyrics, you're just playing a bunch of notes. We are the soundtracks behind the script that's going on. With the lyrics being the script, the music becomes the story of the song."

I know that Rudy and I would have an incredible chemistry in the studio, because it is a rare understanding he brings forth in what he just said about making music. For example, as a producer, once the musical concept for an album was agreed upon and I knew the feel I wanted for the project, it came time to put together the musicians. The first person I booked was always the drummer—he was the key to what the band would sound like when all was said and done. The very next thing on the list would be to describe to him the overall feel I was looking for and then ask him who he would like to join him on bass.

I was building my musical house on a firm foundation. If the drummer and bass player are in sync, then I could replace every other instrument or vocal that was recorded after that. Ask any producer who has tried to replace the drum track after a song is recorded, and he'll send you to the thesaurus to check out all the synonyms for the word *nightmare*. There is something special that happens between a bass player and a drummer that is unique to their craft. When they lock into a groove, you can tell they are in such a special place that World War III could come along and they wouldn't even look up until the song was over.

Rudy's understanding of the drummer's role in a band was made real to me by a great drummer, Ringo Starr. I was privileged to sit in the studio with The Beatles during the recording of the *Let It Be* album, and as I observed the interplay while they were putting down tracks, I realized the talent that made him such a great drummer *and* the perfect drummer for that band. He knew how to stay out of the way of the singer and play around the lyrics and not over them. He always honored the intent of the song. As strange as it may sound because he was in a real hard rockin' band, I still think of him as being a lyrical drummer.

That's life in a nutshell. God writes the melody and gives us the lyrics. Our hearts set the beat, our voices provide the soundtrack, and a song of life is created. Between the rhythm and the melody of that life is a bridge. Giving one's life over to God takes an unwavering faith and trust to walk the walk across that bridge.

Rudy took that first step long ago when God brought his family out of Cuba. Since then he's been living his faith journey by being the example he wants to set for others, albeit quietly. It's a journey that has taken him by surprise, but God's plan for him was better than any he could have constructed himself.

Okay, this has been pretty straight ahead so far, but there's so much more.

Rudy began building his resume as a professional musician after graduating high school. His first paying gig was in 1969, after his high school graduation. His band, Sylvester, got its first nightclub job backing up R&B singer Jeb Stewart, at the Topless Tomboy Club in North Miami. While not exactly the kind of glittering engagement he'd hoped for, the seven forty-five-minute sets six nights a week helped Rudy expand his musical horizons and chops playing R&B and funk. He says there were other perks as well. "Sharing the dressing room with the friendly topless dancers exposed my raging hormones to an exhilarating lifestyle."

That lifestyle came to an abrupt halt in 1974 as disco began ruling the airwaves. Rudy tells the sad tale of his friend Victor, a musician who came up in the ranks with Rudy. When disco hit America, almost all of Miami's rock clubs dried up. Owners demanded that musicians wear matching polyester suits—most likely of the powder-blue persuasion and white shirts with frilly ruffles—plus they told the bands to play only Top 40 tunes. So, Rudy decided to move to New York in search of more rock-friendly pastures, and he invited Victor to join him. However, Victor decided that he wasn't going anywhere.

"Man, are you kidding? I'm doing better than ever," Victor said, turning to a bartender and ordering his usual vodka tonic. "I got me a steady gig, all the hot chicks I want, a new Corvette, and my own pad on the beach where the party never ends. I don't ever want to leave Miami. I've got it made here."

Seven years later, when Rudy passed through town as Ozzy Osbourne's bassist, Victor was singing a different tune. Victor's girlfriend had gotten pregnant, they had married, and then they had divorced. Then it became time to pay the piper.

"She took me to the cleaners, man," Victor told Rudy. "She took the kid, the condo, my Corvette. Everything. Gigs got thin and I was really broke, so I started dealing and got popped. I'm still paying my attorney bills. You know, sometimes I wonder if I had taken you up on your offer to leave Miami ... I don't know, maybe things would have turned out different."

It's crystal clear to Rudy what would have become of him had he stayed in Miami—and he thanks his Father in heaven for His guidance and protection.

Rudy toured the eastern seaboard for a few years and also spent time on the shores of Los Angeles. It was there, in October 1978, that he joined Quiet Riot with gifted guitarist Randy Rhoads and lead singer Kevin DuBrow. The group rocked the LA scene hard. Despite a contract with Sony and record releases in Japan, the group didn't find much success beyond the Sunset Strip. They quietly disbanded in November 1979, when Rhoads joined Ozzy Osbourne. Rudy found employment with Angel, a glam-rock band whose heyday was definitely in the rearview mirror. Rudy caught them at the tail end of their history, after they were let go by Casablanca Records.

He also gigged on and off with Kevin Dubrow's new band, DuBrow, in various clubs around Los Angeles, but nothing was clicking. Rudy felt like he had come to a dead end. He found himself very alone and nearly destitute. He had just turned thirty and was sleeping on DuBrow's Sherman Oaks apartment floor. Everything seemed hopeless, but then he got a phone call from Rhoads, telling him that Ozzy Osbourne wanted him to audition for his band. It was the job that would change his life. The struggle to make it musically had worn him down and was making him feel like "it's over," but just before that phone call he had a sudden realization not to give in to that feeling. Rudy hadn't bottomed out, and his faith was stronger than ever before. "I never gave up. That was the whole point of my epiphany. I wasn't saying, 'Boy, if I don't make it in six months from now or a year from now, I'm going back to Miami or do whatever.' Instead I said, 'No, no. I believe. I believe that if I'm meant to do this, it will happen.' But, if it didn't, that was not going to change my relationship with God."

As I got more into Rudy's head, I liked the orderly way the furniture was arranged in there. It is very coordinated and consistent in form. It had not been rearranged since childhood, in my estimation. Rudy boils everything down to a proper relationship with God, and that is the first place he goes to sit down and put up his feet to think things over. It appears he never ran out the door in a panic, looking for answers someplace else. He knew who *the* Drummer was in his life and had found a groove to lock into when the big stuff came along.

It wasn't lost on Rudy that most people considered Ozzy evil incarnate due to his onstage persona. More than his music, rock's "Prince of Darkness" had become best known for biting the head off an unconscious bat during a concert. Perhaps it was his band's name just as much as it was the bat incident. Ozzy, born John Michael Osbourne on December 3, 1948, in the English West Midlands, may have gleaned a gentler image in the early days if his band had been named something other than Black Sabbath and he didn't bite the disabled creature while on tour in the heart of the midwestern Bible Belt. His Bat Out of Hell tour pigeonholed him as a somewhat demonic rocker with no affinity for life. Rudy knew differently. "Ozzy is one of the most caring, funny, loving people that I've met in my whole career. It's a miracle that I went from sleeping on the floor to being in his band. This was God's will, you know? It can't be bad, because it's a gift."

Now I imagine considering what Rudy just said about Ozzy Osborne to be true could be a bit hard for most people—it was for me. I have no way of knowing otherwise because I have zero knowledge of Ozzy the man and cannot debate it on that level. Because Rudy has been consistent in everything else and has been a model in his spiritual judgments, from my standpoint, I find I am open to what he says about Mr. Osbourne.

When I was with Waylon, he could scare the birds away with his appearance. When I would tell people what a pussycat he was in real life, they would just give me a blank stare like I was daft and then discount everything else I said after that. But—and I admit that this is a rough analogy—when God sent the prophet Samuel to select Israel's next king from the seven sons of Jesse, everyone was surprised that he picked David, who certainly didn't look like a king at the time. In guiding

Samuel in making his choice, God let us know that He doesn't see people the way we do. He knows their hearts. I am not suggesting Rudy is God and Ozzy would make a good king, but Rudy knew Ozzy in ways that we will never comprehend.

Ozzy's "evil" persona did pull a Christ-in-the-desert temptation bit when they first met. Rudy relied on that same Christ for discernment when Randy Rhoads warned him not to accept any drugs or alcohol from Ozzy. Being tested was nothing new to Rudy. "You think Los Angeles is sinful? No. Miami, Florida, is the most sinful place in the country. It's not that it's that evil, but it's one of the most sensual places in the world. It has a very seedy energy. If I were a pleasure-seeking individual who wanted to drink, do drugs, meet chicks, carry on with behavior that is associated with being a rock star, then I would have stayed in Miami."

After a bit of grateful trepidation, Rudy passed Ozzy's bizarre new employee interview ritual and came on board as his bass player. He had no illusions of the life he was about to enter and totally understood why Ozzy tested him.

Rudy explains: "I had no track record. I had never been with another major touring band, right?" (Quiet Riot was an LA band that didn't have their breakout success until Rudy came back in 1982, and it was a year later before they became a phenomenon. He was only with Angel in the studio and that album got dropped, so even though he had tons of valuable experience, this gig put things on another level.) "Ozzy and Sharon Osbourne had no idea who I was. They went on Randy Rhoads' recommendation. They wanted to know, what if I turned into a drug addict or an alcoholic in the middle of the tour? What if I turn into somebody who's not going to be responsible on stage? They had to find out themselves. They tested me because they wanted to know about my character."

Ozzy first offered him some vodka, and Rudy declined. Then Ozzy sat on the couch next to Rudy and pulled out some cocaine and asked if he "wanted a toot." When Rudy said, "No thanks, man," Ozzy shrugged his shoulders and said, "Okay, just means more for me then."

To say Ozzy was a character was a gross understatement. The ever-present alcohol and drugs, his well-documented off- and onstage antics, and his well-publicized bouts with depression didn't help his image in the media. Sharon even had him institutionalized once for psychiatric evaluation. In a nutshell, it sounds like Ozzy decided he wanted to have the luxury of screwing up, if and when he wanted to, but he wasn't going to allow other band members to be screwups. It was his band and his money. He could only afford to have one bizzaro in the band, and it was going to be him. Rudy could have easily fallen into the same trap, but he was smart to lean on faith and friends, learning from others' experiences so as not to make the same mistakes. "Sharon was hoping I would drink just enough just to keep Ozzy company, but I knew after a couple weeks that would either kill me or destroy any future I had. After so many years of trying to make it, I decided I wasn't going to go that route. You have to stay focused in this business."

Drugs, alcohol, and a notorious front man notwithstanding, Rudy describes his days with Ozzy as more like the classic TV show *Happy Days* than the rampant aggressive behavior that is the norm for today's hard-rock bands. Three and a half decades ago, he says, times were different, kinder, not as shocking and "in your face" as today's music world.

"The world is too edgy now. Way edgy. Kids are edgy. When we were teenagers, we didn't have that edge like the average teenager has today. Today they are just trying to shield themselves from everything that is going on around them: all the information, all the aggression that is going on in the world. We were not aware when we were teens what was going on in the Middle East or that so many people hated us for our beliefs. Back then we didn't have to deal with all that. We were more sheltered, and we didn't realize that we were shielded. We could be a bit more innocent, a little kinder to each other. Now it's difficult for kids to be that way.

"Our lifestyle in the band back then was different; we would go from town to town, check into a hotel, and then, 'Hey, let's go to the mall.'

You know, just hang out, because the malls in those days were fun; they weren't dangerous like it is today. You can actually get in trouble going to the mall these days. People go out to the parking lot now and face kidnappings or shootings. So, yeah, my world with Ozzy was different. We treated each other with kindness: Randy, me, Sharon, Tommy, and Ozzy."

I love it that Rudy used the word *innocent* in recounting his time with Ozzy and road life with the band. I am sure every time he uses the words *Ozzy* and *innocent* in the same sentence, he gets this back-of-the-neck scratching and sideways look. I have never been in close association with bands or artists who live on the road where there isn't a sense of family, a looking out for one another, a sharing and caring … a first responder attitude when one of the team faces a major trial. I am not saying we didn't cheat at Crazy Eights or smoke in the boy's room while on the road, but the outward appearance to the public is typically different than what goes on inside the rooms and hearts of these people.

That's not to say that everything was smooth sailing back when. Ozzy's shenanigans and temptations on the road kept Rudy on his toes both temporally and spiritually. When he got the Ozzy gig, he promised God that he would only glorify Him, not what the rock lifestyle afforded. "I knew from day one that if I had not had that epiphany before I joined Ozzy, my career would not have been the same. No way! Not at all! I mean, not just because of the opportunities, but because of the way that I would have treated my gifts. I would have never been so focused on the reality of where they came from—gifts from God. That's why when I was playing with Ozzy, I never saw it as, 'Oooh, I'm playing with this guy who is really into the bad-boy thing.' I knew that anything that God was going to bring my way was going to be good—a good thing."

But all good things end—or at least transform themselves into paths we never expected to take.

March 19, 1982. Rudy's second major personal loss.

It was a morning that changed his life and a definite game-changer for everyone in the band and crew. After pulling nearly an all-nighter in Knoxville, Tennessee, they embarked on a 655-mile bus trip to the Calhoun Brothers Touring Bus headquarters in Flying Baron Estates, just outside Leesburg, Florida, on their way to a gig in Orlando. The band's golden-brown and white tour bus had a malfunctioning air conditioner, and they needed to pick up a few spare parts. The band's bus driver, Andy Aycock, owned a home in Flying Baron Estates on adjacent property to the Calhoun Brothers facility. He wanted to spend some time with his wife, Wanda, and try to mend their troubled relationship. Upon arrival at Calhoun's place, the band parked their bus approximately sixty feet from a Georgian-style mansion, which also bordered a private airstrip.

Without the permission of owner Mike Partin, Andy, an ex-commercial pilot, commandeered a small, single-engine 1955 Beechcraft Bonanza F35 and took keyboardist Don Airey and tour manager Jake Duncan for a flight around 8 a.m. for some local sightseeing. Andy then dropped the two off and picked up two more passengers—Randy Rhoads and Rachel Youngblood, the band's fifty-eight-year-old seamstress and cook. Randy had asked Rudy to join him, but Rudy, not exactly bright eyed and bushy tailed, declined, falling back into a deep sleep. It was a quiet, pretty Florida morning.

During the second flight, around 9 a.m., Andy made at least three low passes at treetop level so he could "buzz" the tour bus. On the fourth attempt, he wasn't so lucky. According to eyewitnesses, the plane was flying approximately ten feet above the ground at speeds of 140 and 180 miles per hour. The left wing of the plane clipped the rear of the bus, causing a six-foot gash through the roof, and then the plane spiraled out of control. The aircraft crossed over the bus and severed a large pine tree before crashing through the north wall and roof of the estate's garage. The Beechcraft exploded and burned on impact, which also incinerated two cars parked in the garage. The bodies were burned beyond recognition.

Rachel was dead. Andy was dead.

Randy. Was dead.

Toxicology reports later revealed that Andy had traces of cocaine in his system. Ozzy confirmed a day later in a sworn affidavit to authorities that he had seen his driver snorting the drug the night before the crash. Randy only had nicotine in his system.

Different people deal with grief in different ways. Randy Rhoads' death didn't shake Rudy's steadfast faith. He wondered, though, how Ozzy would deal with such a loss. Rudy learned early on that religion isn't something that can be forced; you can't simply influence someone into becoming a believer. They have to experience that revelation on their own. "From my experience, people really have to open up themselves to want to believe. Essentially everybody wants to believe in something. But it has to happen at the right time and the right place."

In the words of Thomas Paine, "What we obtain too cheap, we esteem too lightly: it is dearness only that gives everything its value."

I have always said that God is the greatest economist of all time and He will use all the events of our lives—good, bad, or indifferent—to His good purpose, once we turn everything over to Him and recognize His lordship in our lives. As deep as the pain was for Rudy to lose his dear friend in such a tragic manner, he knew amongst the rubble, in time, he would find God's heart and purpose. The bond between road band members is deep and unexpected. There *is* something spiritual about the connection they experience when they unite in songs and share in the excitement of the live stage together. But it's not only the extreme high moments that are shared, it's also the drudgery hours on the bus, the shoddy hotels, the bad food, and the weird people along the way that makes them fall in love with each other. Even the guys they do not like in the band rate a special place in their heart because they share such a broad spectrum of emotions. These friendships don't come cheap. They are extremely valuable, and they are dearly missed when taken away.

After waiting and wading through many phone calls explaining what had happened, Rudy set off on his own once the police allowed him and the other survivors to leave the property. He happened onto a church down the road from the crash site and walked in. That's where he saw

Ozzy on his knees praying near the altar. No one else was there—save the "Prince of Darkness" bemoaning his grief to the Lord.

Rudy had his own theory about the crash. Andy's wife, Wanda, was standing in the doorway of the bus and watched it all unfold. It was common knowledge among the band that their marriage was on the rocks. Andy was very upset about it and couldn't control his emotions. Rudy believes that Andy saw Wanda standing at the door of the bus and aimed the plane at her. That just made sense to Rudy. More sense than what the fireman told Rudy at the crash site that day when he wanted to rush to his friend's aid in the garage where the aircraft had crashed:

"Don't go in there, son. Remember him as you last saw him."

Rudy cried himself to sleep that night and slowly worked through the agony of Randy's terrible death. "I never questioned my faith during that whole time. I tried to figure things out, to make sense of things. I grieved and somehow learned to live with the passing of a friend—somebody whom I owed my career to, someone who I believe saved our lives by turning the plane from crashing into the bus when we were sleeping and just clipping it instead."

A good description of Rudy and Randy's relationship can be found in Proverbs 18:24 (NLT). It states: "There are 'friends' who destroy each other, but a real friend sticks closer than a brother." The road and their music had built a bond between them that's hard for people outside of that oddly intricate world to understand.

At Randy's memorial service, Rudy was filled with guilt, grief, "what ifs," and shock. Ozzy's hands were shaking, and he was inconsolable. "You know, I just don't understand it," Ozzy said to everyone within earshot. "I drink myself into bloody oblivion every night, I get stoned out of my mind and abuse myself all these years, and the guy who kept his nose clean is the one who buys the bloody farm. I just don't get it. Why him and not me?"

There have been too many books and sermons written in answer to this age-old question, so there will be no lengthy attempt at proffering an involved answer to the question on these pages. He is God, and when I got that straight I realized He doesn't have to explain things to me. His thoughts and ways are higher than mine, and if He can create heaven and earth in a few days, I am sure His other ideas are logical too. His Word says I am supposed to trust Him in all things, so…

Rudy handled his grief, what he termed his "deepest stage of depression," by deciding whether or not he wanted to stay with Ozzy's band. "After Randy's crash, in order to survive every single show we did, I shut down emotionally. I shielded myself. I started playing notes, not music. I became a robot on stage. Randy's death affected everybody. If Ozzy could've left Ozzy, I think he would have because he knew from that point on he had to keep playing without Randy—on the same stage doing the same show, same production, same set, same everything—without him. We canceled six dates to take time out for the memorial service, but then we had to resume the tour only ten days after his death. That was incredibly hard … almost impossible, night after night. For Ozzy, it was an emotional trip every time he opened his mouth to sing."

Rudy finished out the tour but left Ozzy in September 1982, rejoining his former band Quiet Riot, where their chart-topping album *Metal Health* sold more than 10 million copies, making it the first heavy-metal debut record to reach the number-one spot on the *Billboard* 200. With God as his agent, as Rudy likes to put it, he found himself blessed to be involved in several successful bands and projects. His services continue to be very much in demand.

Rudy admits that he doesn't listen much to modern music because he finds it "much less musical" than the classic stuff and because "there's so much anger, despair, so much negativity in it … I don't need that in my life." So he looks for opportunities where he can make a positive difference in people's lives. Forever the encourager, Rudy is a natural teacher and mentor. "One of the things I am involved in is the Rock 'n' Roll Fantasy Camp in Las Vegas. I meet the new generation, kids, and teach them how to be more musical, because they have very little current references when learning musical skills or musicality. They've branched so far away from the roots of what we call the Rock and Roll Tree. There's just no connection with blues, R&B, and gospel. That's a problem."

Rudy is right; it was different in the "good ole days" when it came to the music. I keep going back to the way it was developed before the attorneys, the accountants, the quest for larger and larger amounts of money, and the image-makers took over. There was less machinery involved, both technical and financial. There was less "We can fix that in the mix" or "Don't worry about your vocal, we can adjust your pitch with the equipment." Back then the attitude was, "Let's work on it until we can get it right." If I want to get a blank stare and mental dismissal from most beginners in the music business today, I can always start with, "You know you've got to work long and hard and earn your dues, man!"

Rudy's also right when he says everyone plays an important role in society. "To me, a rock star could be anybody. It's someone who fulfills their goals. That person who is at their best 24/7, no matter what they do in life. It could be a doctor, a lawyer, a writer, the guy at Subway making the best sandwich possible, or the guy at Home Depot who can find the size of a certain screw in an instant. People think of rock stars as guys who can have as many chicks as they want, can drink like a fish, do a bunch of drugs, and be an ass on a daily basis. No, to me, that is a rock and roll casualty. A rock star is someone like Bruce Springsteen, Bono, Sting, people who take their musical accomplishments and then turn around and help others. That's what I do in these camps. I help people find their inner tree—I always use the tree as a metaphor because it's very simple. A tree starts out as a seed, is planted, and then grows. It can provide oxygen, shade, fruit, nests for birds, or refuge from the rain. A tree knows not to try and be anything but a tree. Human beings are meant to be the same way. We're all supposed to be humans; we're supposed to help others, be kind, share, and teach. The thing about humans is it takes us a little longer to get there, whereas a tree knows immediately what must be done."

Rudy's long-ago promise to put God first, to glorify His name, carried him through both the losses and the blessings of life, and there have been a lot of blessings. His deeper relationship with God. His thirty-year marriage to Rebecca. His voice of reason. His music. His gift of sharing with others.

Throughout it all, Rudy always kept one thing in perspective:

"I'm joining the band; the band is not joining me. I have played with many tremendous musicians who every time they join a group, they want to change the chemistry to make it comfortable for whatever style of music they do. In my case, I realize that the band is already established and they need certain qualities from me that's going to add to the group or seamlessly fill that hole that the previous musician left. I look at it as filling that hole perfectly so there's no seam. I don't just plug into certain areas and make it patchy; because I am who I am it has to be as seamless as possible."

Seamless. Most of us don't take paths that aren't patchy, full of holes to drop through, or forks that take us nowhere—misguided journeys that eventually make us search for how to get back to where we need to be. Rudy's generosity of spirit led him, maybe not always on a seamless path through life, but one destined to tear down walls that keep people apart. People everywhere who have the same needs but maybe different paths to fulfillment, like the tour of life Rudy shared with Ozzy and Randy—two very talented, caring men on different paths toward God. Randy got there first.

Randy reached out and brought Rudy into some pretty good bands before … I bet he has a real showstopper that needs a great bass player, just waiting for him when they get together in heaven. Now that will be seamless!

JOHN FORD COLEY

England Dan & John Ford Coley

England Dan & John Ford Coley waved the soft-rock banner loudly in the 1970s, releasing several platinum and gold records in their decade-long partnership. Their four Top 10 hits—"I'd Really Love to See You Tonight," "Nights Are Forever," "It's So Sad to Belong," and "Love Is the Answer"—are staples of classic rock radio.

SEVEN

LOVE IS THE ANSWER

JOHN FORD COLEY | England Dan & John Ford Coley

The only thing greater than the great state of Texas is its people. You don't have to ride a horse to be a cowboy in Texas—just look, talk, and feel like one as you mosey about town. It's funny how they have the rare ability to take Southern hospitality and then put a steel guitar to it. During my five years with Waylon, I found it curious that he talked differently when Willie was around.

Texans love who they are and where they come from. John Ford Coley is no exception. Besides the dead-giveaway accent and manners, this singer usually sports something to do with Texas on his baseball cap or T-shirt whether he's on stage or not.

Born John Edward Colley on October 13, 1948, he grew up in a middle-class neighborhood in Dallas, Texas, called Pleasant Grove. John's parents were professionals, and family, music, and church were mainstays in the Colley household. So were good old-fashioned manners.

"Being raised in the South is entirely different than most places," says Coley, speaking from his South Carolina residence. "Honor is an extremely important facet of life in the South. How you treat people is significant; manners and showing respect were ingrained in me as a kid. So was going to church."

As a Southern Baptist, John spent serious time in the house of the Lord. "My family was very devoted and if those church doors were open, they were always there. They sang in the choir, and hearing those old hymns today will still drop me to my knees quicker than anything. They actually did what Proverbs 22:6 instructed them to do, and that is to 'train up a child in the way he should go, and when he is old he will not depart from it'" (NKJV).

While the music was heavenly, the message delivered from the pulpit wasn't so divine and drove fear into John's imaginative mind during his formative years. "When I was a child, the thing that upset me was that when Christ came back, bodies were going to be rising up over our local Safeway store. There would be murders, mayhem, earthquakes, fire, famine, and people killing one another. It scared me to death. Then they would comment, 'I just can't wait until Jesus comes back,' and I would think, *after all you've described, are you out of your mind?* Eventually I ran from that fear into the arms of another religion and spent twenty-eight years there. I do applaud the enthusiasm of those preachers, but their manners and methods of just using the fear of God and not His love was a turnoff. They would browbeat you with the Bible, and that pushed me away instead of drawing me in."

This is not the first time this scenario has been brought forth in our stories, and as we hear this repetitive theme it becomes apparent there was a lot of collateral damage done to John's generation. The spiritual paths of many of the artists we interviewed became very rocky because of this experience. Much of it came out of the '50s, and it's so surprising that such a frightful message was being brought forth during such a wonderful era. Give me heaven or the '50s; I am sure they are pretty much alike.

Like John, as a young lad, every time I left Sunday church I was sure I was going to hell before I got to my house. I knew when I left my hometown at seventeen the one thing I was not going to look for was a church.

I wanted to enjoy life, and I don't mean I wanted to rape, murder, and steal—just not live under condemnation. I didn't feel I had had enough time to be so bad that I was doomed to the pit for eternity. But according to my pastor, I was headed for hell for getting up in the morning and doing normal things. I can't remember if I was ever taught how to experience joy—you know, have some good clean fun without shoveling flaming ashes forever.

When John wasn't obsessing about Christ's return, nuclear war, or eternal damnation, he was a normal kid who enjoyed sports, music, and television. "I was raised on Buck Owens, the Grand Ole Opry, Lawrence Welk, church music, opera, and Irish music. My parents wouldn't let me watch *Gunsmoke* or *Have Gun – Will Travel* on Saturday nights unless I watched *Sing Along with Mitch* with Mitch Miller and *The Lawrence Welk Show* first. Later on I got into doo-wop, Elvis, The Beatles, The Beach Boys, Buffalo Springfield, and rock and roll. It was a very entertaining time because there was an array of eclectic music being offered to American audiences, and I ate it up. I had to be a part of it, so I got involved in it and that was a real thrill for me."

Playing music came naturally to John and by age sixteen, he learned to play the guitar and then stepped up his game by becoming a classically trained pianist. In 1965, John met Danny Wayland Seals, a meeting that changed his life. Seals attended the same high school and was the younger brother of Jim Seals of the soft-rock duo Seals & Croft. John says it was not exactly mutual admiration at first sight when it came to Dan Seals. "Dan was playing saxophone in the Playboys Five and when one of their guitar players left, Dan wanted to replace him with another guitar player, but everyone else wanted a keyboard player. I got the gig over Dan's objections, and at first we mixed like oil and water. We didn't get along, and the only thing we had in common was music and being in a band together."

The relationship changed over time while they were riding to gigs singing Everly Brothers and Righteous Brothers songs, learning their craft and perfecting their harmonies. There's something special when two artists who don't necessarily get along sing together and their voices meld in a special way. This is another theme that repeats itself as these stories unfold—some artists compare it to a spiritual experience because it is so moving. This feeling is very akin to falling in love with someone and that feeling you get the first time you touch—it sends shivers through your whole being. When musicians experience this emotion, it too is like falling in love in that they don't care about anything else: facts, figures, or common sense. They just want to be with that person so they can keep the feeling alive.

The Playboys Five were performing at a Dallas hotel one night, when a touring country singer caught their act. He invited them to Nashville to record a series of demos, but insisted they change their name to The Chimeras for the recording session. The boys were still in their teens and Nashville was the big time—this was going to be their big break, so they agreed to the name change. "When we got ready to record, we were told that the producers didn't want us to play, only sing. They had a regular house band, which included legendary Charlie McCoy on harmonica. I remember how exciting it was for us to see Chet Atkins walking through the studio while we were there. They said they loved us, thought we were 'cute,' and sounded good for our age. I was having the time of my life. I ate a salad with French dressing for the first time and thought, *now I'm a man of the world and I'm gonna be a star*, because they kept telling us that. They sent us home, saying they'll connect with us soon … *very* soon they promised. Then they proceeded to steal our songs. Welcome to the big time."

Ah … Nashville is thrilling—it sparkles, it pulsates, it enchants, it mesmerizes, it buzzes with excitement, and one thing is for sure—it seldom sleeps. Its mystique reaches out to talented and passionate souls from all corners of our country. Along its hallowed streets, in its famous studios, and deep within its legendary backrooms, the magnificent and the merciless await—some are there to bless the wide-eyed singers, songwriters, and pickers who wander into its creative arms while others are lurking to pick their bones dry. Innocent dreamers drift into those places hoping for stardom but often walk out starving instead; it all depends on who gets to them first. Instead of the magnificent men of Music Row, it appears John and Dan stumbled into the pit of the merciless thugs that prey on the innocent and naive. It's called "Music Biz 101," and instead of "Welcome to the big time" it was "Whoa, we just got scammed."

John and Dan had better luck with Theze Few, their new band, which included Ovid Stevens, Doc Woolbright, and Buddy Lay, who was drafted and replaced by Zeke Durell. The group's auspicious debut was the grand opening of a local Goodwill store, and they happily split the twenty-five-dollar payday. Eventually Theze Few became Southwest F.O.B. ("Free On Board"), added Randy Bates to the band, and developed into a killer sonic brigade, playing parties, sock hops, teen clubs, and even strip joints. John said he discovered a lot of broken hearts in those venues. "What I found through all that was a compassion for people. I saw that they were lost and instead of judging them, I felt compassion because of that loneliness."

By 1967, John had grown a mustache, let his hair get longer, and switched his blue jeans for bell-bottoms. Paisley shirts and moccasins were the rage, and the band's blue stage pants with the zippers on the side landed in the dumpster. It was John's senior year, and he was finally one of the "groovy people." The folks at his church thought differently and felt he was in the express lane to hell. "I remember Christians would come up to us, hand us religious tracts, and say, 'You're one of Satan's children leading our kids astray.' I'd take their tracts, thank them, wad 'em up, and throw 'em on the ground. I wanted nothing to do with those people, and that behavior kept me away from the church until I was about fifty."

The Southwest F.O.B., mostly influenced by acid rock, featured a good amount of R&B in their musical repertoire. They played Otis Redding, Sam and Dave, Steve Cropper, and Wilson Pickett, and they developed a large following in Texas. Their sound was a slice of '60s-style pop-psyche perfection and drew the attention of Stax/Volt Records, based in Memphis, Tennessee. Stax was predominantly a black label and had opened a subsidiary called Hip Records. The only other white act on the roster was a group called The Nobody Else, who later became known as Black Oak Arkansas. Hip Records released Southwest F.O.B.'s *Smell of Incense* in September 1968. The title song made it to number fifty-six on the national charts. The cover featured four naked young women sitting together in a steamy glass box. "The album jacket was a surprise to the band. I recall our manager Rich saying it wasn't something I could show at my Sunday school. He was right."

It was also something they couldn't show to the public, as shopkeepers refused to stock the record. *Smell of Incense* never had a chance. I can relate from firsthand experience, as US manager of Apple Records and having been on the cutting edge of John and Yoko's 1968 *Unfinished Music No. 1: Two Virgins* album. Its cover featured a full frontal nude picture of John and Yoko—not a pretty sight, by the way. EMI, The Beatles' parent label in the United Kingdom, and Capitol in the United States refused to distribute the record. In order to placate John and Yoko, we allowed them to offer the album to other labels. It was eventually distributed by Track in the United Kingdom and by Tetragrammaton in America. How times have changed—it had to be sold in a brown paper bag and kept behind the counter. Although it did have the Beatles magic dust, it also didn't sell well, reaching 124 on the US charts. The most interesting part for me was sitting in a London hotel room on a couch with John and Yoko showing me different versions of the nude pictures they were deciding on for their cover. It wasn't exactly like choosing which sunrise photo should be used for an Easter church bulletin.

Undaunted by the failure of *Smell of Incense*, Southwest F.O.B. pressed forward. They opened for national touring acts like Three Dog Night, Paul Revere and The Raiders, Johnny Rivers, The Standells, and Poco. The group peaked when they opened the 1969 Texas International

Pop Festival featuring Led Zeppelin. It was the first major rock festival in Texas, held two weeks after the legendary Woodstock festival in Woodstock, New York. John remembers hearing the roar of the crowd much better than seeing them. "It was hard to see the audience because of a thick haze of smoke. I've ever seen smoke like that in my entire life, and I lived in Los Angeles and endured years of smog. It was an exciting time and a learning experience. It exposed me to an adventure I had never experienced before."

John's Southern Baptist upbringing kept him grounded during those drug-happy '60s and '70s. Seals' father once warned them, "Alcohol, dope, and fast women killed ever country singer there ever was." John and Dan never got sucked into that lifestyle even though some of their band mates did. Some of the band members' drug use grated on John's nerves as well as the ever-revolving membership. "We kept changing band members, and drugs were popping up more and more in the group. Our new bass player went nuts because of it. One time Dan had to stop him from beating up his girlfriend for not sharing her stash with him. I was beginning to lose any sensitivity or compassion for this group and didn't care if they killed one another. Bass players were easy to find. Dan and I wanted out because the time to leave was long overdue."

Now billed as Colley and Wayland, the acoustic duo found work in local folk clubs and began performing their own songs. Duos were hitting it big after The Everly Brothers paved the way. Other duos followed in their footsteps; Simon & Garfunkel, Peter and Gordon, Sam & Dave, Seals & Crofts, and The Carpenters all gained prominence in the industry. Their music stood out, but now they needed a catchy name to match. This was the era when unusual band names were in vogue—Strawberry Alarm Clock, Iron Butterfly, The Mothers of Invention, Pink Floyd, Jefferson Airplane, Grateful Dead, etc. so "The John & Dan Duo" wasn't going get people talking.

It was Jimmy Seals, Dan's older brother, who suggested "England Dan & John Ford Coley." When the British Invasion was in full effect a few years before, Dan affected a fake British accent that earned him the moniker "England Dan." Not to be outdone, John changed his middle name and used "Ford" after the Confederate Col. John Salmon 'Rip' Ford and shortened his last name to Coley. "The name caught on, but once when we were playing with Bread, we were reviewed as 'English Don & John Portfolio.'"

Their name not only flowed well but also was unusual enough to garner a second look from programmers, reviewers, promoters, and the general public. With the name finally settled, they had no difficulty finding a record deal thanks to musician Louie Shelton, a top session guitarist in Los Angeles who played with Jimmy Seals in the Seals & Crofts band. Shelton heard the duo perform at The Ice House in Pasadena and liked what he heard. He asked them to send him a demo tape, which he immediately passed on to Herb Alpert at A&M Records.

"They're a cross between Simon & Garfunkel and the Bee Gees," Shelton told Alpert. The description didn't peak Alpert's interest, but he did promise to listen to the tape. He decided to listen during a morning shave. Once he pressed play, he never finished the shave and called Shelton.

"Get 'em out here," Alpert said. That was May 1971.

England Dan & John Ford Coley recorded a pair of LPs, a self-titled debut album and *Fables*, both produced by Shelton, which resulted in very modest sales. The two albums and singles, recorded with some of LA's finest session players, featured a somewhat rougher, textured version of the mellow sound for which they would later become known.

When it came to touring, they worked with some of the best—Chicago, Bread, Three Dog Night, Carole King, Fleetwood Mac, and Elton John, who requested they wear cowboy hats on stage to accompany their boots, out of his love for all things Texas. They happily obliged.

Los Angeles was then as it is now: the mecca for alternative religions. It was a time when Jesus Freaks, gurus, Moonies, Krishnas, vegans, and New Age followers comingled and coagulated. They seemed harmless, seeking a form of God consciousness—the "free love" and "we are one" syndrome. At first John was reticent because something deep inside was going against the grain of his heart and soul. "Getting involved with an alternative religion simply was not on my agenda. I was about as interested in that as I was in jumping out of an airplane."

Introduced to the Baha'i faith by Dan Seals, John was taught that all religions lead to God and are acceptable. That teaching, along with the proposition that Revelation was actually a symbolic occurrence that had already taken place, appealed greatly to John. "After I heard that explanation, I went, 'You mean I'm not going to have to go through all that stuff in Revelation? No earthquakes, fires, death, and destruction? Okay, I'm in. Yeah, man, where do I sign up?' Looking back, I can see where I ran from the fear of the Baptist church into the arms of something that solved long-held fears. Dan's ideas had a profound impact on the way I thought about God and religion. One of the biggest principles within that teaching was that we were to independently investigate all truths for ourselves. I jumped headlong into that mindset and spent twenty-eight years there."

I went through the same thought process that John did during this time. Baptists, Lutherans, Methodists, Presbyterians, and the rest of the good and godly Protestant denominations had a tendency to make dwelling within God's loving mercy and grace sound more like a day on the chain gang rather than a gentle basking in the beauty and wonder of His love. So in our addled pride and sometimes drug-driven madness, we sought the easy way out. We were babies in a cruel world, and we still wanted to be loved and coddled by our moms within the shelter of our rural upbringing. We didn't want to hurt anymore—that's what we were escaping with our fingers on the frets and songs on our hearts, so like sponges we soaked up the New Age philosophies that said more to us than "If it feels good, do it." They offered something pleasant like, "You *are* good, so do it and feel good like you deserve." All the years of frustration and being beaten down were removed with a toke and a teaching that said we were okay for a change. I personally can cut all of us who bought into that bit a lot of slack, because when you boil it down, we *were* seeking God all along. We came rolling out of our constrained hills with a lot of suppression, and this new freedom to love and let go felt really good. God is the greatest of all economists, though, and not one of John's twenty-eight years was wasted on His eternal calendar.

John will not talk down about his former religion, citing that it had several good qualities and the people he met were kind, loving, and supportive. "It helped keep me in check, because there were certain things that the Baha'i faith frowned upon—adultery, drugs, alcohol. We were in the public eye and if we violated these belief systems, no one would take our faith or us seriously. The bottom line is if you don't know who you are when you get out on the road, you're in big trouble. I'm not saying it didn't happen to me—because it did, and my ego got me in a lot of trouble."

The two men had to lean on their faith when A&M dropped them in 1974—the same year John visited Israel for the first time. John recalls an incident from his youth: "I was eight years old when I attended vacation Bible school, and the church leaders had my class visit one of the orthodox synagogues in town. I still vividly remember the two rabbis rocking back and forth while standing in front of the ark in their tallits, long ear locks, and beards, while reading the prayers from the siddur. There must have been a minyan (a quorum of ten Jewish male adults required for certain religious obligations) that day in the synagogue, because the rabbis opened the ark and showed us the Torah scrolls. I was smitten right then and there and didn't know why. I do remember that I felt something very powerful tug deeply at my soul."

Here he was, almost two decades later, in the land that had captivated him as a child. John could feel the historical roots coming up out of the ground and attaching to his soul. "Visiting Elijah's cave on Mt. Carmel, where he had defeated the priests of Jezebel; the fortress of St. Jeanne d'Arc, and the Acca prison site where Napoleon's cannon balls are still embedded in the city walls when his army attacked that holiest city of the Baha'i faith. There, many of the Jewish resistance heroes during the War of Independence in 1947 and 1948 were imprisoned, beaten, and hanged by the British-controlled Palestine, as it was called at that time. It was from this prison that the huge escape occurred in 1947 so prominently displayed in the movie *Exodus*. Why was I here in Israel? I didn't know why."

My guess is that the Lord was the tour guide for John's stirring trip. I can never separate the words *tapestry* and *God's wondrous ways* when I hear dramatic and poignant stories like this. John was bewildered because everything that had happened in his life had been woven into this moment—a moment that was not a brief episode but actually a taste of his eternal purpose. I can envision God stepping back, admiring His work while looking at John, in that old place, observing the evident stirring inside His beloved child, and saying to Himself, "This is good—I can take a break for a while and watch where John goes from here." This was not a happenstance or a stop on a wasted trail—it was all about God's love and Him having a good time with His good news. But the Grand Weaver was not finished yet.

When John returned to Los Angeles, he and Dan knocked around for a while, toured here and there, called in favors, and did everything they could to keep the dream afloat. John was of the show business belief, "If at first you don't succeed, you're simply not vicious enough to play the game."

They finally caught a break in 1976. That's when their manager, Susan Joseph, heard a demo of a new song called "I'd Really Love to See You Tonight," penned by Mississippi-based composer Parker McGee. They weren't crazy about the song because they felt it was a bit too feminine. But at Susan's insistence, they cut a demo and went label shopping. Bob Greenberg, an executive at Atlantic Records, turned it down. But Doug Morris and Dick Vanderbilt of Atlantic subsidiary label Big Tree Records heard it through the wall of an adjoining office and offered them a singles contract. Their thinking was if the song was a hit, the single would be the cornerstone of a new album. The song was released in July 1976 and peaked at number two on *Billboard*, kept out of the top slot by Wild Cherry's "Play That Funky Music." Their first Big Tree album, "Nights Are Forever," was cut in Nashville in less than thirty days and was the label's first RIAA-certified gold album. "I've always felt God's had His hand on this record—I'm too old to believe in coincidences. Things have a reason and a lot of the time we don't have the understanding or wisdom to grasp the wisdom of God's timing."

Like John, I believe God's timing is impeccable and that I am strictly on a "need to know" basis with Him. I have a feeling on that day when He reveals life's most mysterious things, we will be amazed by how simple the explanation is—in *His* world.

Between 1976 and 1979, everything was coming up roses, gold, and platinum. England Dan & John Ford Coley had notched six Top 40 hits, triple platinum album sales, and a Grammy nomination. Their best known songs included "I'd Really Love to See You Tonight" and "Nights Are Forever" in 1976; "It's So Sad to Belong" and "Gone Too Far" in 1977; "We'll Never Have to Say Goodbye Again" in 1978; and "Love Is the Answer" in 1979. They appeared on Johnny Carson and *The Midnight Special*, toured in private jets, hung with fellow celebrities, and tried to enjoy their fame, which felt like riding a meteor. "It's a hard business. When you're hot, everybody wants you. Then, on your way down, no one cares because there are new acts to be marketed and exploited. Being a recording act epitomizes the old adage about being 'the fastest gun in the West.' You're constantly looking over your shoulder because someone's always gunning to take your spot."

Somebody waiting to take over your position is not new or specific to the recording industry. In fact, as cutthroat as the music business may be, it is typically more dependent on talent and ability than most occupations. I'm not suggesting there will be no backstabbing, schmoozing, or manipulating, but once you wheedle your way to a pivotal position you need to have the goods. Artists may be able to climb over people, but the one thing they cannot control is the public. Once they have clamored their way into a recording studio or onto a concert stage, they have to deliver. No one can force the fans to buy a concert ticket or download their tunes.

Getting back to John's cowboy analogy, you do have to have the fastest horse and the loudest gun in order to shoot up the charts—and it is a horse race. Once you enter that bareknuckle fray, you have to accept the rules of the entertainment game: every man for himself. Oh wait, I already said that—it sounds just like every other business. But the main difference that separates musicians and entertainers from other businesses is by nature the players tend to be more sensitive, more driven, and more insecure. Their battles become very personal, and betrayal is waiting around every corner, so paranoia, suspicion, and distrust soon become the new normal and in some cases drown out the beautiful music being made. I often joke that after thirty years in the biz I developed the keenest sense of paranoia known to man. To this day when someone says hello, I wonder, *what did they mean by that?*

John was well on his way to becoming burned out and coldhearted.

England Dan & John Ford Coley became so successful that they leased a plane for touring in order to avoid the hassles of flying commercial. During one tour, as their plane sped down the runway, the copilot, Jack Brunner, heard the band screaming that the engine was on fire. Brunner immediately pressed a button that shot foam on both engines, dousing the fire before the plane got off the ground. Pilot Robert Fowler released the hatch door, and everyone ran out except for John, Dan, and their publicist, Nancy, who stayed in their seats. Later Fowler confirmed what they already knew—it was a close call.

"If the plane had gotten off the ground, we'd have crashed and we'd all be dead now, just like Jim Croce and Buddy Holly," he told them.

While the proclamation should have sent chills down their spines, John had become so disconnected from reality that even a near-death experience didn't rattle him. He remembers sitting there nonplussed, thinking, "*Either you die or you don't. I've got someplace to go, so when can we get another plane?* I was truly amazed at how detached I was. Dan and Nancy felt the same way, so we got on another plane and flew to our next date."

By the end of the 1970s, England Dan and John Ford Coley began to unravel. Musically they were sandwiched in between the disco boom and the undercurrent of punk rock/new wave. Their brand of harmony-based, melodic pop rock was losing ground with radio and the record-buying public. To show how desperate things can become to stay on top, their new manager, Marcia—with Dan Seals' blessing—talked about peddling a "John is gay" story to the tabloids to generate headlines. John shot that down quickly, citing that it was not only false, but he had a wife and young daughter and parents who might get upset. His denial miffed Dan and Marcia and spelled the beginning of the end. "Marcia and Dan would discuss what was going to happen in our career but never discussed anything with me. Dan would just tell me what the two of them had decided. I resented this and because of my constant objections we each ended up with different management."

The management decision to play the gay card to get attention for a dying band is the perfect example of how twisted, desperate, and actually demented things had become in their separate reality. Just think what an abstract plan that was—*Gee, I bet people will buy our records and come to our concerts now... not to hear our music, but so they can listen to and see a gay guy.* Talk about marketing genius! They'd have been better off working with what made them successful: their talent and creativity. I am not much of a percentage guy, but as I look back on my time working with managers, I realize now many of them did more harm than good. Bands typically have simple motives: make music and make money. Some managers have only one motive: make money, forgetting the part that makes it all happen.

Following the release of a greatest hits album in 1980, the pair went their separate ways. Seals launched a successful solo career in country music, topping the country charts eleven times, most notably with "Meet Me in Montana," a duet with Marie Osmond, in 1985. No one was happier for his success than John. "Dan had one of the finest voices I've ever heard. He could sing R&B, rock, country, soft ballads, always with his own style. He was a phenomenal sax player and played great guitar. He could play chords upside down I couldn't begin to make standing up. I am really proud of Dan because he established a successful career on his own in country music."

John returned to A&M in late 1980 to produce an album, *Leslie, Kelly & John Ford Coley*, with Leslie and Kelly Bulkin. In addition to being musical partners, the trio were practitioners of the Baha'i faith. Unfortunately their single, "Come Back to Me," and the album slipped quietly into obscurity. John then tried his hand at writing songs for the silver screen and even took up acting, appearing in the 1987 feature film *Scenes From the Goldmine*, and in 1989, *Dream a Little Dream*, starring Corey Feldman and Corey Haim. He also played the part of a felon on an episode of *America's Most Wanted* and did such a convincing job that they caught the culprit in less than three hours after the episode aired.

John says despite the outward appearance of success, the 1980s were a tough time financially and emotionally. "I was one lost guy. My music career had ended and I also got divorced, which played havoc with me. Then the Internal Revenue Service came after Dan and me because of unpaid taxes, and they really nailed us. I was still playing and writing songs, but they weren't being published or recorded. Spiritually I was sinking and trying to hold it together, but nothing seemed to generate any success. I can look back now and see that nothing I did had God's blessing. It was a very long, dry period in an ever-growing and vast wilderness."

First God knocks gently on our door, and if we don't answer after repeated attempts, He sometimes knocks us to the ground. Not because He is a cruel God but because He wants the best for us. Being an entertainer is such a self-centered undertaking, it is sometimes hard to see beyond the damaged desire for personal success. You get so full of yourself that there is no room left for God, no matter how obvious it becomes that we need Him and His grace. He doesn't break our legs to get our attention, but sometimes He steps back and watches our hearts get broken or lets us go broke until His Word finally breaks through. There is always the danger that continued denial of His sovereign control could cause our hearts to become hardened to a point of no return.

An egocentric life leads to accepting the accolades of success as validation of our genius while the bad things are blamed on God. Over time the reality gap gets wider and wider, and as resentment builds we dig the pit even deeper until we realize we are in over our head. It gets very quiet down there, and that's when we are able to hear His voice and let His light shine through the darkness. We finally get it, reach out, and He lifts us up into His waiting arms.

But one day a bright light appeared in John's life. It was 1983, and her name was Dana Peters. The two met in Oceanside, California, married in 1986, and started a family. Their life was simple. It was about raising horses, advocating for children in the court system, and playing occasional gigs. It remained that way for almost a decade.

In the summer of 1997, John received a phone call from his publishing administrator in Nashville, asking him a series of strange questions concerning New York City and a recent series of interviews there. John was informed that someone in Long Island, New York, had claimed his identity and was performing in nightclubs under his name. The imposter was so brazen that he appeared on radio and cable television shows and had even progressed to the point of landing a booking agent. He also had written rubber checks with John's name affixed. John hired an attorney, sent a cease and desist letter, and filed a complaint with the Long Island district attorney's office. "Before long, I was receiving tapes from the police of cable TV shows he had been performing on as John Ford Coley. He had a long face with a salt-and-pepper beard. He wore this 'Old Salty Dog' sailing cap and had hands the size of the state of Oklahoma. His East Coast accent was so thick that anybody could tell he wasn't from Texas or anywhere close to the South. Then I heard him sing. He actually sounded pretty good, in a 1960s Las Vegas kind of way. I actually felt sorry for the guy."

Law enforcement arrested the imposter, forty-five-year-old Bruce F. Setzer of Central Islip, New York. He was charged with fraud, petty larceny, and criminal impersonation—all misdemeanors. The arrest made national headlines, including *The Daily Show With Jon Stewart* on Comedy Central. After the furor died down, Setzer was at it again, so Real TV flew John to New York to confront him in person. But Setzer got wind of the sting and finally fled for good. John decided to begin performing again in order to reestablish his name. He felt Nashville would be a good place to restart his career and raise his family. Nashville being in the South, it didn't take long for John to get invited to church. The person extending the invitation was singer-songwriter Paul Overstreet, and the church was The Oasis.

At the time, John felt the last place he'd find God was in a church, because of what he had experienced in his youth. But he wanted to appease Overstreet and get him off his back. "I really wanted nothing to do with it [church], but Paul kept pushing. Finally I said, 'Paul, I'll tell ya what … if I come to church with you, will you shut the hell up and leave me alone?' He said, 'Yeah, I'll leave you alone.' So my family and I finally went. As we arrived, we could see people singing with their arms raised in the air. My wife was holding on to my arm for dear life and asking me, 'What in the world have you gotten us into?' I looked at my kids and said, 'Okay, no matter what color the Kool-Aid is, don't drink it.' I then told Dana that we'd sit in the back, close to the door, in the event they started passing out snakes or killing chickens."

But what took place that day was something John hadn't expected—he ran into the presence of God. "So we sat in the back and got hit by the Holy Spirit. I mean it drove me to my knees. I'd never felt like that before.

It's hard to explain because it's a very overwhelming feeling. I could feel the presence of God, and I felt like He was saying, 'Okay, you're fine. Everything's going to be alright. I'm going to take care of you.' For about two months, we kept going back to that church, sitting in the back and crying."

God, in His perfect timing, had just sewn the final tassel on the tapestry He had been weaving for years. The dry times, the broken dreams, the duplicities, the disappointments, and years on the wrong road had finally taken its toll. Without knowing, John had been stripped of all his resistances and become as soft and raw as a newborn baby that day. And what do babies do when they are born, or as in John's case, born again? They cry. It is a cry for life, it is a cry for a new beginning, and it is a cry that is satisfied by God's loving embrace. What happened to John and Dana that day has the wonder factor of being something that is unexplainable, yet so real, that nothing can ever compete with it for sheer joy and peace. It is hard to explain because it involves mammoth things like eternity, unconditional love, peace that passes all understanding, foreknowing, omniscience, and old things made new. At the same time it is bathed in simplicity—*Jesus loves me this I know*. You are finally home, and you are forgiven, redeemed, and wonderfully brand-new. Looking back, John finally understood what all the dryness and darkness had been leading to—it was this moment. Who wouldn't cry over something so incredible?

John's story is also a testament to prayer. For years his parents prayed for him to return to church and trusted God to do His job. "Unfortunately neither of my parents lived to see the day when I came back, but I'm sure they are rejoicing in God's kingdom today. They knew I still believed in Yeshua [the Hebrew name of Jesus] all those years, but I had to search out answers for myself. There were answers I had accepted for so many years that suddenly ceased to make sense."

John found the answers he was looking for when he dove headfirst into the Bible. He prayed hard to God: *I'm not interested in dogma, doctrine, or man-made religious theology. I only want to know the truth of what You are and how to be in relationship with You. Show me how to find it. Reveal it to me. Put me in contact with those that deeply search and want to know.* John says, "You have to understand something—I was pretty upset at the time. I felt I had missed God for twenty-eight years, and I became very driven to know and understand the biblical Scriptures. I wanted to get back to the foundation, so I went back to the beginning of the Bible, the Torah. I studied in both the synagogue and the church. The more I questioned, the more God revealed to me. The more I asked, debated, argued, and challenged, the more I learned. I made some people quite angry, while others loved it and when they saw me they knew we were going deep in the Word, not accepting something until I could understand it, looking up the Hebrew, Greek, and Aramaic words ... Eastern versus Western thought. I finally got my passion back for the Word of God. From so much study of the Torah, the New Testament simply opened up and finally made perfect sense to me. I came home one day from the synagogue and told my wife that finally, I felt that I was beginning to get a foundation in the Word of God. The next day we went to church, and as I sat there I felt the Spirit of the Lord say to me, 'The way you were raised, where you are now, and where I am taking you is like reading a book of a thousand pages, but only starting on page 800. If you do not have any idea of what the first 799 pages say, how do you possibly think you're going to understand pages 800 through 1,000?' I was stunned. Dana also got hungry. When the kids went to school, she literally spent the entire day in the Bible, studying, looking up, and finding information. He put a deep desire in her to know Him, and her relationship with God developed as a result."

One day while reading Psalms 51, an undercurrent of anger inside John revealed itself. "As I read the Bible more and more, the teachings of my former religion made less sense to me. I got to the part where David said, 'Create me in a clean heart and renew a right spirit within me.' That was the straw that broke the camel's back for me. I wrote to the Baha'i leaders and said, 'Guys, thank you very much. It's been wonderful, but I'm gone.' They wrote back thanking me for my service and said if I ever changed my mind, feel free to contact them again. They were kind and loving about it."

John's departure meant very limited contact with Dan Seals, who was still involved in that faith. But though they hadn't seen each other since 1983 and phone calls had been sporadic over the years, John felt the need to reach out and mend fences when he heard that Dan had been diagnosed with mantle cell lymphoma and was terminally ill. "I had been trying to talk to Dan for a couple of years, but it didn't work. There were hard feelings, but at that point I said, 'This is ridiculous.' We were good friends for many years, grew up together, and traveled the world together. We were brothers in arms for a long, exciting time. So we did talk and decided it was nonsense to hold onto bitterness and agreed to let it go. All the stupid politics that went down in our career and the machinations of other people involved went by the wayside. It was such wonderful closure for me because I felt everything was complete and nothing left unsaid."

Seals died the following day, on March 25, 2009. He was sixty-one.

Today John continues to tour on a regular basis and plays close to fifty dates a year, including visits to Australia and the Philippines, where he is especially beloved. He is still writing songs, telling jokes and stories, and plays his music in secular venues for people. "Although I'm heavily involved in both, I don't talk about politics or religion from the stage. People don't come to hear that. They come to hear music. I try to get everybody out of their daily grind, to just come in and laugh a little bit. All that stuff is waiting for them when they leave, so I try to help them escape for a little while."

He takes the same approach when his church ministers to the homeless and less fortunate. "For me, it's not about what you say, but what you do, and as Francis of Assisi says, 'Preach the gospel at all times and when necessary use words.' I enjoy finding out where they're from or how long they've been out there. Sometimes Scripture isn't what they need at the moment. They simply need someone to care about them, talk to them as humans not a number. Yeshua says, 'I came to save that which was lost,' which can have many different meanings from the lost of Israel to the lost in the church and the lost outside the church. We all get lost, we all need help from the highest to the lowest and have a need to return to God. He wants us to build a relationship. I prefer to be with hungry people because it keeps my fire lit. For me it's all about kindness. There are so many avenues God will open up if you're open to them, and He will work through you."

Like the Grammy-nominated duo's last big hit, John now knows the answer to almost every great mystery that life has to offer. "Love *is* the answer!"

DEZ DICKERSON

Prince

With Dez Dickerson at his side, Prince became a household name, selling more than one hundred million albums, earning seven Grammys, a Golden Globe, and an Academy Award. Sporting his trademark rising sun headband, Dez was Prince's dazzling lead guitarist from 1978 to 1983, and his solo on "Little Red Corvette" ranked number sixty-four on *Guitar World*'s list of 100 Greatest Guitar Solos.

EIGHT

PARTIES WEREN'T MEANT TO LAST

DEZ DICKERSON | Prince

Dez Dickerson and I grew up in very different eras. Our cultural environments were polar opposites, but through our respective rock and roll paths, we ended up in the same place when it came to our faith. The one thing we know we had in common growing up was a lot of snow in the hard winters where we once lived.

I have always believed there's a shared DNA in music people. People in our business sense one another across the room, especially if we are the only ones there who have travelled that very unique long and winding road. We become like magnets, and in a short time we'll be drawn to the same spot. We can smell the music on each other, the analog tapes, the digital "ones and zeros," the slapback echo that has dominated our lives.

Growing up in Lewiston, Idaho (population 12,000), I wasn't exposed to much diversity and culture—unless you consider cowboys diverse. I was seventeen years old when I first met someone of African American descent. His name was Joe Jackson. Because of my sheltered existence, I had developed zero prejudices, so when I shook hands with Joe, I was not only curious but also intrigued by our apparent differences. I wanted to know as much as I could about him. I admit even though my queries to him were innocent, some were probably not that welcome or appropriate. Growing up next to the Nez Perce Indian reservation gave me an appreciation for people different than me—in fact, the more different the person, the more exciting they were to me. This curiosity may be why I chose to go to college to earn a Bachelor of Science degree in foreign trade. I wanted to visit other people, talk to them, learn their languages, eat their food, and drink their beer.

So here's Joe Jackson from Oakland, California, who had been sent to the minors to play baseball for our local farm team in Lewiston. Joe was the only black man in seven counties, and I could feel his loneliness. Sure, we had our good old boy rednecks like every other rural town, and you could tell Joe was very cautious. Like a puppy dog, I pursued a friendship, and it wasn't long before there were some people who not only shunned Joe but also separated themselves from me. I remember sitting in the stands at a high school football game with him and hearing people in the rows behind us yelling racial slurs at a black player from a visiting team just for our benefit. We finally had to leave the game—Joe in self-preservation mode and me in confusion. The hurt I saw in his eyes was something I had never experienced before. He was such a cool guy, and he even knew one of The Platters, a famous R&B group from the '50s. When I found out he knew somebody famous, I wouldn't have cared if he were florescent pink. We left the ballpark and here I am, a kid about as white as anyone could be, trying to ease a cultural pain that was completely beyond my understanding. As I reflect upon my naïveté, I would love to hear back the words I used to try to make him feel better. I fear I failed miserably.

When I entered the music industry, I loved the lack of prejudice at its core. I knew that a flashy guitar solo has no color on a record. The most talented person, regardless of race or ethnicity, always got the job. Race has never been an issue for me and I sensed immediately it wasn't an issue for Dez, who was raised in the suburbs of Minneapolis.

"Minneapolis was then as it is now, predominantly white. There's a huge Scandinavian influence with lots of Norwegians and Swedes, and even musically," Dez reminisces as we sit across from each other in my Nashville hotel room. "I remember even back in the '60s a lot of bands were multiracial … I'm talking rock bands, show bands, funk bands, whatever. Some of the funkiest players I've worked with were white. Race was never an issue. It was always the music."

So here's Dez and me looking across a million miles of confusion and hearing the same central song. I learned discomfort around different ethnic backgrounds over the years and miss the innocence I once had about the whole matter. I eventually became a bit guarded, wondering if a black associate didn't like me because I was white and because "my people" had treated "their people" badly in the past. That's what I liked about Dez—that vibe was never on the table.

Dez told me that as a child, it was always about God in the Dickerson household. He lived near Pilgrim Baptist Church, the largest in the Minneapolis region, with a membership teetering around five thousand. "It was a magnet for everything in the African American community at that time. I went to church, Sunday school, vacation Bible school, weddings, funerals, meals, everything. I was a typical church kid. I remember when I was around five or six years old and singing 'Jesus Loves Me' in Sunday school. I had this sense wash over me that this is really true … that Jesus is real and does love me."

Dez's mother, Charlene, was the spiritual catalyst when it came to matters of family faith and was in the leadership of the church, while Dez's father, Maurice, had a more hands-off approach. "My dad grew up in a religious family, and maybe not in the positive way that Mom was. He had stuff forced on him and later rebelled … his attitude was, 'Yeah, I believe, but I want nothing to do with the church.'"

Neither did Charlene after a political dispute in their church erupted, and so the Dickersons (sans Maurice) began attending a local Lutheran church, a place where Dez admits he felt no connection. "It was a huge denominational and doctrinal change, and I noticed it was a more laid-back approach. The service was shorter. The people weren't as close. We weren't as connected. I had reached the point where music captivated my interest and religion fell to the wayside."

"Belonging" to a church can be a very delicate matter for a family. Mom may like the liturgy, sister Suzie may like the youth pastor, brother Bob's into the music, and Dad's after the cookies and coffee in the foyer. But when these are the attractions, and not Jesus, and the church changes one of them, then the whole experience begins to disintegrate, eventually driving followers away.

Dez had another religious experience, but it had nothing to do with God. "I remember brushing my teeth in the mirror one morning and experienced that same sensation that washed over me as a youth when I sang 'Jesus Loves Me.' It wasn't as dramatic, and it wasn't an audible voice, but when I looked in the mirror I heard this inner voice tell me, 'You're going to learn to play the guitar, you're going to be very good at it, and that's what you're going to do with your life.'"

That notion didn't come straight out of the blue. Maurice was an accomplished musician, and one of Dez's earliest memories was waking up in the middle of the night to the sound of Maurice's saxophone in the downstairs living room. "Dad started travelling at age eleven and played for years. He quit because he had to raise a family. He loved jazz and had an audiophile stereo system before it was cool. I grew up hearing Miles Davis, Aretha Franklin, B.B. King, and King Curtis."

Like Dez, I loved jazz. It was our rebellion music until Bill Haley and His Comets came along to divert us white guys into something else. And for those people who don't quite get jazz as a basis to our musical heritage and its appeal, just listen to The Oscar Peterson Trio play "I Love's You Porgy" and tell me you don't notice something real cool.

Outside the home, Dez got a taste of Beatlemania on *The Ed Sullivan Show*. A few months later, he and a friend went to see the theatrical release of *A Hard Day's Night*. It was a game-changer. "We were the only two black kids in our neighborhood who were into rock and roll. The theater was jam-packed—90 percent of them were screaming girls. I couldn't even hear the dialogue in the movie, but I went out into the lobby and bought the single of "A Hard Day's Night." I was so profoundly impacted by that moment, I knew exactly what I was going to do from that day on."

As the '60s progressed and music got heavier and more progressive, so did Dez's dedication to music. He was inspired by Cream, Hendrix, Led Zeppelin, Robin Trower, Black Sabbath, Deep Purple, and Grand Funk Railroad. "I literally imitated Grand Funk's lead singer, Mark Farner. He wore a vest with no shirt, a black armband, and green crushed velvet pants. Somehow I managed to find a pair of those. Musically I was colorblind and ethnically neutral. I didn't feel like I had to play rhythm and blues because I was black. The opposite was also true when it came to rock. I didn't feel like the music was off limits because I wasn't white. I found the whole idea of race in music profoundly stupid. If you look at certain artists throughout history, even going back to Mozart and Van Gogh, they had this overriding sense of having their own GPS. It wasn't about trying to fit in, because I never fit into a mold. The funny thing is, when I started talking I didn't sound like my parents. I didn't sound like my relatives. I didn't sound, talk black, and my race never defined me. It's weird, but I've always been this way." These wisdoms are what defines Dez to me—not only did he become a genius in his craft, but he mixed that with a street sense about his God-given identity and God's intention as to how we were made to relate to one another as brothers and sisters on this planet. If we all could just get over ourselves…

Music brought out the perfectionist in Dez, who spent hours honing his craft on his Gibson guitar. His new passion did not go unnoticed by family members. "I'd practice a minimum of six hours a day, and it got to the point my parents became genuinely concerned for me. I remember discussions about, 'Do we seek help for him?' I wouldn't say it was an obsession, but I was committed to learning everything I could. I had set certain goals for myself. I'd listen to songs on the record player and try to play them note for note. I told myself if I could learn 'Crossroads' by Cream from beginning to end, I would know for sure this was what I was supposed to be doing. It sort of became my 'touch tune.'"

When Dez was tuning into the music, he consciously turned the volume down on God. He broke his mother's heart at age sixteen when he told her that he didn't want to go to church any longer. "You have to know my mom to know that was a bold move on my part. She stands about five foot one, but she's a mighty person. She was very cool and wise about my decision and said, 'Well, okay, if that's the way you feel.' So I opted out of the whole church thing as a teenager and began to pursue what was by then my true religion: 'The Church of Dez Becoming Rich and Famous.' Everything else became secondary in my life, and I do mean everything!"

I believe Dez made my writing job easier by staying true to a pattern that I have suggested throughout these stories. No matter how we defined it, explained it, described it, or justified this decision to break away from our geographical, cultural, and family mode, it was mainly because we wanted to prove something. I don't know where it comes from, but when an inborn talent mixes with an outward desire to escape the mundane, people like Dez and almost everyone else in this book see something out there, way out there, that will validate them as somebody or something more than how their beginnings defined them. Some guys need to show their dad they are their own man, while others want to break Mom's apron strings that they feel are wrapped around their wonderful necks. Some have to leave to prove they are more than the common existence they have been told to accept in life. It's like when you see a deer raise its nostrils to the wind and begin sniffing—they know there's something out there, either to embrace or run from.

While the good Lord allowed Dez to have free will for the next decade, he says he experienced "spikes of conviction" every now and then. "I remember playing in Aberdeen, South Dakota, for six nights in a row. The owner put the band in an apartment above the club. An evangelical organization was out on the sidewalk with bullhorns, doing the fire and brimstone thing and at first, I remember having this twinge of guilt. Soon that feeling was replaced by a flood of anger because it was people like them who made me bolt from the church in the first place. So I burrowed into my resistance for several years."

Ironically, Dez's first band was called Sky Church—naturally, he was the leader. He admits he wasn't always the most diplomatic member, but no one cared more about the music than Dez. "I was OCD about the whole thing. Every note had to be perfect. I'd be in bands where I was better than the drummer. I'd hear someone play the wrong note, and it would drive me crazy. I'd stop what I was doing, put my guitar down, walk over, and take over their instrument and say, 'This is how it goes.' I was in some great bands but none ever survived. I was the only one who ended up making a living."

Minneapolis/St. Paul was one of the few places in the country where working musicians could earn a living. The Twin Cities has always had a vibrant music scene, and the region's punk/funk/disco/rock/R&B scene flourished in the late '70s thanks in large part to a diminutive and painfully shy artist named Prince.

Prince Nelson Rogers, aka Prince, was a tour-de-force. He could write, dance, sing, perform, arrange, produce, and he played almost all of the instruments on his recordings. He was one of those rare artists who could do everything. As an unknown teenager with no previous track record, he demanded and got total creative control. "Prince was like an urban legend in Minneapolis. Everybody had heard of him, but no one had seen him play any shows. Owen Husney, who owned The Ad Company, an advertising agency that marketed local musicians, managed him. Husney strategically packaged Prince and shopped around for a record deal. He was getting interest before Prince played his first live show. I had been on the scene for years and never seen him play, but everybody seemed to have heard of this guy. It was unreal."

Husney's approach was clever and worked well in an industry that thrived on The Next Big Thing. He pitted all of the record labels against one another until he squeezed a three-record deal from Warner Brothers, who wanted the first album within six months. A touring band needed to be assembled.

Every once in a while, a manager comes along with real vision and a unique inner knowledge of how to spot talent and market that talent. They pull off things that no one else can conceive. It is like the story about a manager named Helen Noga who spotted Johnny Mathis and knew he could probably become one of the most famous love song crooners of all time. Her management deal structure with Johnny was unheard of and became legendary. Probably Colonel Parker and Elvis Presley's relationship are the only ones in the same category as far as being unique and wildly successful. As the story goes, Helen asked Johnny if he would rather have half of millions of dollars or all of thousands of dollars. He answered, "Of course, I like the million-dollar bit." She said, "Fine, sign with me, and I will take that other half." He did and she did just what she said she would do—she made him famous and they made millions of dollars, which they split down the middle. As is customary in this industry, Johnny eventually took Helen to court because he felt her middle and his middle were not in the same place.

In the winter of 1978, Dez answered an audacious ad placed by Husney in the *Twin Cities Reader*, a local entertainment paper. ("Warner Bros. recording artist seeks guitarist and keyboard player…") The audition was held at a rehearsal space at Del's Tire Mart on the west bank of the Mississippi, near the University of Minnesota campus. Dez showed up at the appointed time in his lime-green Plymouth Sebring, the latest in a series of muscle cars Dez had owned since he was sixteen. However, Prince, bassist Andre Anderson, and drummer Bobby Rivkin showed up two and a half hours late. Prince didn't apologize for his tardiness, nor did he speak directly to Dez. He took his place behind an Oberheim polyphonic synthesizer and Hohner Clavinet keyboard and began playing. He nodded slightly to Dez, who cut one of his blistering solos and then quickly returned to the rhythm. Fifteen minutes later, Dez left because of a prior commitment. His brief performance was enough for Prince, who liked what he heard. "He asked me some very mature questions for a nineteen-year-old guy. He wanted to know my musical tastes, influences, my work ethic, and my career goals. I was very honest with him—I wanted to front my own band as I had done in the past. I then took off for Wisconsin to play a gig. I began getting calls from Prince, asking me to come to his house and learn a couple of his songs. About three weeks into this, I walk in and Owen is standing in the kitchen and hands me a check. He didn't say a word, just hands me the check. I guess when I took it, it meant I had the job."

Prince wasn't an overnight success; his ascension was slow according to industry standards. Even though he had an ironclad agreement with Warner Brothers, they were ready to wash their hands of him after album sales didn't meet their expectations. Prince defied categorization, and the label didn't know how to promote him. His sexually explicit lyrics and incorporation of dance, funk, R&B, and rock music clearly baffled the execs. Dez says it all changed when *Rolling Stone* wrote a glowing review of his second album, *Dirty Mind* (1980). "I remember the day the review came out, because Prince had asked me to go to lunch with him at this Indian restaurant he loved. I was three years older than him, and I ended up being kind of like his older brother. He didn't trust the managers that much, didn't trust the record people at all, but he trusted me. He was very down because he felt like the ax was going to fall at any moment. Then in the middle of our lunch, he opened the magazine, read this review, and his face lit up. A critic's darling was born, and that review changed the tide. Finally, the record label decided to get behind the record and fully promote it. So from there, things changed dramatically."

Contrary to popular belief, adversity is not the greatest test of character. Nothing tests character like overnight success, says Dez. "It was like this vertical takeoff, and suddenly there are more people around you. 'Oh, we have roadies now? Oh, we have bodyguards too?' And they're there for a reason too. We experienced mini riots; we couldn't walk down the street, and they had to cordon off the floor of our hotel. What this does to your head is beyond description, and what it does to the human psyche is a whole other thing. There's this internal mechanism that unconsciously begins to take form, and your equilibrium gets so skewed that you find yourself doing and saying things that aren't you. You become your own press release. It's difficult to articulate if you haven't experienced it."

Fame is a complicated narcotic. Deep down you know that it has nothing to do with reality, but after your first hit, pardon the pun, you like the high so much that you can't stop toking on its allure. Fame is fleeting, and this is what makes it easy to define in the framework of drugs. The word *fleeting* in this context means coming down from an artificial high, and that part of the process is not only bad but inevitable. Because it is usually wrapped in money, fame draws unto itself many unpredictable situations and strange people. French poet Victor Hugo described this best when he was asked about fame:

"Fame must have enemies, as light must have gnats."

For almost a decade, Dez had been a faithful disciple of his dream, adhering to every doctrine of self—eating, drinking, sleeping, and pursuing stardom with all his might. He thought, as many do, that stardom would be his salvation. But when he looked in the mirror, he wondered, *I should be the happiest guy in the world—my dream is coming true, so why do I feel so empty*?

I marvel at Dez's and my reflective similarities—like us, it's not always black and white but instead it's colorless, vapid, void, and tragic all at once. I am compounding images with side-by-side observations because it is important to understand one of the purposes of this book. There's emptiness at the end of the fame and fortune rainbow when it is all about self. Most of us will admit the price we paid for admission wasn't worth the bad movie that unfolded before our eyes. To double up on Dez's observation ... I was sitting at the desk of my home office in the Hollywood Hills one beautiful afternoon and couldn't figure out what was wrong. I had a number-one record on the charts, a large estate in the Hills, a movie actress wife, and was routinely cavorting with the rich and famous. I remember getting up from my desk and walking out through French doors to a private patio that looked out over Laurel Canyon, and I stared out into that heightened space feeling empty and confused. Years later at a church speaking engagement in Southern California, the host pastor, during a question and answer segment, asked me if I have ever looked back to a time when I could identify what I was missing without Christ in my life. It blew me away because that moment from decades ago flashed immediately in my mind. I knew what that empty space was, and I smiled at God's beautiful, subtle ways of letting us know that He has always been with us—even when we had turned our back on Him by taking advantage of His wonderful gift of free will. A gift intended for much higher purposes.

When Dez was in the studio or by himself, he could usually quell his conscience, but he found that a more difficult proposition out on the road. "There were nights I'd look out into the audience and see a kid no older than eight or nine and think, *That could be* my *child out there. What are we teaching them?* Sometimes on our days off from the road, I'd watch a Christian TV show, looking for answers—some peace. Some nights as we gathered in a circle and prayed before a show, I'd wonder, *Who are we praying to? The God I learned about would not approve of what we're doing.*

Dez was most likely referring to Prince's material on *Dirty Mind*, a mash-up of religion and extreme sexuality. It was a gender and race-bending album that was unsafe for children's ears and I'm sure, arched a few eyebrows of many adults. It was a message that Dez wasn't sure he fully endorsed. When the road to fame is officially set out upon, it is hard to recognize the twists and turns that lead you away from that God-given center that has been placed inside by the pastors and moms of the past. The bends in the road are so subtle that it takes a while sometimes to realize you are drifting off the shoulder and into the, once again pardon the expression, weeds. At some point, the fortunate ones on this magic carpet ride begin sensing that something is not matching up with what is good and true inside. This awareness can drive a person crazy because it is the beginning of the luster coming off the crown that has been sought after for so long. The dedication to seeking fame begins to turn on you, and it happens as subtly as the whole journey did when it started leaving the original destination behind. Dez was beginning to get it and had an inkling that he was on the old proverbial road to nowhere … man!

One night in December 1980, when Dez was sitting alone in his living room, he felt as if he were in the presence of God just as he experienced as a child. He says God showed him that night why he felt empty and that his greatest need was to know Him, the love that He had for Dez, and the love He wanted Dez to have for others. He showed Dez that he didn't need to be rich, powerful, or a star—he simply needed to be forgiven. "He showed me my whole life in a moment of time, like reliving it all in an instant. He gave me a choice—I could continue to live my life my way, or I could surrender my life to Him, trusting that He knew best what to do with it. It was the easiest choice I've ever made. I couldn't see how I could possibly say no. I don't remember what I prayed or how I responded—all I know is that, when I did, I instantly felt different. The weight of the world came off me, and, for the first time in my life, I believed I was experiencing real peace."

After his born-again experience, Dez began reading the Bible on a daily basis and decided after nine years of dating that it was time to marry his girlfriend, Becki. They were married in June 1981 at the Lutheran Church of the Redeemer in St. Paul before family, relatives, old schoolmates, and band mates. Dez remembers the only day he was happier was the birth of their son, Jordan, who came along five years later.

Dez's renewed spirituality also invigorated his attitude about the band, and everything was fun again. He added a gallon of milk to the rider and arranged to get back to the hotel ahead of the rest of the band so he could read the Bible until he fell asleep. Inner peace was all well and good, but Dez had to strap on the body armor, because he was about to go into battle as Prince became a household name in 1983, thanks to a trio of radio-friendly hits—"Little Red Corvette," "1999," and "Delirious"—plus a little invention called MTV.

Curiously, this is around the time our paths crossed. Prince and his band were on the precipice of superstardom while I was trying to hold on to what little I had left.

I was grasping at straws around this time—and yes, some of those straws were used for snorting cocaine. My successful tenure as a producer with the Outlaw movement should have been a powerful credential, but a strange thing happened as a result. When the breakup between Waylon and me happened, he controlled that small community of renegade artists and I found myself on the outside of that genre. In the process of defying the good old boy structure in Nashville, I had picked a bed (The Outlaws) that I was no longer able to sleep in. Mainstream Nashville was able to get even and not let me back into their fold. I had brought rock and roll production to Nashville, and that is what made The Outlaws records sing. The irony is that I had entered the Nashville fray as the rock producer from Los Angeles, but when I returned to Tinsel Town I was now cast as a country producer. Regardless of my success, I was not what the labels were looking for to produce their pop acts. I had a few opportunities with hot rock artists like Nick Gilder ("Hot Child in the City") and big names like David Cassidy, but I couldn't seem to get back on the charts in a meaningful manner. I did get a big break with David Geffen's record company when someone in the A&R department at the label heard some demos I made with a band of sizzling Cubans named OXO. Geffen got in a bidding war with A&M and finally won with a half-million-dollar album deal. The budget for the album was $250,000, and this was back in the early 1980s. The leader of OXO was fascinated with another Geffen artist, John Lennon, and felt this was a natural fit for all of us, which was why he chose Geffen over A&M.

I began producing OXO at Sunset Sound Studios on Sunset Boulevard in Hollywood, sharing the three-studio complex for months with a hot new band from Minneapolis called Prince. The two main studios we were recording in spilled out into a protected courtyard with a basketball area and a pinball machine room off to one side. Bands, producers, engineers, artists, gofers, etc. would hang out there between takes and breaks.

This was always a fun aspect of recording in multi-studio environments. When I was producing Waylon, we would be in Hollywood's Sound Labs Studio B and next door in Studio A would be Olivia Newton John or Hall and Oates. The mixture between the different music cultures was entertaining, and watching Olivia's and Waylon's drummers in the midst of a heated pinball contest was a study in hilarity as they expressed their cultural opinions in exciting moments of defeat and victory. It was very different with the Prince/OXO sessions.

There we were, two decidedly diverse ethnic groups who would seem to find a commonality in this fact and the cutting nature of their music, but nothing clicked between the two bands. Prince may have never said hello to anyone. I am sure Dez and I shot baskets or played pinball machines side by side during those days, but my remembrance of him is vague.

He wasn't there all the time, and as is consistent with the Prince experience at the studio, he seemed like a nice guy but aloof. Now that I know what he was going through, it would have probably been a good thing if he and I had sat down for a chat. Often close friendships between members of neighboring bands are made in the intense atmosphere of making albums, but this time, it didn't happen. The obvious discussion of God's perfect timing would take place at a later time.

There was an introverted intensity that kept us separated. I was wrapped up in what I knew could be my last major shot at getting back into the good graces of the LA music scene—if I blew it with Geffen, then I promise you … it was blown! OXO was caught up in the passion of making their record, while Prince projected an air of aloofness.

Dez was going through his own personal dilemmas, walking various tightropes of faith and fame while dancing to the spiritual/moral/psychological complexities of working on the "sexplosive" Vanity 6 recordings at the same time. Our ships had crossed troubled waters at Sunset Sound, but in a way we passed in the dark without really touching on each other. He was getting a grasp on his new walk with the Lord, and I was hanging on for dear life to an existence that wanted nothing to do with our Creator.

Dez and Prince went on their way into their story, and our debut record on Geffen Records was a Top 30 hit called "Whirly Girl" that died a painful death. The moment the record charted, the group began breaking up. Politics and power struggles erupted between management and Geffen, which left me out in the cold again. *Ahh, there's that special splendor that surrounds bands when they get a hit record raising its head again!*

So while that was my trip at the time, here's what Dez says about his: "The thing about fame is if you don't watch out, it'll make you break your own rules. Being a new Christian, without anyone around to follow me in this new life, I was like a plane flying on instruments in a dense fog—if your instruments were off, you were in danger. Fame started to change me, and I didn't know it. It wasn't a radical overnight change. No, it was slow and subtle. I wasn't aware I had been giving up tiny little pieces of my self-worth, until one day these pieces added up to the point that I had become someone I didn't know anymore." (For reference and confirmation, check every other chapter in this book.)

Dez's desire to have a solo career began kicking in, and he fashioned himself as a sort of "rock star for Jesus" to counterbalance some of Prince's sexually charged lyrics and the lewd nature of their music. The timing also coincided with a new band contract that, while it offered some royalty participation, didn't seem to be commensurate with their collective contribution to making Prince a star. Prince declined to negotiate and took the contract off the table. Ill feelings took hold, and tensions slowly increased despite the fact that they were becoming more popular by the day. A huge fissure was created when Prince was photographed with

Vanity 6 on the cover of *Rolling Stone* instead of his band, which Dez took personally.

As the tour rolled on, the venues got bigger, and so did the tour buses and entourages. Prince, however, rolled on down the highway with Vanity and other crewmembers, but not the band. He also demanded his own dressing room and only saw the band moments before show time. Dez believes the show changed from funky and spontaneous rock and roll to rehearsed Vegas-style schmaltz. When Dez voiced his concerns to Prince, he felt like it was the first time Prince had ever been patronizing to him.

Dez's resentments began to manifest, so he demanded his own dressing room. And remember that famous milk rider that Dez placed in the contract? Well, that was replaced with a bottle of Blue Nun wine, and Dez began partying like it was 1999. One day during sound check, he grabbed a boom stand and went after keyboardist Matt Fink, fully intending to do bodily harm. Fink was lucky that crewmembers held Dez back until he calmed down, or else the keyboardist might have been looking for new ivories. Dez recalls, "For the first year, you're in what I call this grace bubble. Everything is new and wonderful, but then conflict arises. You have renewed thinking and begin making decisions based on who you think you are at that point. It's as if there was this internal countdown taking place. I could feel it. I started unconsciously acting out in certain ways. I began sabotaging myself. In a way I was letting myself know it was time to exit."

And then there were the fans. Multitudes of them clamoring at Prince and the band, causing riots, holding up traffic, and presenting security issues. Dez remains astounded at the lengths some fans would go to meet or have relationship with him. "One female fan wanted to leave her husband and marry me—never mind the fact that I was already married and didn't know her from Adam. Another young lady wrote asking if she could move in with Becki and me."

Being the toast of the town, Dez met the Who's Who of the music, entertainment, and sports world—Mick Jagger, Keith Richards, Bob

Seger, Stevie Wonder, Magic Johnson, Jim Brown, Bruce Springsteen, Joe Perry, John Belushi, and members of the Jackson 5. One night during a show in Michigan, Dez looked over his shoulder behind the monitor mixer and saw the unmistakable silhouette of his rock hero—Mark Farner of Grand Funk Railroad.

Despite flashes of excitement, life on the road became almost unbearable with its demands and monotony. There were a lot of new faces and many bandwagon jumpers. Manipulation, self-promotion, and bad intentions were constant battles Dez and others had to wade through. The old guard was slipping away. "During that time I developed what I called the 'concentric circle theory.' Relationships in every artist's career are like sets of concentric circles, traveling outward from the artist at the center. The odd dynamic is, the further out from the center, the bigger people's egos were. When you were part of the contingent that paid the dues and sweat the bullets it took to give them a bandwagon to jump on, it was irritating."

Dez is describing here the bane of making it big in the music business. It is the talent and hard work of a small group of people that create the success, and when outsiders begin weaving their way into the fabric of the phenomenon, that's when relationships start unraveling. Morally this fabric gets stretched to its limits, and once clear visions become blurred. It's the original band united against the world at one time, and then a shift occurs and members splinter into separate entities with diverse goals. Next a maze develops around the band, and in order to move into the center of the maze where the goodies are, the original members had to deal with Victor Hugo's "gnats" who decided to shoot their way into that center, leaving a lot of spent souls in their wake. One by one, outside private interests begin culling the herd, and one band becomes many enterprises. A rotting process begins, the corpses don't go away, and the smell of deception and backbiting makes the whole place uninhabitable after a while. The concentric circles begin to close in, and soon there's a new center. It's not about the band and the music anymore—it is about egos and money and position and notoriety and self-doting fragments. The invading strangers become familiar, and old mates become strangers.

It got to the point that Dez brought his beloved Blue Nun onstage with him for "medicinal purposes" to regulate his emotions. In place of the cups of water he had his tech normally place on his amp and in various parts of the stage, they were now filled with wine. The embers of Dez's discontent burst into a full blaze of outrage when the band conquered New York City's Radio City Music Hall. After the performance, Prince left the rest of the band standing on the street in front of the venue while he hopped into a limo and sped away. The band had to hail a cab to their hotel, the Parker Meridien, but Dez seethed the entire ride and told himself, *I'm done!*

As much as Dez valued the opportunity he had been given, it was clear things weren't going to change and it was up to him to change them. He started the journey as a young veteran of the local Twin Cities music scene. He had become, next to Prince, the most visible member of the band, with his rising sun headband and blistering licks (his solo on "Little Red Corvette" was named one of the Top 100 Guitar Solos of all time by *Guitar World* magazine).

The 1999 tour was the top grossing tour of 1983, with more than $10 million in gross receipts. The band received a bonus of ten thousand dollars apiece for their services. The song "1999" went double platinum the following year, but the band did not receive any royalties. Dez and Becki drove cross-country from Minneapolis to Los Angeles, visiting friends and relatives and decompressing from the circus life of the road. When they finally arrived in Los Angeles, Prince summoned Dez back to Minneapolis to talk about Dez's future role in the band. Prince was planning his next big move, a feature film called *Purple Rain*. However, that required a three-year commitment from Dez. Prince offered Dez two alternatives: commit to another three years or, if he committed to two, Prince would see to it that his managers would get Dez a record deal.

Dez told him he'd need to think about his offer, but he knew he didn't have it in him to continue with the charade. He was depleted in every way: spiritually, emotionally, creatively, and mentally. He says it was an easy decision to make. "Becki and I talked about it, we cried, and then we knew what we needed to do. I had to leave. I couldn't do it anymore. It was five years of my life—it was the best of times, and it was the worst of times. Sure, there are things, had I known then what I know now, that I would have done differently. But I wouldn't trade what we lived for anything, warts and all. Some people still wonder why I left when I did, but anyone that knows me knows better. It was just a season—a significant one, but a season. The only thing worse than missing your opportunities in life is to hang around too long. We have a good relationship today, but a relationship with Prince is different than what you'd normally think. It's probably why Prince has a more antagonistic relationship with the people who stayed the longest and why I'm the only one in the band he's never sued or threatened to sue."

As Dez so famously sang on the song "1999," "Parties weren't meant to last."

Prince's parting gift to Dez was a cameo in his 1984 movie *Purple Rain* with Dez's new group the Modernaires. However, their song was not released as a single or on the film's soundtrack—perhaps Prince's way of keeping Dez in check. The Modernaires experienced a short burst of success when they supported Billy Idol on his 1984 *Rebel Yell* tour. They later morphed into the Dez Dickerson Band. The group, even without a record deal, began booking headliner shows for big money. Then Dez suddenly pulled up stakes and quit. "I was getting this sense of déjà vu in that I'd be touring in hopes of getting a record deal, and it seemed like another uphill climb. I had this sense I needed to stop. So I came off the road, cancelled all of our dates, and boom—it was over. The Lord basically told me I needed to get off the road and into a church. Clearly God had an agenda for me."

The road can be a magical place, but much like catching on to a magic trick, Dez recognized the deception involved in its allure. He saw it for what it was: fantasyland in a carry-on bag. What really drew him up short was understanding that the longer he stayed on that track, the farther he was getting away from his fellowship with the Lord. Dez was now a seeker, and God revealed to him that he was on the verge of getting lost. God did this because He is a good God. He sent His Holy Spirit to tap Dez on the shoulder and gently say to him, "Hey, this way, not that way, for my way is *the* way to a better place."

The special place God had in mind for Dez, Becki, and their newborn son, Jordan, was The Word, a nondenominational gospel church. The Dickersons studied the Bible, forged friendships, became youth pastors, and Dez fielded many offers from churches to give his testimony. He became an ordained minister in 1988 and occasionally freelanced on other artists' albums, such as Aretha Franklin, but money was tight. In 1989, he received a phone call from his agent, John Hule, to coheadline with another Christian artist, Judson Spence, who was trying to drum up label interest in Nashville. The tour was a success, Judson subsequently signed with Atlantic Records, and Dez connected with major players in the Christian music business. "For about six months, Becki and I had what I call a 'progressive dealing of God,' and that's the only way I can describe it. We knew we were supposed to move to Nashville, and it got to the point where it was almost comical. We kept getting these bizarre confirmations we couldn't miss if we tried. I had a meeting with a group of people to talk about a label that I wanted to start, and they offered me a position that didn't yet exist with their company. At this point I'm broker than broke; broker than the Ten Commandments, but we were faithful to God."

Dez accepted a job as vice president of A&R with the Christian music label Star Song Communications in 1990 and moved to Nashville. That's when we met up again, at Bethel Chapel on Granny White Pike and Old Hickory Boulevard.

It wasn't always Debbie and Pat Boone time with Dez and me. There was a shared experience where we were not exactly walking down Mary Poppins Lane singing "You Light Up My Life." We met and became friends at Bethel, but there was a reserve in Dez that let me know—and I understood this stance—that his guard was still up from his experiences with industry types. We were both at an incredibly intense time in our walk with God, and Bethel was an on-fire church with a pastor who understood people like us. It was a place where the famous and infamous mingled with both the wipeouts and winners. It was the perfect place for us to lay down our pasts and rejoice in our new futures. An exciting thing happened during this period that caused our relationship to change from being coworshipers to also becoming coworkers.

Darrell Harris, who was the president of Star Song and Dez's boss, hired me to produce the legendary Imperial's *Big God* album. Dez's professional duties at the label placed him in the position of being the executive producer on the project. In this scenario, the artist is the top dog but at the same time beholden to the record company's desires. Next comes the producer, who although having the responsibility of running the creative aspects of the sessions, will typically have an executive producer who oversees the project, making sure creative needs and business needs are running side by side. Armond Morales, who was the founder and leader of The Imperials, had a pretty good idea of how he saw content and concept for the album.

Now, Dez has previously described his nature when it comes to making music, so I am not drawing my own picture here. In his overseeing of the project, Armond began feeling that Dez was offering a little too much input, and Armond, being an old-timer, began having a problem with this. Dez was bringing his constant quest for perfection into a room where Armond was used to mapping out the legendary Imperials' way of going about things. Long story short … Armond wanted either no executive producer or a different executive producer who was not quite as hands-on. He wanted to work with his producer and the band without any distractions. Job descriptions dictate that it is the producer's job to handle matters such as these between label and artist, so I was asked to go to Darrell Harris and ask for a new rep from the record company. It was a "sticky wicket" as the British would say—I had to protect Armond and keep the label on board at the same time. I was also hoping to foster a deeper personal relationship with Dez at that time.

I think Dez thought that the conflict had to do with him and me, but it didn't—except for the fact that I was able to observe the friction and knew the clashing creative energies could eventually cause problems for the project. Changes were made, politics were satisfied, and Dez and I never talked it out at the time. The issue just laid there all these years. It felt so good when I called Dez about being a part of the book and he didn't hesitate to accept and share his story. Stuff like that project, things that seemed so important at the time, rightfully and eventually dissolved under the weight and wisdom of God's time and ways. I welcomed the opportunity for us to sit down and work on the book together without all the scattered dynamics of our younger years getting in the way.

Dez amazes me in that he continually reinvents himself. Today he manages record label and branding companies Pavilion Entertainment and Pavilion Synergies, coordinates events, runs a social marketing agency, builds brands for companies and artists, and moderates panels at music conferences. Somehow, he still finds time to remain a vessel for God. As Dez sees it, "Jesus described himself as the person who would leave the ninety-nine to go after the one. One of the things that I realize that's key to what I am here for is, I'm one of the guys He sends after the one. Even though I love pastoring and teaching and being involved in church ministry, I find I'm most alive when I'm in that place where church people aren't present, organ music isn't playing in the background, and God creates a divine appointment. There's something even more powerful than a Sunday morning experience in church, and that is a one-on-one experience on a street corner or in a restaurant. For me, that's the sweet spot. So even though I am doing all of these things in business, entertainment, and that whole marketplace, I'm just His guy at large."

So in a nutshell, God used us just as He planned from the beginning. He watched over us, laughed at us, cried for us, helped us, disciplined and corrected us. He let us gather the accolades of crowds, and He taught us what lonely was like. He showed us what dopes we could be, and He also showered us with His grace and mercy. In our moments of madness, He stood by and let us go our own way with His gift of free will. When we finally ran out of bad ideas, He joined us in our quiet times, loved on us, and told us how unique and special we were. We came to know in this process that we are at best a pile of filthy rags compared to His magnificence; but when God lifts us up out of our rag pile and tells us that we are beautiful, we are beautiful indeed. Dez and I came from two entirely different places, different colors and smells, different times, and different worlds. And though we traveled down different paths, we ended up in the same place. We can now sit down together, identical twins in God's eyes—knowing the heat's off, finding comfort in the fact that we have come in from the cold and are now able to openly share our stories, scars, and trophies. All our worldly differences disappear when we look into each other's eyes and see the same thing—God's light beaming back. Then we smile and agree—wow, it is so good that the early part of the trip is over.

Now instead of saying let's party we say … let's pray.

SHANE EVANS

Collective Soul

Collective Soul dominated 1990s rock and alternative radio, charting an astounding seven number-one hits, nineteen Top 40 singles, and ten million in worldwide sales. Hook-laden guitar anthems, powerfully melodic songs, and Shane's powerful backbeat propelled them to international stardom and put their hometown of Stockbridge, Georgia, on the map.

NINE

SHINE

SHANE EVANS | Collective Soul

Shane Evans should be pushing daisies or wearing a toe tag. He admits he has almost met his maker at least half a dozen times in his relatively short life.

As an original cofounder of super group Collective Soul, Evans found himself on the same mortal trajectory as departed drummers Keith Moon, John Bonham, and Dennis Wilson. Like those who preceded him, Shane was swimming in a decadent ocean of booze, drugs, women, and loving the "high life," when rock and roll took a decidedly unexpected turn in the new millennium and yanked the carpet out from underneath him. Imagine Shane's surprise when his band mates, who were buddies since childhood, took a stand and fired him for his lifestyle choices.

I find there is an uncomfortable irony in someone getting fired for a lifestyle that promotes excess—something that is standard procedure in the music industry. Especially when much of the support group (fans) that lifts these discharged malcontents up on a pedestal not only glorifies bad boy action but also emulates and expects it. In fact, in many cases that's what fans pay for, and the artists find that is actually a big part of what they are getting paid for. And how could the band, longtime friends, pals to the end, fire their childhood buddy at a time like this—after years of hard work and camaraderie and dreaming the same dream for so long?

I am purposely digging a literary hole here because I do want to bury myself in the absurd so that as I dig myself out there can be clarity found in the madness once all the muck and slime is scraped off. Hopefully I will answer these questions by the end of this saga.

As a young man, when my career soared in the entertainment business, I not only observed this phenomenon but also became caught up in it myself. In all humility I can say I am an authority on this subject. So let's start at the bottom of the pit and work our way through this.

I had never met Shane in person when I began working on his story, but I knew him better than most people I have spent a substantial amount of time with over the years. I know his story, his pain, his glory, and his redemption. I've sat in the seat beside him on the tour bus and the equipment van. I turned my back on him when his excesses became too much and got in my way. I've hugged him and loved him because of the deep-down part of him that is so special. I cursed him when I saw how he could turn his back on people that cared for him. I stood up for him when others attacked him, because we were bound by loyalty to our cause. I applauded him when he knocked it out of the park with his creativity. I wept for him as I watched him throw away his dreams for a toke, a hit, or other siren call.

If I could put a corkscrew down inside him and pull out that thing that resides there called talent and passion, I could share the beauty that lives within. In time, though, I would become frustrated because once again I would have to watch a God-given gift covered up by excesses, insecurities, and self-destruction to the point that the endowment eventually became imperceptible. I had never met Shane until this book, but yes—I knew him well.

Shane reminds me of the actor who plays the lead in a remake of a classic movie. It is the same script with a new leading man and a new supporting cast. The problem is that our star is, pardon the expression, doing the same lines that so many have done before, the aforementioned Moon, Bonham, and Wilson for example. The movie ends but the drama continues. The show is a success, the players become famous, the crowds idolize them, and they soak up the adulation as if it were health food—then freebies, foibles, and fantasies become too much for one of the members and they succumb to self-indulgence. Finally a faded, confused, and stoned velvet Elvis is asked to leave the building and he can't figure out why.

So here we have Shane (he's in his forties and I'm—well, let's just say I have dental fillings older than him), and I find our stories follow similar paths and parallels. Music might change over time, but the trials and tribulations of people in the industry remain constant.

Like most people born in the Deep South, Shane Evans was introduced to Jesus Christ at a very young age. It was no accident, because where he grew up is called the "Bible Belt." The problem is sometimes that belt is cinched up so tight that it chokes the spoon-fed Jesus right out of a person.

But then there was this special lady in his life—Shane's maternal grandmother, Martha Dean Bowen, a jack-of-all-trades who worked day and night to feed her children. "As a kid, 'Mama Dean' told me and my brother about miracles that had taken place throughout her life and how Jesus constantly watched over her. One time she said her car stalled out on the railroad track as a train was approaching. She tried all that she could to start the car back up. She said when she had no other choice she closed her eyes and prayed to Jesus to save her. Moments later, the car was mysteriously on the other side of the tracks as the train whistled by. She believed to her dying day that God somehow moved her toward safety.

"Mama Dean was also married three times and didn't have an easy life. She had prayed one night to make Jesus real to her and said sometime in the night a light appeared at the end of her bed, and it got brighter and brighter. It was Jesus. She said He made His presence known and let her know how much He loved her. When telling these stories, her whole being changed and she radiated. There was this strength in her voice. I heard it and definitely picked up on that vibe as a kid.

"I went to church, I walked down the aisle to receive my salvation at age thirteen, I professed I was a sinner, but once a person receives his salvation it's vital to have someone mentor you. The Baptist church at the time was more interested in saving souls than mentoring them, and I can look back now and see that I needed someone to guide and shepherd me."

With no shepherd to guide him, Shane got lost in the wilderness. He eventually found a new guiding force, and its lure was as powerful as Shane's first altar call. Its name was rock and roll. The Police, R.E.M., Rush, The Cars, and Van Halen (a group he toured with almost fifteen years later) were Shane's first musical influences growing up in the small town of Stockbridge, Georgia, in the late '70s and early '80s. Then he discovered AC/DC, a group of hard-charging rockers from Down Under, and all bets were off. "Most kids my age were listening to groups like the Bee Gees, ABBA, or KISS at the time. Nothing against those groups, but I didn't see anything real there like I did with AC/DC. I would buy *Hit Parader*, *Circus*, and *CREEM* magazines all the time. The one picture that resonated with me was some cover photo of Angus Young in his black schoolboy cap and clothes, snarled face, ripping up those chords, and snotting all over his guitar. I said to myself, *dude, that's what I want to be!* I wanted to be the center of attention, onstage and under the spotlight, and be seen snotting all over a guitar."

Shane didn't get exactly what he wanted, but he did get the rock and roll dream. He didn't get a chance to snot all over his guitar, but he did pick up a pair of drumsticks, and along with Ed and Dean Roland, Will Turpin, and Ross Childress, banged his way to stardom.

The sudden success experienced by Collective Soul was one of the 1990s big music stories. Their debut album, *Hints, Allegations and Things Left Unsaid* was nothing more than a collection of demos. It was originally released in 1993 by an Atlanta indie label and featured "Shine," a song that resonated with college radio stations in the south. "WJRR in Orlando was playing the song like crazy, and we were on our way to a gig. We were all in this van, and we happened to catch WJRR's Top 10 countdown in the parking lot of a Denny's. They announced that 'Shine' was the number-two song of the week, right behind a song from Rush. We all looked at each other and got out of the van and began jumping up and down. It was then I realized there was a much bigger world beyond Stockbridge, Georgia, and great things were in store for us."

After *Hints* sold close to forty thousand copies (not bad for an independent release), Atlantic Records signed the quintet to a five-record deal. Wisely, Atlantic reissued both the single (which shot straight to number one) and album (which sold two million copies) and thought they had the next Beatles.

It's easy for me to draw parallels between the music of Collective Soul and The Beatles based on what I hear in their music. Like the Fab Four, they wrote melodic guitar-based songs, buoyed by Ed Roland's blend of Lennon lyrics and McCartney-esque melody. Plus the band had a team ear for making commercial music. They admit The Beatles were a major influence, but I like to make a distinction between being influenced by someone and mimicking or copying. The Beatles opened a very wide door of musical adventure and creativity to a waiting world of young musicians-to-be. It was a combination of subtleties and "in your face" songs and production, more than the industry had ever known. In the process they gave those that followed a plethora of tools and suggestions to work with.

If you copy The Beatles, you are a cover band. If you are influenced by them, then you are a student of their craft and can work from their essence, creating new sounds and word plays. Someone obviously influenced The Beatles, and they admit to that. They loved the American rockabilly artists Buddy Holly, Gene Vincent, and Carl Perkins, as well as the early R&B groups from the South. Ringo loved our country music, especially Buck

Owens, and for years I sent him every new country record I could get my hands on. I will sometimes hear a band today that is heavily influenced by The Beatles but sound nothing like them—i.e., Collective Soul.

When you listen to their cover of John Lennon's "Jealous Guy," you get the idea these guys understand the whole Beatles thing. They took the sensitivity of Lennon's lyrics and the sweetness of his melody and then, while maintaining both the word and music integrity, they gave the song a whole new vibe. What is so curious about this is that they used Beatle-infused arrangements and production techniques and totally pulled it off. It was as if they were paying homage to The Beatles in the way they used their inspiration, and yet through their unique creative touch, they made it their own.

Collective Soul's hook-laden guitar anthems and powerfully melodic songs propelled them to international stardom and multiplatinum status. The quintet charted an astounding seven number-one radio hits and nineteen Top 40 singles in a seven-year period (1994–2001) and received more airtime on the radio than any other band of its era—Nirvana, Pearl Jam, R.E.M., Soundgarden, and Oasis weren't even close.

Now imagine Shane's situation—you go from living in your parents' basement to playing Woodstock '94 in front of 250,000 people—at the ripe old age of twenty-three. Everything is coming up roses: multiplatinum-selling records, sold-out concert dates, world tours, cover stories, photo sessions, video shoots, meeting your musical idols, dating women way out of your league, and eating dinners with powerful record executives at five-star restaurants.

I feel drawn to quote myself once again, because when I look at the life of a young man three decades younger than myself, it seems to call for these kind of reflections … or should I say repetitions. This is from my first book, *The Beatles, the Bible, and Bodega Bay*:

Billboard magazine was my Bible,
The record charts my God

Prestigious positions my purpose.
The Holy Grail was a "Grammy"
The best table at the Brown Derby—the promised land.

What I am about to say here may be debatable, but if it were possible to do clinical research, I believe the resultant percentages would prove me right. So many successful artists, and I am not speaking of everyone but a large number of the passionate doers in the creative arts, have come from either hard country places, backwoods environments, mean streets, ghettos, broken homes, dire upbringings, or challenging circumstances. They experience restrictions, denials, hunger of many sorts, and a lack of loving care and instruction in their tender years. They were forced to make their way through life without a lot of good foundational teaching—everything from how to hold your fork to investing your money to how to treat your woman. This hurt and hunger plants a drive to overcome, to get even, to prove that they are more than common and will not be denied or put down any longer.

It is hard to hold back someone who *has* been held back without them coming out of the other end with a little edge to their mental makeup. They have been restrained long enough and become obsessed with making up for lost time. Being accustomed to coming from behind does have a useful side effect—it fosters appetite and desire for competition. Inborn talent becomes their escape, their narcotic, the only thing that gives them relief from their upbringings. Then this ability that has been driven by passion and pain bursts forth one day and suddenly finds its place. It can be in a work place, a football field, a science project, an art studio, or a rock and roll band. The place may be different, but the result is the same: an arresting birth of talent that demands people take notice.

The way it worked in my case was that music was in my head the first day I heard Lefty Frizzell sing "If You've Got the Money, I've Got the Time" on an old radio in the northern Idaho panhandle. I wanted more out of life than working in a sawmill and freezing on those cold winter nights just south of the Canadian border. I didn't want to be what I was told I was meant to be. So I got on a bus to California when I was seventeen and never looked back. I fought my way past those that didn't have the grit I had because they had been fed a little better than I had been growing up. I found that made me a little hungrier than them and I wanted a good meal more than they did. Okay, this may be a little too poetic, but I can tell something got in Shane's gut early on that developed that kind of craving in him.

So now let's continue—our type finally fights to the top in short order, but here is where it all falls apart. We were so dressed for battle, and so engrossed in the competition, that when it came time to celebrate our success, we didn't have anything to wear to the victory banquet. We were unprepared for the fine meal, the pretty waitresses, and expensive libations. (When I was a kid and went to a church picnic, I stuffed my pockets and myself because I had never seen so many goodies in one place. Of course, just like Shane, I got sick from the overindulgence.) We discover we missed out on the part about understanding success *and* what to do when it comes our way. The speed of success allows no learning curve or time for maturity in order to navigate all that success brings. Then the old records begin playing in the back of our minds, the ones about our unworthiness and our commonness, and we begin to worry that someone will find out that we aren't really as great as everyone says we are. Fast success's biggest nemesis is weak foundations and self-assurance. Shane's situation may not have been that dramatic in the years leading up to his achievement, but he was unprepared for what lay ahead.

Aside from these realities, these scenarios, however glamorous they may sound, are hell-bent for trouble. Shane says it was a gradual shift in values. "I used to have normal patterns before we became famous. You know—go to school or work, go to bed, get up, do this, and have a life. But when 'Shine' hit it big, it was like being on a permanent vacation. My home was the road, and somehow I had to sleep on a big fifty-foot chunk of metal that's moving seventy-five miles an hour, which is not so easy when you have a generator that's resonating about 110 decibels in your ear. So you could drink a bottle of Jack Daniels to put you to sleep, but I was never really a drinker. The alternative is to go to a doctor and get some pills and take care of the problem. I also hated flying and getting up in front of thousands of people, but there are pills for that too. You find yourself in this realm where everything's an easy fix for everything, whatever it takes to keep the machine rolling. And that's how it starts."

Marijuana was also a powerful addiction for Shane, which he smoked on a daily basis throughout his late teens and all through his twenties. Pot eventually led to Ecstasy, cocaine, crystal meth, and even heroin. "They say that pot really isn't a gateway drug, but it was for me. We tend to categorize things, and I considered cocaine and crystal meth to be hard drugs, so I didn't mess with them in the beginning. But things changed for me when I started doing Ecstasy. I didn't understand at the time that my serotonin gland was being squeezed and this is why it was making me feel great. I thought it was a miracle drug, and so that's when my perception of hard drugs started to change. And even though I wasn't much of a drinker in the beginning, that changed too."

Ironically, Shane was the most flamboyant and outgoing member of the group and felt he had to live up to the image of the stereotypical crazy drummer. He was the guy with the first tattoo, the life of the party, the one in the band who broke all the rules first. "Our first manager was very strict, and he had this crazy set of rules, which included no women on the bus or in the hotel room. I just sat there thinking, *Wait a minute ... this is rock and roll. This is part of the reason we got into music. Something's not making sense here.* It's all at our fingertips, and we're not allowed to participate. So of course, I'm the first guy to break the rules, and I was always in the dog house."

Like all addicts, Shane was an excellent escape artist, and money helped fuel his bad-boy behavior. "Money gives you the power to run away from everything. 'You don't like me? Okay. Well, guess what? I'll just fly to Las Vegas for the weekend. You don't have to like me. I'll just be gone.' When you get to a certain level of stardom, who are you going to listen to? Who's going to tell you what to do? No one was going to tell me what to do or how to behave. Not when we got that first taste of success. Your ego just gets so inflated because one week you're this small-town country boy, and the next minute Steven Tyler is visiting our dressing room and telling us, 'I really like that song, "Shine."' He's talking to us about *our* music, and you look around the room and go, 'Man, this is *crazy*.'"

Despite years of substance abuse, Shane can clearly pinpoint what drove him to slowly self-destruct. "My tendency to isolate started to evolve and looking back, I see this young man with a very low self-image and confidence. In the band, I saw myself as the weird one, the ugly one, and the one musician who was the least talented. I always had to do more to get myself known or seen, but the root of it was based on the fear of rejection and not being sure of myself. My spirituality was out the window a long time before that, but the crazy thing is that I felt God was with me the whole time. Through grace and mercy, He protected me even when I couldn't protect me from myself."

As I observe Shane's journey, it verifies how timeless God's love and shelter is. Like Shane, I can't believe how often God safeguarded me, covered me, and kept my bad self from harm. Not only that, but He kept me from getting in trouble for things that could have jeopardized my reputation, witness, and ability to achieve a somewhat normal life in later years. God loved me so much! I am sure it was hard to turn His back so He wouldn't have to watch what I was doing while He was shielding me from harm. He is a caring God, a Father who loves His children at all ends of the spectrum and will only let them stray so far.

Collective Soul continued to roll on in the wake of the mammoth success of "Shine," racking up hits and selling millions of records. But no matter who you are in the music industry, the ride is always a tricky one, and because of the tremendous pulls and pressures, in many cases it's almost always easier to break up than stay together. An eighteen-month lawsuit with a manager that took them to the brink, a lost fortune estimated in the millions, endless tours, affairs, divorces, a record label split, and the departure of their lead guitarist, Ross Childress, left Collective Soul with emotional dents in their armor. These wide-eyed Southern boys had spent almost seven years on the road or in the studio without a break, and they were fried. They limped back to their home state, beaten, battered, a lot more cynical, and a lot less innocent.

They decided in 2001 to take a few years off to recharge their batteries, which is when Shane decided to move to Los Angeles with his girlfriend. "I had all of these big ideas—I wanted to take acting lessons, score a movie, write my own music, just do my own thing. But then an incident in the band occurred, and the poop really hit the fan. Our singer, Ed Roland, was going through a divorce, and I left him at a time when he needed me most. Ed was always a dear, close friend, who was so good to me, but I justified my actions by telling myself that things were already in motion for me in Los Angeles. I think that must have driven a wedge in our relationship, but that was typical of me back then—to run away when things got tough." (This type of thinking falls into the timeworn "Hey man, nothing personal—it's just business, man, ya know. Hey, but I love you bro—let's do lunch sometime.")

After their self-imposed hiatus, Collective Soul was in the midst of a comeback album (*Youth*) and worldwide tour in the fall of 2004, when the wheels started coming off the ride for Shane. "We weren't productive for a few years, and my financial situation began to steadily decline. I was living near the beach in Santa Monica and took a bath on my house after 9/11. When I moved back to Atlanta, I discovered my roommate was heavily into crystal meth. I asked him if I did it, would it make me go crazy? He said no, so I said, 'Alright, then bring me some.'"

Shane discovered meth was an evil and insidious drug that was highly addictive and all-consuming. "It's a horrible cycle because you're up for three days, down for two days, and then up and then down. It's never ending and you start accepting it as normal. At first it gives you this tremendous drive but then little by little, you start noticing the bad decisions you make, like getting into relationships that will never work or blowing off your bills and obligations. Eventually you get to this point where you just don't care anymore. You develop this 'screw it' attitude, and that extended to Collective Soul. I got a few warnings from a couple of band members that I was messing up, but I'd usually say, 'Dude … whatever.'"

New Jersey State Troopers didn't share Shane's blasé attitude toward drugs when a security officer at the Trump Marina Hotel Casino in Atlantic City opened up a package addressed to the hotel on November 27, 2004. Tucked inside the package were Shane's bills and a gift from his drug-dealing roommate. In the post-9/11 era, envelopes containing white powdery substances were heavily frowned upon by hotel security and law enforcement. Police were summoned and mayhem ensued. "The funny thing is my roommate had addressed the package to the hotel and didn't put it to my attention, so when I went down to the delivery dock to ask for it, they told me I didn't have a delivery. So I was like, alright, I'm going to go to Taco Bell and grab some food.

"When I came back, I saw four or five hazmat dudes getting out of a van and casino guards blocking the hotel exits. I'm watching this episode unfold, and when I turn around, two men in black suits walk up to me and introduce themselves as the state police. They take me down into some dark room below the casino where I'm positive they beat people for cheating … I feel like I'm in some mafia movie, because they shine this bright light in my face and start grilling me. I play dumb. The agent tells me they thought it was possibly anthrax, but they sprayed it with a chemical and discovered it was a quarter ounce of crystal meth. 'Were you expecting this package?' he asked. Naturally, I feigned surprise. 'What? Crystal meth? No, not me, man. I hope no one got hurt.' He said, 'Look, I'm not going to arrest you. I know your band is playing here tonight. I don't care about your drug problem. I care about terrorism, but what upsets me the most is the resources that were burned here today.' I started thinking I was off the hook, but it didn't take long for the band, the crew, and management to find out what happened."

Shane performed flawlessly that night, but his days in Collective Soul were numbered. He noticed that no one in the group talked to him about the incident, nor did they talk to him for a long stretch of time, which frayed his nerves.

Ed and Dean Roland's father passed away a few weeks later, and a dark cloud loomed over the group. When Shane returned to Los Angeles, his addiction flared up again, causing Ed to try and save Shane from himself. "Ed tried calling to drag me back into the studio so I'd be productive, but I wouldn't even answer my phone. I had built what I thought was a paradise in my basement. I had a studio down there, living quarters, a bedroom, kitchen, and this extravagant bar that looked like it belonged in a nightclub. I thought I had built my own playground, but what I really did was build my own prison. It was a prison because I couldn't leave. I wouldn't eat for days at a time, and I just didn't want to go anywhere."

Shane did go to Atlanta to attend a band meeting in early January 2005 to discuss their goals for the upcoming year, which included an expanded tour and a two-set CD and DVD with the Atlanta Symphony Youth Orchestra. The meeting, however, turned out to be an intervention for Shane, who was asked to attend a twenty-eight-day rehab facility in Nashville. He agreed because he knew he was skating on thin ice, but unfortunately, it didn't take. "When it was over, like most addicts I thought, *Okay, I did the rehab thing. I'm good now, might as well celebrate—I can handle it now.* It was an obligation I needed to get out of the way in order to maintain my status with the band, and I went right back to the drugs and drink.

"A big part of the problem was that I had developed a lot of resentments. I formed opinions of other people's motives, money structures within the band because I'd heard stories about other musicians getting percentages of certain things, and it made me angry that I wasn't getting my fair share. Things began building up inside me, but if I had drugs, I could get high and not have to deal with those things. I used again."

Shane had run out of chances. Collective Soul took a group vote and booted him out of the band—an action he admits made him resentful for many years. However, with the wisdom of sobriety, he understands why it had to be done. "Those guys tried to help me but didn't know what to do. They were caught in a place where they had families and had to support them. My behavior and activities were jeopardizing their livelihood. It put the band's reputation in peril at times. It wasn't fair to them. For me, I was in denial and didn't see myself as having a problem. I was trying to maintain my drug habit and play in a rock band that was touring the world, instead of working things out."

Soon thereafter, he received an email from the group's manager, whom Shane barely knew, notifying him that his services were no longer required and that he was being replaced. It devastated him, and he grabbed his favorite Les Paul guitar and smashed it to bits. He spent the next few hours crying and seeking consolation at his parents' home. Shane's problems were only beginning as a string of incidents, bad luck, and bad choices sent him into a tailspin. His mother's demise from complications of diabetes, the accidental death of a girlfriend, and a pair of DUI arrests pushed him into further despair. He even experimented with heroin. "I isolated myself from my family and friends and began hanging out with all of the wrong people. I just disappeared, man. I missed the funeral services of both of my grandmothers, including Mama Dean. After my mom passed away, I saw my family collapse. It all stemmed from my bitterness and being prideful—too prideful to go to anyone and communicate how I was feeling. I told myself I'd figure it out, but all I did was figure out a way to get high, until it all started to catch up with me."

Shane said he spent a few years crashing at people's homes, couches, and drug dens, and witnessed "plenty of perversion and criminal activity." He was completely off the grid for a year, and his family and former band mates couldn't find him; they were hoping and praying that he was still alive. He said he hit rock bottom while living on the run from police at a run-down Atlanta-area motel, ironically called the Whit's Inn. After his father refused to let him come home, Shane believes he was two days away from being homeless. It's a feeling I was all too familiar with.

There is something devastating about knowing you have to consider homelessness, especially when being stoned no longer hides you from the truth—that it's because of your life choices and not anyone else's fault that you have found yourself in that predicament. I was luckier than Shane in that I was beginning to sort things out when that sad time came. I was facing the reality of the consequences of my bad choices, and I had accepted my situation. There was nothing confusing about what was going down with me at the time. But as you read Shane's account, you can merge our almost-homeless stories in terms of God's definite involvement in the introspections involved. In our stories there is no need to change names to protect the innocent, because we will both admit that is wasn't our innocence that brought us to this point. I know now God let me go broke so that I could be broken.

By the time I was facing homelessness, I had already experienced that moment and not only was looking for a place to sleep but was in the process of seeking His face. I was so pitiful and pathetic back then. When I look back and picture myself doing what I was doing when I was totally off course, I wish I could run back in time and give myself a hug. I was hurting so badly, and like Shane I knew that underneath it all I really wasn't that bad—just lost. Imagine this, even though I was forced into finally facing the hard facts of my life, I had actually determined that I was not going to be like other homeless people. My pride had been deeply damaged, but my vanity was still intact. I could not accept my situation in its totality, so I went to a nice part of town to be homeless. I wasn't going to go to downtown Nashville and sleep on the streets around the Rescue Mission like *those other people*!

I began scouting out nice little parks in more upscale neighborhoods, you know the ones with well-kept grass and little dugouts and sheltered benches where there were street lights to keep it bright and safe from riffraff. I scoped out a couple of places where no one would expect a homeless person to be sleeping, and I also secured a place under the stairs of a garage to store my stuff a few blocks away. It was a place where I could go to change clothes and organize my day. Looking back I see how God was totally in charge of everything going on with me.

It blows me away that on the very same day I had accepted I was going to be homeless I received a message I had a producing job, mixing some demo recordings. Three days' work at $500 a day flat fee—if I wanted it. I know now that God wanted me to see what it was going to be like to become homeless, but once He was sure I understood the concept, He let me skip ahead. Because of the studio gig I had enough to put a deposit and two months' rent on a $350-a-month apartment close to Music Row in Nashville. I was thrilled. I had no car, but hauling my stuff was no problem because all I had was three cardboard boxes and three suitcases to my name. The time that followed was one of the best periods of my entire life.

God slowly stripped Shane of everything, and he felt the walls closing in on him in the summer of 2009. He finally fell to his knees and asked for grace. "God just boxed me in and basically said, 'Surrender or die.' I had nothing—no car, no driver's license, no ID, no credit cards, no laptop, no cell phone, no money. Just a couple of bags and boxes of clothes and possessions. Basically junk. I dropped to my knees and said, 'Lord, I've run from you for far too long, and there have been so many times I could have blessed your kingdom but didn't. I never tithed when I made money, and in my heart I know I should have. Please, Lord, forgive me. I give it all to you right now. I need you Lord. I need you to show yourself to me.' I repented over and over, and I finally heard Him speak. 'Aren't you tired? Aren't you tired, Shane? Surrender.' That's the word I kept hearing over and over. 'Surrender … Surrender … Surrender.'"

God is such a good God. In the terror of those moments, He pours His sweetness over us, filling us with a warmth and safeness that we have forgotten could exist in our lives. It's a glimpse of His eventual peace—that peace we have read about—the one that passes all understanding. What we feel in that moment is more than our joy—we sense His joy. His greatest pleasure is loving on us and beginning the process of restoration in our lives. I'm sure God went to bed with a smile on His face that night after hearing Shane say back to him, "I surrender, Lord."

Thanks to his local public library, Shane was able to use a computer and find a rehab center that included spiritual counseling. Shane says AA didn't work for him because he needed a clearer definition of his "higher power." AA says it can be whatever or whoever you want it to be, but Shane needed more. It was a yearlong program, but it was either that or jail. "God granted me enough grace to surrender, but you wouldn't believe the amount of shame I had to deal with. I was in this band that was very successful and toured the world and had made all this money and totally squandered it. People looked at me like, 'Are you stupid? How could you do that? How could you lose so much?' and they'd look at me to see if I was being treated differently. Those first few months at the treatment facility were very difficult."

Through the grace of God, Shane remained strong and pulled through three years of intense counseling and self-examination. With a clear head, he had a much better understanding of his situation and what he calls "stinking thinking." "At the time there was a lot of resentment toward Collective Soul because I felt like it was their fault I was no longer in the band, but when I finally got to a place and realized it was my fault—my choice to use drugs, my choice not to be in a relationship with those guys, to not care about the music as much as I did in the past—then I was able to take ownership of it, and healing could take place."

The healing has taken a long time—almost ten years, to be exact. It's been a long road for this talented musician, who continues to be humbled by God. Shane accepts the wreckage of his past and was forced to deal with the consequences of his former actions—he didn't possess a driver's license for several years, did not own a car or house, and never socked anything away for a rainy day. His financial fortune from the heydays of Collective Soul is all gone, but Shane has persevered and remains faithful to God. He has rebounded both personally and spiritually in a way that is nothing short of miraculous.

Shane ended his eight-year hiatus from the recording industry in late 2013, when he was hired by Christian singer-songwriter Jason Fowler to drum on his solo debut album, *Letters From the Inside*. The two men used to get high together, and now God has put them together again to serve an even *higher* purpose. They are on the worship team at their home church and counsel teens on their Rock, Recovery, and Redemption.

God also rewarded Shane with a beautiful Christian mate in Kelsey Hamilton. The two were married on February 5, 2014, in Atlanta. The newlyweds then took the next logical step—they formed a band, Beauty for Ashes, and rushed right into the studio!

Shane believes the next step is to make amends to members of Collective Soul and apologize for his past behavior. "I'm in a place now where I can pursue a relationship or make peace with them. I love those guys and always will. They're my brothers, my best friends. We haven't spent time together yet to get to know each other again, but I want to. I owe them that and it's important to me.

"The thing I miss most about my days with Collective Soul isn't the fame, fortune, or the perks of stardom. It's travelling around the world with four of my best friends, cutting up with each other, having a laugh, and enjoying the great bond we shared."

I see Shane Evans as a person who is no longer running away from his demons, but a man running into God's loving arms. He has been faithful to God and His Word, and God has been faithful in return. Through faith, sobriety, and a steely determination to honor his grandmother, Mama Dean, Shane Evans has finally become the man he's always wanted to be … but it took several decades to get there.

When I was an executive at Capitol Records, I had to fire one of my best employees and someone who had become a very good friend over the years. He was in a free fall of destructive life choices—choices that the job he held under my supervision allowed him to continue acting out. These were choices that would eventually take everyone around him down. He was stunned that I would do such a thing to an old friend. I flew into Chicago from Hollywood on a weekend to do this because it was personal. I went in and out in one day. I remember staring out the window of the late-night return flight, feeling sick to my stomach.

Almost forty years later, I was on a book promotion tour and appearing on an all-night radio show out of Minneapolis. That same night, he was driving across Wisconsin, returning from a business trip, alone and listening to that program in his car to help keep him awake. It was around 3 a.m. and it was a call-in show—he dialed the station from his cell phone and told the listening audience and me that for many years he had wanted to thank me for firing him. It was a rough go for a long time, he said, but it not only saved his life but also saved his family and his career.

I asked in the beginning of this chapter how could Shane's band mates fire their close friend. I believe it is because they loved him. I applaud them for having the guts to do something that painful. Shane knows that now too, and I know that their story is going to have a beautiful tag ending.

God is love and God is light. I find a special closing irony in Shane's story—and this time the irony is one of comfort. Collective Soul's biggest hit is "Shine." Let that rattle around in your rock and roll head for a while.

NEDRA ROSS

The Ronettes

The first bad girls of rock, the Ronettes were racially indefinable and one of the most exciting acts of their era. Before The Beatles invaded the United States or The Supremes busted out of Detroit, The Ronettes ruled the airwaves in the early '60s with a string of girl-group classics and mini rock operas produced by the legendary Phil Spector.

TEN

THE RIGHT RONETTE

NEDRA ROSS | The Ronettes

It's always good to touch base with Nedra Ross. Her infectious laugh and natural lightheartedness never fail to make you smile, and you will always feel better than you did before you called. Conversations these days are lighthearted because she tends not to discuss her musical past that much; instead, her words are about where she is today in her spiritual walk with Christ. When things teeter toward becoming a little too serious, she switches the subject to lighter issues, joking about when her hair went gray, and how she hopes Uncle Sam continues sending her those generous social security checks before the government runs out of money.

Nedra, cofounder and original member of the classic all-girl trio The Ronettes, is forever etched in my mind as the youthful and exotic teen with the towering beehive hairdo and Cleopatra eyeliner. I think about the musical and cultural impact that the multiracial Ronettes had when they exploded on the scene in the early '60s. They were the first bad girls of rock and roll, racially indefinable, and one of the most exciting acts of their era. Bruce Springsteen, Billy Joel, Eddie Money, and Brian Wilson (who said "Be My Baby" inspired him to write "Don't Worry Baby") have often cited The Ronettes as a major influence on their music. It's no wonder the legendary trio was inducted into the Rock and Roll Hall of Fame in 2007.

These three young ladies—Nedra Talley and her cousins Estelle and Veronica 'Ronnie' Bennett—were a combustible mix of sexy and sweet, vulnerable and tough, appealing to record buyers of both genders. Before The Beatles invaded our shores or The Supremes busted out of Detroit, The Ronettes ruled the transatlantic airwaves from August 1963 through December 1964, with a string of classics such as "Baby I Love You," "Walking in the Rain," and the watershed "Be My Baby." These mini operas, produced by Phil Spector, were monumental and memorable productions.

The Ronettes became the perfect centerpiece for Spector's "Wall of Sound." To those of us in the industry, it was a mind-boggling sonic phenomenon. It was like seeing color TV for the first time after watching black and white for so many years. Phil added a new, invigorating dimension to recorded sound, and when his influence played into the hands of other producers who tried to accomplish a similar sound, the result was quite interesting—even very creative by accident. In order to compete by mimicking the Wall of Sound, music makers and recording engineers invented new recording techniques and unique sounds of their own to the point where they became innovators themselves. When the lay people heard Spector's massive arrangements, they were not that analytical—they just liked it because it was fresh and different. It is interesting to listen to his records today—I sometimes wonder how such a muddled sound could be so exciting. But it was amazing for the times, and he was so clever as a producer. He would cram all this music into a record, yet the vocals were out in front and easy to understand. Consequently, the listener got a lot of music, but most importantly they could identify with the lyrics because they could hear them. Phil made a lot of noise but left an open space in his recordings where you could get to know the artist.

At one time, The Ronettes were so big that The Rolling Stones opened for them on their first tour of England in 1963. Later they toured with The Beatles after the Fab Four demanded the teenage trio. Those heady days, Nedra tells me, were a long way from Sugar Hill on the west side of New York.

Nedra smiles when she reads fabricated stories about The Ronettes coming out of the crime-ridden, mean streets of New York's Spanish Harlem. She is proud of her tight-knit family, her upbringing, and that she grew up in a nice neighborhood across the street from City College, shielded by her large family and God's protective hand. It also didn't hurt that her grandfather, John Mobley, was a Baptist minister.

"We were raised in the Convent Baptist Church on Convent Avenue and 145th Street, and Sundays were totally dedicated to the Lord," Nedra says from her southern Virginia home. "We went to church in the morning, came back home after service, had a late lunch, then back to church in the afternoon. Back home, and then back to church by seven o'clock at night. Sundays were for the Lord."

All the other days were set aside for "Mama," Nedra's maternal grandmother. Also known as Susie Mobley, Mama ran the household after her husband, John, passed away in 1947, when Nedra was barely a year old. Mama cooked, cleaned, disciplined, doted, and prayed. "Mama wasn't someone who talked about church—she lived it. God was in her heart and she did a lot of praying. All her boys went to war, and every one of them came home. I know it was because Mama continually prayed for them."

Mama was the glue that kept the family together and held tight to her loved ones. "Mama and Papa had fourteen kids and numerous grandchildren. Every day after school, us kids headed over to Mama's house. We needed to be with her because basking in her love was everything. There was the constant smell of homemade cooking at Mama's. There were cousins to play with, aunts and uncles to visit with, baseball games on the radio, records playing. On Saturday nights, Mama would roll up the carpet in the living room and everybody would perform. Every branch of the family was represented. We'd sing, tap, tell jokes, dance, play records, having a good time and enjoying each other's company. It was a loud family too. Some of my uncles had yodeling contests. You couldn't be shy if you wanted to join in, so the way to be heard was to be louder and a pitch higher than the others. The volume could be deafening at times."

Nedra says even though Ronnie and Estelle Bennett were sisters, she was especially close to Ronnie. "We told each other everything, shared everything, including a toilet seat. If she had to pee, I had to pee. We sat on the toilet at the same time butt to butt, cheek to cheek. I remember one time when we were going to Florida on vacation and Ronnie couldn't go. I cried my eyes out. I didn't know how I would make it without her."

The talent level in the Mobley family ran deep, and those Saturday nights were a great proving ground for Nedra and her cousins. They mimicked records by Patti Page, Rosemary Clooney, Dinah Washington, Billie Holliday, Lena Horne, and The Andrews Sisters, who Nedra claims were The Ronettes' biggest influence. This was a surprising bit of musical news to me—wow, The Andrews Sisters and The Ronettes being similar in sound? Brian Wilson made it clear that his major vocal influence was the Four Freshman, and seeing that similarity is a no-brainer, but The Andrews Sisters and The Ronettes? I did check out some old Andrews Sisters records and although I don't hear the two groups sounding alike, I can see where The Ronettes zeroed in on tight harmonies the way the vintage Andrews Sisters did.

The three songbirds didn't just look cute and sound good—they were exceptional in every department. Recognizing their potential, Nedra's mother, Susan Talley, enrolled them in singing lessons, paid for rehearsals, and knocked on doors until they opened. "Behind every dream there are people behind you who are the driving force. For The Ronettes, that was my mom. She was energetic, a mover, a shaker, and very aggressive. She had more drive than I did because I didn't have that passionate ambition to be somebody. She thought big for a woman at that time. She was also a great singer in her day, once auditioning for Duke Ellington, who let her down graciously. Harry Belafonte also had an opening for a touring singer and Mommy wanted it badly, but Mama Mobley absolutely refused. Mommy was only seventeen or eighteen at the time and had to live her dream through me and Ronnie and Estelle."

The dream was temporarily sidetracked with Mama Mobley's death in 1959. It was not only devastating for fourteen-year-old Nedra, but it was a spiritually seminal moment for the family. "Mama's death took the starch out of all of us. I remember Estelle being especially devastated because she had just purchased some knee warmers for Mama and never got to give them to her before her death."

It may appear to be a small thing on the surface, but it was a big deal to Estelle because she was looking forward to giving something to someone who had given so much of herself to the grateful teenager. "She [Estelle] was screaming, like she would never be able to go on. At the funeral I went up and touched Mama, and she was hard. I knew she was gone, but I didn't have that true understanding of heaven and that one day she would be waiting for me. It was the first time I had dealt with death. Mama's passing emotionally wiped everyone out. After her death, our family couldn't go back into that church because we could not handle the memory of Mama lying in a casket there. She was the foundation that held everyone together, and this was too much. It tore us apart from the church."

Knocked down, but certainly not knocked out, Susan became even more determined to see the girls succeed. Billed as the Darling Sisters, they played sock hops, parties, and bar mitzvahs for about a year, honing their act and tightening their harmonies. A break came in the form of Phillip Halikus, a talent agent who conducted business at the Brill Building, which housed many major music publishers in New York. Halikus recognized their talent and set up an audition with producer Stu Phillips of Colpix Records, a subsidiary of Columbia. Halikus signed the three young ladies—all teens—to a contract. They recorded an album as Ronnie and the Relatives, but Halikus failed to find songs that captured the sultry innocence of the group. While they waited for a hit, they developed their live act and changed their name to The Ronettes.

By 1961, they had become featured entertainers at the famed Peppermint Lounge in Manhattan. They were also employed by rock and roll impresario and WINS-AM disc jockey Murray "the K" Kaufman as his "dancing girls" for the holiday revue shows he hosted at the Fox Theater in Brooklyn. Kaufman's multiracial all-star bills featured acts like Stevie Wonder, Jan and Dean, Dionne Warwick, Smokey Robinson, Bobby Vee, Tom Jones, The Temptations, and The Shirelles. However, The Ronettes inched their way to the top. They did it by teasing their hair higher, adding darker eyeliner, wearing spiked heels, and increasing the slits in their oriental dresses. Nedra says they didn't have a hit record at the time to grab the attention of the audience, so they were forced to make a stylistic impression.

"The Ronettes were about what girls wanted to be and what guys dreamed about," Nedra says.

Scott Ross, who worked with Murray Kaufman as an assistant music director at WINS, had history with all three Ronettes. "Scott came to a lot of Murray's shows. I remember when I first saw him. I thought he was cute. He saw these three girls, and I could tell he really liked me. But he was shrewd, and you could see his mind working as he asked us for our ages. He found out that I was sixteen, Ronnie was eighteen, and Estelle was twenty. He was twenty-two. Back then guys went to jail for hooking up with 'jailbait' [i.e., girls under eighteen]. So he and Ronnie went out two times, and he knew their personalities weren't going to click. He also went out on a double date with Estelle and me and Brian Jones of The Rolling Stones. So he's the only guy that has ever gone out with all three Ronettes. His claim to fame," Nedra laughs.

The Ronettes also met producer Phil Spector backstage at one of their Brooklyn Fox shows. He told Susan Talley he wanted to sign them on the spot to his Philles Records label. When he discovered they had an existing contract with Colpix, Spector and Susan came up with a solution.

"We were all underage when we signed the contract, so Mommy told them we were tired of the music industry and going back to school. She basically lied to them, and they tore up the contract."

Teamed with Spector, The Ronettes recorded "Be My Baby," a song *Rolling Stone* magazine listed number twenty-two out of the 500 Greatest Songs of All Time, calling it a "Rosetta stone for studio pioneers such as The Beatles and Brian Wilson."

Spector rehearsed with the group for several weeks at Mira Sound Studios in New York. They finished recording "Be My Baby" at Los Angeles' Gold Star Studios, a legendary studio where Spector created his famed "Wall of Sound." A meticulous producer, Spector made The Ronettes do forty-two takes before he was satisfied. Aided by a room full of seasoned studio musicians, a full orchestra, and backup singers (including Sonny and Cher and Darlene Love), the 2:40 tune was a heartfelt Kennedy-era paean of love, lust, and seduction, which included the recreation of a thunderstorm and the most memorable drum track in rock history, thanks to Hal Blaine.

"Be My Baby" was a real Linda Blair head twister the first time anyone heard it. That record had an incredible influence on people, things, and places, in the manner of *Sgt. Pepper*'s groundbreaking sound and production. Phil Spector became a celebrated producer; his Wall of Sound made recording history. Hal Blaine became the standard bearer for the ultimate in drumming style and technique (when any of us LA producers would have a messed-up drum track, we would always call in Hal Blaine to make it right). Plus, Gold Star became Mecca—artists, engineers, and producers came from everywhere so they could say they recorded there. Hearing that Wall of Sound in those days was like hearing *Pet Sounds, Sgt. Pepper* or *Dark Side of the Moon* for the first time. I remember the impact, but I can't remember exactly where I was the first time I heard Phil's production. I do, however, remember seven of us being crammed into a Cadillac Eldorado hardtop convertible, smoking joints in the parking lot of Pasadena's Ice House, listening to The Beatles' masterpiece recording *Sgt. Pepper's Lonely Hearts Club Band* for the first time. Nobody said a word, and when it was over we all piled out of the car for air and tried to gather ourselves together from the sonic shock we had just experienced. That's the kind of emotional response "Be My Baby" generated from a wall of new fans.

Those days and those landmark recordings, like the ones by The Beatles and the Phil Spector–produced Ronettes, were seminal moments for people in the music "biz." We sensed something and had an inner knowing that we were going to be partaking in new musical horizons and adventures. For the teens, it wasn't quite that complicated, but they were just as excited and sensed a shift. As the dance shows used to ask—"Yeah, but can you dance to it?" The kids loudly answered in unison, "Yes we can!" They could not only dance to The Ronettes but they loved to listen to them, look at them, and fantasize about them. And yes, that includes yours truly.

When Nedra heard the final product, she wanted to cry. "I thought, *Oh my god, this is ... this is it. This is big!* I felt we just entered a new realm. It was a sound no one had captured before. It was more than just rock and roll. It took on a new dimension. I knew after that song we were going to be famous." That fall, the song hit number two in the United States and number four in the United Kingdom and sold more than two million copies. In actuality, they had a number-one record, but many times in the industry, another blockbuster record that is climbing the charts at the same time will grab that coveted position and hold it for the fleeting moments that another record could have made the spot.

More hits followed as well as sold-out concert tours, television appearances, and endorsements. They were also courted by some high-profile suitors, including members of The Beatles and The Rolling Stones. "The Beatles gave us a welcoming party when we were in the UK, and we had a great time. We laughed, literally ran around the apartment playing some dumb game. I can't even remember what it was. It was all innocent fun."

Nedra's eighteenth birthday was a particularly bright moment as the Stones, who were the openers, brought her a cake after one of their shows. "It was our first time in England, and everything was so new to us. The accents, the nightclubs, the crowds, and the British rock music. We were used to looking nice for our shows, and about an hour before our start time the Stones would be hanging around our dressing room. We said, 'Don't you guys need to get dressed or something?' They said, 'We are dressed.' We were used to The Temptations, Smokey Robinson and The Miracles, Motown, guys in shark-skinned suits and ties, dressed to the nines. The Stones looked rumpled, like they'd stayed in their clothes from the night before. They looked rough. It was a whole other world back there."

Picture what it was like for me when I ventured to the United Kingdom in the 1960s and into the heart and heat of the mind-boggling music scene there. London made Los Angeles look like Mayberry when it came to the creative energy coming out of that place. Not only was the music that was pouring out of the clubs, studios, and auditoriums mixed with an abundance of fresh ideas, but the young people who crawled out of the British version of our backwoods and backstreets looked like something I had never seen. The clothes they wore, the way they were tailored, and the way they put their outfits together was bizarre. One band would look like Savile Row had carefully outfitted them, while others looked as if they borrowed something from a drunken uncle. It was not so much about what they were wearing but the way they pulled it off.

The big thing that happened to most of us coming across the "pond" from the States was the surprise we experienced when we got there the first time. Everything was just as we imagined it would be—the pubs, the food, the accents, the black cabs, the terminologies (elevator/lift, car hood/bonnet, girls/birds, TV/telly, bathroom/the loo, goodbye/ta ta, damn/bloody etc.). It was like going back in time. Everywhere else I had been was never as I imagined when I got there, but to this day London is and always will be … London!

Nedra says, though, life was always normal back at the Talley household. "My mother would never allow me to get a big head. Once I returned home I was expected to do my chores and be a big sister to my brother. Looking back, this allowed me to keep humble and conduct a normal life."

It's hard to picture big stars and famous people being normal like Nedra just described, but like the old saying goes, everyone puts on their designer jeans one shaved leg at a time. If someone would have walked into the kitchen during my Apple days, while George Harrison was cooking up some vegetables for our lunch, they might have been taken aback by the image. It is said you can take the boy out of Liverpool but you can't take the "pool" out of that boy; well, in Nedra's case, you could take the girl to London, but when she got back home, dishes needed to be done, floors needed to be vacuumed, and beds needed to be made.

When producing an album or promoting an artist, I always loved visiting their homes and watching their moms make them eat their veggies or seeing their dads make them clean the gutters. The blessed ones are those who have those common places to go back to, whether it is to flaunt their success, lick their wounds, or just nestle in the arms of loved ones. The ones who typically become messed up by fame are often those who escaped bad situations by using their talents to get away, but when they achieved success, they had no place to go back to in order to regain their normalness. Most entertainers I worked with over the years grew up common—that was their real identity and the actual person I grew to know over time. They took off their makeup after the show, put on jeans and a T-shirt, and made a PB&J sandwich for dinner. Nedra's foundation was so strong that no matter what happened in the future, deep down she knew the past was going to take care of her. She could always go home.

The center of the rock and roll world, especially in Nedra's case, one filled with the Stones and The Beatles, is not a real place—it is a separate reality, and Nedra knew there were times she needed to step away. Now, picking Scott Ross as her beau may have not been a real down-home idea, but we will get into that! (In fact, if you want to get a true understanding of this unusual guy, read his book *Scott Free*.)

Having experienced the fame merry-go-round for about a four-year period, the lifestyle was beginning to fray Nedra's nerves. So were the politics and power plays. Early into The Ronettes' success, Spector stepped outside of his marriage and began courting Ronnie. Nedra says it spelled the beginning of the end for the group. "I remember being very firm with Ronnie about Phil and I told her, 'Ronnie, he's married. You can't do this. This is wrong … absolutely wrong. God is not going to bless this.' Back then you didn't live with a guy much less date a married man. Ronnie started pulling back on me, not fully disclosing what was going on because she knew it was not right. That's when I noticed the cracks beginning to show in our personal relationship, and we began to grow apart."

Nedra also noticed something else seeping into their professional relationship. Photo shoots revealed Ronnie in a more prominent light; album covers featured the lead vocalist front and center wearing different clothing than the others. Most interview requests were funneled to Ronnie first. These were behind-the-scenes workings of Phil Spector to draw him closer to Ronnie, who didn't seem to disapprove. Ronnie hinted about a possible new arrangement. Nedra recalls, "Everybody in the music industry knows favoritism leads to some sort of professional advantage. Once Diana Ross got together with Berry Gordy, it went from The Supremes to Diana Ross and The Supremes. As far as I was concerned, it was always going to be The Ronettes. But it wasn't long before Ronnie said, 'Well, I sweat more than you do when we dance.' I said, 'We will not be comparing your glands to my glands. Just because you sweat more than me doesn't mean that you work any harder. The Ronettes are a trio, and everything is a third. The day it stops becoming a third, I will not be here.'"

Issues with Spector surfaced when he limited Ronnie's outings and performances, something that had never happened before. During the summer of '66, on The Beatles' last US tour during the month of August, the lads from Liverpool had specifically requested The Ronettes as their opening act. Spector would not allow Ronnie to go because of his insecurities, which reflected his increasing control over her life. Ronnie acquiesced, and The Ronettes were forced to make some adjustments. Nedra sang lead vocals while Estelle and their cousin, Elaine Mayes, took the second and third harmonies for the tour. By this time, Nedra was growing weary of the constant drama and began experiencing serious spiritual rumblings.

One of my absolute favorite Scriptures is Philippians 2:13 (I especially like the Living Bible's translation): "For God is at work within you, helping you want to obey him, and then helping you do what he wants" (TLB). What strikes me about this very profound word is that I can see this happening with Nedra. Like her, I can see my whole adult life chronicled in a single sentence. If there were a progress bar running beneath that Scripture, I would be able to watch my movement as I have traveled along my individual spiritual path—a spiritual path that had no resemblance to me being spiritual. The whole time I was living a crazy life, I could feel something tugging at my heart. I knew something wasn't right deep down inside. God was trying to talk to me, but I had built up so much resistance, so many walls, and pushed back this gnawing feeling to the point that He was having a real tough time getting through. I had traveled so far away from the seeds planted in my youth that He had to plow too many stones and hard ground to get to my soul. He "was at work within both of us" for quite a while.

Fortunately for Nedra, she offered much softer and fertile ground for the Master Gardener. She soon realized who was behind what was happening in her heart and knew she needed to go home in more ways than one. She was riding an emotional bullet train, and her spiritual sound barrier was getting ready to be broken. I envy her for catching on so quickly—it is never easy, but though she may have felt she was coming from behind in this matter, she was, as it turns out, way ahead of the game.

The Ronettes had fulfilled all of their contracts by early 1967, and the group disbanded. Nedra knew she wanted a different life than her two cousins, who wanted to continue their careers. While Ronnie and Estelle dreamed of individual stardom and solo careers, Nedra dreamed of a husband, a family, and perhaps a chance to settle down. When she bumped into Scott Ross again, she cleverly applied some reverse psychology to nab her man. "I hadn't seen Scott for a while and when we caught up with each other, I told him I was thinking of getting married. He said, 'Married? You shouldn't get married. Don't do it! Don't do it.' So he's trying to talk me out of marriage, and I had no one to marry. I just wanted to see what his response would be. When I saw he was fighting for me not to get married, it clued me in to how he felt about me." Nedra chuckles. "When I kissed Scott for the first time, I saw stars. Honestly! 'Bing-bang' just like those movie cartoons with the *POW!* and steam coming out of my ears. I still remember that first kiss. You need some things to hold on to when times get tough."

Admittedly, Scott was no choirboy. He had been arrested for drug possession (marijuana, hashish, and LSD), which got picked up by the local papers. As a result, he lost his prized job at WINS—blackballed by the radio industry at age twenty-six. Because he could no longer pay his bills, his car was repossessed. And right around the same time, an old girlfriend claimed she was pregnant. Let's put it this way—if Scott would have put an ad in a singles column listing what he had to offer at that point in his life, no girl in her right mind would have answered. But Uncle Sam felt Scott's attributes, as negative as they might be, were good enough for him to qualify for service in Vietnam. The draft board ordered him to report to Hagerstown, Maryland, for a physical. Sensing he was at his lowest, Nedra stood by her man. They boarded a Greyhound bus and ventured south to Hagerstown, where Scott grew up and his mother still resided. Once inside her home, Scott unburdened his soul to his mother while rolling joints in front of her. She suggested they join her for church that evening. A sensible suggestion to anyone going through a dark period, but for Scott, the idea was ludicrous.

We should probably take a sidebar at this point: Scott Ross was raised in a God-fearing home in his native land of Scotland. His father, Charles, was a lay preacher in the Apostolic church in Glasgow, and his mother, Marjorie, was a strong, matriarchal figure, spiritually yoked with her husband. At the age of five, Scott got down on his knees on his parents' linoleum-tiled kitchen floor and accepted Jesus Christ as his Lord and Savior. Life was storybook-good in Scotland, until Charles immigrated his family to the States. Scott arrived on our shores sporting a kilt, a funny accent, and smelling a little rank from his transatlantic journey. His welcome wagon to this country was a group of neighborhood roughs who disliked Scott's fashion sense and ragged on him about his "skirt." Scott's mettle was constantly tested. But he was tough and pugnacious, and his fists were lightning quick. He learned to strike fast when provoked and often became the aggressor when situations grew tense.

Now Scott and I have known each other for a long time, but I couldn't believe it when I heard this. When I was five years old, my family was uprooted from their proper Pennsylvania Dutch culture in a small town not far from Wilkes-Barre/Scranton. Because of my baby brother's asthma they were forced to move to a dry climate, and northern Idaho was chosen. My dad became a lumberjack because that was the only work he could find in a hurry. In a dramatic life change, we suddenly found ourselves living in a sawmill town. Where I grew up in Pennsylvania, the attire for a proper young lad in school was the basic Little Lord Fauntleroy outfit—dark-blue short pants, patent leather shoes with long socks, a matching jacket, proper white shirt with ruffled collar, all topped off with a frilly tie and a bouncy haircut. It was the way to be dressed, and I would have probably been beaten up by the Pennsylvania kids if my parents didn't dress me proper like they were. When we moved to Idaho, my mother sent me off to first grade in those digs, and my beautiful blue and white outfit came home red, white, and blue. These were tough kids in torn Levis and plaid hand-me-down work shirts—they bloodied my nose before the first bell. I was small for my age, but before the first semester was over I learned how to fight. Like Scott, I discovered if you see it coming, you'd better get in the first punch and make it good because that may be your only shot with a bigger guy. (Big guys only pick on little guys, never bigger guys. I never had someone smaller than me pick a fight with me.)

Scott grew cynical by his teens and loathed religious hypocrisy. He'd listen to the faithful in church talk about how they were delivered from their nicotine habits, only to see them sneaking a smoke before the service. He wondered if there was truly a God at all when a church-goer who gave the Ross family shelter attempted to molest him—and not once but several times.

He soon rejected everything the church stood for. Scott's attitude didn't soften in adulthood—he felt everyone who filed through the sanctuary doors and sat on wooden pews was a pious, Bible-toting hypocrite who preached eternal damnation rather than God's love. His path changed course, especially when he discovered booze, pot, and jazz music. He reached his breaking point when the church dumped Charles as their pastor in front of his own congregation in favor of a newer, younger model. That soul-crushing incident probably led to his dad's physical demise and eventual death—something that Scott had never fully pieced together until the writing of this chapter.

Charles's death did not stem the degradation of the Ross family. Congregation members stormed into the Ross household, carting off items they felt belonged to the church. Marjorie, numbed with grief, watched in horrified silence. When Scott saw them reaching for his father's toolbox, he went ballistic and ordered everyone out of the house. However, they issued a final decree before their departure: vacate the premises for the new pastor. Scott eventually found Marjorie a place in a low-income government housing project, but the humiliating experience was further proof of what Scott already believed—Christians stank to high heaven. Those insensitive actions helped drive him into rebellion against God in what he termed "the prodigal years."

Now he was back in the town that drove his father into the grave and his mother into the projects, and Scott remained deeply embittered. Going to church was the last thing on his mind; all he wanted to do was smoke some fine herb. After a toke or two, he began to relax, and his mood lightened. Scott thought it might even be fun if he—sporting a chic '70s-style mustache, shoulder-length hair, and suede suit with fringes—walked into this formal lily-white Pentecostal church with his olive-complexioned girlfriend.

What a ruckus that might cause! Scott chuckled to himself.

But the last laugh was on him. Nedra said people were speaking in tongues and one of the messengers wailed a prophetic word from God, "I have directed your steps to this hour. Cast your burdens upon Me, my children, yea, cast them upon Me! There are two people here tonight who are responding even now to My call. Come forward, come forward, My children! Give your hearts to Me this night!"

The words shot through Nedra like a lightning bolt, who whispered, "Scott, that's us! Those two people—that's us. Scott, let's go forward."

Scott wasn't convinced, and the last place he wanted to rededicate his life to the Lord was Hagerstown. "Scott, that's us. Let's go forward."

"No, it's not. It's you."

"Scott, God said two people."

"I'm not going."

"Well, then it's me. One way or the other, I'll go with or without you."

Nedra got up, crossed over Scott, and headed to the altar where she knelt before God. Moments later, Scott was kneeling next to her. As she looked up toward the ceiling, she saw something out of the corner of her eye. More than four decades later, she still recalls that moment with great clarity: "I looked up and saw this old-fashioned slate from school, like a chalkboard. The chalkboard listed all of my sins, and when I blinked and looked up again, they were all erased. All my life I was a good daughter, a good niece, a good sister, a good person, but I had sins that needed to be forgiven. These were major things I had done throughout my lifetime;

things only I knew about, and I just needed forgiveness from the Lord. At that moment, I was a completely changed person. I knew God for God, Jesus as His Son, and that I was a daughter of the King … which is so much better than being a rock and roll star."

When Nedra and Scott returned to his mother's house, he rolled a joint to calm his nerves. He lit it, took a hit, and the smoke suddenly tasted like poison. He gagged and violently coughed up a black ugly substance that took him and Nedra totally by surprise. He ran to the bathroom and vomited. Seems the Lord was beginning to work on "old things passing away."

Scott wasn't at his physical peak when he visited the draft board the next day, but he sure was chatty. When asked if he had ever been arrested, Scott went into great detail about his recent drug bust, the headlines and embarrassment it caused, and how he couldn't seem to get it together. After he was finished, the draft board decided that Scott was unsuitable for the army. Scott's problems dissolved almost overnight, and he and Nedra headed back to New York City. On the bus ride back, Nedra placed in Scott's hands his father's Bible—a book that he now devoured. He spent the next few weeks reading the Scriptures while temptation literally banged on his door. Old friends, musicians, and drug buddies dropped by his apartment with enticements of drugs and alcohol, all of which Scott politely declined. Nedra was tempted as well.

She had one final obligation with The Ronettes: a nine-date tour of Germany. "During the tour, I was sharing my newfound faith with this young, *very* good-looking, blonde-haired, blue-eyed performer in blue jeans, in the back of the bus. After I professed my faith, he looked me straight in the eye and said, 'If you give me two weeks, you will deny everything you believe.' As he was talking, I couldn't help but think of that song, 'Somebody's Knockin' (Devil in Blue Jeans).' Like the devil, he was a very beautiful person coming with a very ugly statement. It was so scary, because I knew if I tried to walk and grow where there was no fertile ground, in a short period of time I would be gone. I knew that there would be a lot of good-looking guys saying, 'Just give me a chance.' Or girls who would say, 'You know, this is the real truth. What you've got right now is not the truth.' Something in my heart said, *Okay, make a choice. I need to grow, and I can't grow here.*

"I had been confronted with a choice; the gauntlet had been thrown down. I knew there was an enemy who could destroy every belief and everything else that counted with the Lord. I could not stay in that circle if I wanted to be with the Lord."

When Nedra returned from Europe, she and Scott knew they had to find a church to keep them equally yoked and focused on the Word. They attended the Rock Church on East 62nd Street and Lexington Avenue almost nightly, and Scott later landed a job as a book clerk. Blessings continued to flow when Scott received a phone call from the woman who claimed to be carrying his child. Sheepishly she explained she was no longer pregnant, and it wasn't an abortion, either—just a big misunderstanding. Relieved of his last burden, Scott pulled Nedra gently into his arms and asked her to marry him. They exchanged nuptials at the Rock Church on March 5, 1967, following the Sunday night service. After they said, "I do," the congregants—garment workers, cleaning ladies, widows, retirees—lined up to shake hands with the newlyweds. When they came to Scott, they handed him fives, dollar bills, quarters, dimes, and nickels. He suspected it was cab fare, subway change, and lunch money for many of them. Afterward, Scott's musician friends treated the couple to a wedding party at The Scene, a nightclub on Eighth Avenue. They were treated to an evening of songs by Tiny Tim and Spanky and Our Gang, who played the entire Ronettes catalog. As the newlyweds took in their surroundings that night, they knew theirs was not going to be a normal married life.

Things took an "adventurous" turn when Scott quit his job and they headed back to Hagerstown, the place he so despised, in an attempt to "get to know God better." Upon his arrival, he offered his services to Pastor Vernon Miles. Think about this for a moment—Scott was a new

Christian, who much like myself jumped head, heart, and hands into this wonderful new experience and immediately began exercising the precepts and the mechanics of how he believed his new faith was supposed to work. Now, there is fine line between obeying God's Word and doing something that outsiders would say is pure lunacy. When you look at the newlyweds' situation, it sounds crazy from an outsider's point of view. They were leaving a vibrant city, the place they called home, and their church. Nedra was leaving her family; Scott was going to a place he hated to take a low-paying job. Their prospects were dim, and it was also the place where Scott's father was run out of church and his mother was kicked out of her home. It was the last place on earth Scott wanted to be, but it's where he eventually found employment and prosperity.

Now what I am about to say is where many theologians will start spinning in their pulpit, but the way I see it and the way Scott did it makes total sense to me. If you are going to be tied to worldly logic and let it dictate every move you make in life, then why bother with God in the first place? I have always said the greatest asset I possessed when I began my climb up the music business ladder was naïveté. I believe when Scott became a Christian the world probably saw his choices as naïve, or better yet, a form of insanity. If there were a Christian dictionary for what earthly words really mean, then the heavenly words defining *naïveté* might possibly be innocence, trust, passion, and abandonment to godly visions. The most beautiful part of being a Christian takes place during those first few years when we simply absorb, believe, trust, accept, and bathe in all the incredible promises and glorious teachings. When this happens, it is so wonderful and so much bigger and better than anything we could have ever imagined. The experience really sparkles when we discover that the self-indulgent invincibility of our youth has been replaced with the undeniable and profound invincibility of God's Word.

Scott would have never thought of these choices, or have the guts to act on them as a nonbeliever, because they would have made no sense in the old days. The thing he grasped right away is that God makes sense in everything He does, and we don't have to understand, we just need to listen. Once again I am led to paraphrase Scripture: His ways are so much cooler than our ways. Scott emptied all the junk and clutter out of his mind and heart, had a clean slate to write on, and was just following in the steps of his heavenly Father—the Teacher of all things good and true.

While Nedra and Scott didn't officially take a vow of poverty, they might as well have considering they subsisted on his small salary. Adding to this pressure was living together for the first time, adjusting to their low-key life after New York City, and discovering who Jesus really is. Becoming Christians seemed to make their lives more desperate. They'd lost touch with most of their friends, were quarreling nonstop, and were broke. Nedra recalls, "Before I was married, I was making good money. I lived in a three-bedroom Riverside Drive apartment, made my mom quit her job, and took good care of her. I paid a maid to clean the place, and I drove a white Chrysler Imperial hardtop around town. I had it all, and I had it good. Even though I was twenty-one when I married Scott, I placed all of my property, income, and savings with her and kept the car at my mother's insistence. She didn't want me to marry Scott. God took us to a point where we were so broke that I had to think about it before I even bought a Pepsi. But, it never made me go, 'There is no God,' because when I did really want one, He provided the soda pop. The way we looked at it, God was our provider and we were safe in His hands. Maybe God felt that living on just a few dollars a week was all we could handle."

God returned their faithfulness when they discovered Nedra was pregnant. Scott was also blessed with a big bump—in pay. They were elated when they saw how God works. After a chance meeting with evangelist Pat Robertson, Scott was offered a music and talk show job at the Christian Broadcasting Network in Portsmouth, Virginia. But in an all-too-familiar pattern, Nedra and Scott's blessings came in tandem with difficult challenges. In this instance, it was a life or death proposition. After the birth of their first daughter, Nedra Kristina, on September 29,

1967, they discovered a problem soon after coming home from the hospital—Nedra Kristina's intestines were twisted and stuck to the lining of her stomach. She required immediate surgery, which was scheduled for October 4. While Scott and Pat Robertson began a round-the-clock prayer campaign with their on-air listeners, Nedra kept a two-way frequency open with the Lord. "I never talked to the Lord like I did that day. I said, 'Jesus, you know me. You saved me. Nedra Kristina is yours. We already committed her to you. If it is possible that I could change places with her, if she is dying, I'd rather you take me. But if you don't, no matter what you do, I will love you no matter what.' I knew He heard me and knew I meant it. That was the first real big test in my walk with the Lord. I'm glad everything turned out well, but I know I would have kept my promise to the Lord. I would have loved Him no matter what happened."

When Nedra said this, I got chills. I know when she looks back on that chat with God that she knows now that He gave her a special gift at that time—and that gift was the blessed assurance that her faith was strong. Without her realizing it, the depths of her love provided her and God with an incredible bonding moment. God knew her faith was real, and even more special, Nedra knew it—because she meant what she said. She knew that she could have never said those words lightly to her Creator. If you ever wonder if you really are a believer, just ask yourself if you could come before the Father and tell Him heart to heart, face to face, that no matter what happens in a deep trial and time of testing, you will not desert Him—that you are staying with Him whether you like the outcome or not. If you have read His Word, you know He has already promised these very same things; He said it, and He always does what He says. It's hard not to love and serve a God like that!

Nedra Kristina came through surgery, thanks to the thousands who prayed for her. Soon son Christian Scott followed in 1971; next came Heather Brooke in 1974, and finally Ryan Christopher in 1980.

As Nedra and Scott's faith grew deeper, so did their responsibilities. *The Scott Ross Show* found a permanent home in upstate New York, where they moved in 1969 to build on CBN's fledgling network of five radio stations. The weekly show was eventually syndicated to 185 stations internationally and won five *Billboard* magazine awards for best syndicated radio show.

Concurrently, Scott and Nedra also founded and pastored a countercultural church in a barn in Freeville, New York, thanks to a call Scott received at the station from listener Peg Hardesty, who had suffered from crippling arthritis. Peg said God had touched her body and totally healed her arthritis after praying along with Scott on the radio. She had received a message from God that she should offer him the use of her barn. Scott didn't know what he would use it for, but in time the message from God grew clearer: start a church.

As Scott began talking about the barn to his radio audience to flesh out the idea for its use, he received many calls from listeners offering help. As the clearing process commenced, Scott envisioned a place where people could gather to listen to live contemporary Christian music. The new organization became a ministry, and the barn was crowned "Love Inn."

Love Inn was the East Coast equivalent of Calvary Church in California, where miracles took place on an almost daily basis. Nedra was by Scott's side, singing, speaking, counseling women, and building relationships. The couple also published a newspaper called *Free Love*, free of charge to those who requested a copy. The paper dealt with current events, the deception of the Unification church and transcendental meditation, plus interviews with artists and musicians who appeared on Scott's show. The ministry also offered "Teach Inn," which were teaching cassettes on various Christian topics. Those endeavors spawned the "Love Inn Book Shoppe," which made music available as LPs, cassettes, and eight-tracks.

Eventually, Love Inn's barn was host to production for *The Scott Ross Show* and a theatre for drama, dance, and music. It also provided a dormitory for full-time workers and a school for the children of the members of the community.

In addition, Love Inn built a recording studio called New Song

Productions, for the sole purpose of producing records for the emerging Christian market. Artists Phil Keaggy and Ted Sandquist became a part of the Love Inn community, and New Song became their record label.

Scott and Nedra brought the Love Inn concept to Schenectady, New York; Albion, New York; Youngstown, Ohio, and Cape Cod, Massachusetts, and later tied into a national group of Covenant churches based out of Ft. Lauderdale, Florida. By the late 1970s, they extended into different parts of the United States and the world.

The Reagan era brought more prosperity to Nedra and Scott. Scott returned to CBN in the early '80s, where he produced and hosted television entertainment features for a national audience and garnered five "Angel" awards for excellence. For three years, he hosted *Scott Ross Straight Talk*, a daily talk show on The Family Channel. Today he serves as a TV producer and liaison for the CBN Network and WorldReach, where he continues to motivate viewers to positive response with his stories on substantive issues.

As for Nedra, once she left The Ronettes, she never looked back. In addition to her work at Love Inn, she opened a chain of restaurants with her mother in New York, Atlanta, and Virginia, and a barbeque sauce line. She also bought several investment properties and managed them, ultimately flipping them for a tidy profit. Who would have guessed that little Nedra Ross would one day reinvent herself as a businesswoman and create a business empire? Spunk is spunk, moxie is moxie, and good people do have a way of coming out just fine in the long run. Scott not only married well—he married *real* good!

Life got even sweeter when, in 2007, The Ronettes were inducted into the Rock and Roll Hall of Fame. Nedra smiles about the night she found out. "Scott asked me, 'Darling, did you hear the good news?' I said, 'What good news?' He said, 'You're inducted!' I let out this scream that rattled the house. And then I broke down and cried. These were emotions and feelings that I had pushed off to the side."

The induction ceremony was the first time the three original Ronettes had been reunited in public in more than forty years. Ronnie attempted to put the group back together after she left Phil Spector in June 1972, divorcing him shortly afterward. Nedra had no interest in reuniting, and Estelle could no longer handle the burden of performing. Her inner demons later manifested in the form of schizophrenia, anorexia, and even homelessness. This time around, though, it was important the three ladies reunite to get closure on issues that had brewed for several years. For Nedra in particular, it was an opportunity to publicly recognize her mother Susan's contributions to the group, something that had been shrouded in the past. Nedra's acceptance speech, totally unplanned and off the cuff, resonated with the audience, including Ronnie and Estelle. "I said to Mommy, 'No matter what, I know what you did. The family knows what you did. The Ronettes know what you did. It may be reported that you didn't do these things, but God knows it.' That night I thanked Mommy and gave her the recognition she deserved. It wasn't to throw barbs at Ronnie or Estelle but simply to say 'thanks.' God knew all those years ago that this special event was going to take place, even though we didn't. We had no idea one day there'd be a Rock and Roll Hall of Fame at the Waldorf Astoria and that this girl from uptown was going to be there accepting this prestigious award. Who could predict such a thing other than God?"

It's hard for me to believe that Nedra Talley—the baby Ronette—is today the same age as her grandmother Mama Moble, the doting grandmother who kept her large family together in her formative years. A lady who Nedra says still looms largely in her life. "Mama was the best grandmother in the world. I cried so many years because my children never got a chance to know her. My son once said, 'Mommy, you talk about Mama like she died a couple of weeks ago, and she died over fifty years ago.' I said, 'Well, I hope that my grandchildren will remember us—Mama, Mommy, and me [Mom] as three people who loved their children with all of their heart. My family is my legacy.' I also have a legacy with people that keep the memories of The Ronettes alive in their hearts. They loved us, and I so appreciate their loyalty and their love. They are family too."

Philippians 4:7 reminds me so much of Nedra because she possesses the peace of God, which passes all understanding. Though it took a while to get there, Nedra and Scott are blessed and draw strength from each other ever day. "We are absolute communicators. We talk and read the Word together from the little devotional the Rock Church gave us forty-five years ago. And if I'm at home and he is at work, we'll call and talk about whatever's necessary. Sometimes the thought of losing Scott crosses my mind and I can't imagine what life would be like without him, even though there were times I was ready to send him to Jesus!" Nedra laughs. "But we've got the blood of Jesus over the doorpost, so there's nothing that's going to come to my house that the Lord won't allow me to handle. But remember one thing: when you ask Jesus into your life, you'd better duck, because 'stuff' is going to happen."

Yes "stuff" does happen, but today Nedra has the "stuff" of the good wife in Proverbs 31, who sets about each day doing the things that please God, family, and friends. As she puts it, "I see myself as the daughter of the King. He's my father and I represent him. Not in an aloof, distant sort of way but as someone who is proud because He is the Ambassador of the kingdom."

* * *

Estelle Bennett died in February 2009.

The Ronettes sued producer Phil Spector in 1988 for $3 million in back royalties. This dragged through the courts until 2001. They received a little more than $100,000 apiece when it was finally settled. Although this was a victory of sorts for The Ronettes, those of us in the industry see it as a feeble payoff far below what the girls had coming.

The important question to consider here is, in the long run, who would you rather be: God-fearing, family-loving, forever-blessed Nedra, who lives in a peaceful world surrounded by a faithful husband of many years, with beautiful children and grandchildren—or Phil Spector, who…

RICHIE FURAY

Buffalo Springfield / Poco

Buffalo Springfield was a wellspring for some of the greatest music of an era, and along with their predecessors, The Byrds, were the major catalyst for the 1960s country folk rock sound. In 1997, Buffalo Springfield was enshrined into the Rock and Roll Hall of Fame. Richie Furay's repeat performance as cofounder of Poco carried on this tradition of great music.

ELEVEN

STOP, CHILDREN, WHAT'S THAT SOUND?

RICHIE FURAY | Buffalo Springfield, Poco

In addition to life-changing experiences of working with The Beatles, Waylon Jennings, and other legendary artists, a musically pivotal moment was when I first became aware of Buffalo Springfield. They were, in my estimation, a wellspring for some of the greatest music of our time. Out of their lyrical harmonics evolved the resonance of bands like Crosby, Stills, Nash and Young, Poco, and The Flying Burrito Brothers to name a few. These bands spawned the great migration away from the old normal in contemporary music. Along with their predecessors, The Byrds, Buffalo Springfield was a major catalyst for the country folk rock sound that has been a perpetually pleasing sound in our ears and hearts since the late '60s.

When the Buffaloes came stampeding into my mind, I was mesmerized by their music and the almost classical depth of their arrangements and ideas. As they dispersed into newer incarnations, I shared meaningful moments with some of the original members. I coproduced my first chart record with Jim Messina, signed bass player Bruce Palmer to a solo deal at MGM, and even convinced Neil Young to let me change his lyrics to "Are You Ready for the Country" for one of Waylon's groundbreaking albums. Dewey Martin, Buffalo Springfield's drummer, was a good friend and carousing partner in the Laurel Canyon days—unfortunately, most of my dear Dewey stories are not suitable for print.

Although we ran in identical circles, Richie Furay and I never connected until this book, but when we talk now it's as old friends. He was among the handful of architects responsible for blending folk and country rock. His creative talent and artistry became evident at an early age—eight years old, to be exact.

It was Christmas 1952 when he asked his parents for a guitar. "I remember going downstairs Christmas morning and seeing this shadow around the tree. 'Wow! I got a guitar,'" Richie recalls. "I picked it up, and it was puke-green with cowboy scenes on it and … it was a *gut string guitar*! I was repulsed. I marched upstairs to my parents' bedroom and said, 'I want a real guitar!' After their initial shock wore off, they bought me a 'real guitar' after the holiday. I picked a Gibson hollow-body electric ES295."

Paul Richard "Richie" Furay, the son of Paul and Naomi Furay, shopkeepers from Yellow Springs, Ohio (population 2,000), was a typical midcentury teen who played sports, enjoyed the outdoors, and was glued to the television set when ABC-TV's *The Adventures of Ozzie & Harriet* aired every week. "I still have this picture in my mind of Ricky Nelson singing 'Be Bop Baby' with his acoustic guitar to a baby in a crib. Then there was a sudden scene transition, and Ricky was belting out the same song at a high school dance with guitarist James Burton. Suddenly it hit me: *I've gotta do this!* That was my moment," Richie recalls, speaking to me from his Colorado residence.

Going to church on Sundays was also woven into the fabric of Richie's life, but not a big deal. "It would be safe to say in the 1950s, most families went to church—it was what you did. There was no personal relationship with Jesus Christ. I was 'confirmed' as a child but never knew what that meant or what difference it made and never invited Christ into my life. I assumed I would go to heaven because I was a good person. In reality, I didn't have a clue how to get there."

Richie aptly described the family dynamic of the '40s and '50s growing up in America. Church was an obligation, not a spiritual experience. At our house, it started with Saturday night baths; putting on our "church" clothes the next morning; driving to church as a shiny family; sitting stiffly in the pews between our folks so they could keep us quiet within the boredom; singing from the hymnal book; listening to the pastor's message; fidgeting until we were released for Sunday school, and then "religiously" waiting for it to be over. Once out the door and on our way home, we were good to go. It was a sweet normality for families, having that stable ritual as part of your life. Our days were orderly and life was simple. We learned discipline, respect, and goodness. There was a mother, a father, God, and 2.76 kids.

As far as Richie was concerned, life was going according to plan ... until he received word his forty-five-year-old father died from an aortic aneurysm. Richie had just turned thirteen. "With my dad's death, everything changed. I knew my life would never be the same. What impacted me was knowing I would never really get to know him."

Richie discovered that music filled that void and soothed his soul. He traded in his hollow-body Gibson for a Martin D28 and saw instant results: he won a talent show at his college, and a fire was lit—Richie had a new calling.

Soon Richie joined forces with fraternity brothers Bob Harmelink and Nels Gustafson and formed The Monks. They made the rounds at parties and campus events, usually performing for the fun of it. For most bands it is not only the desire for applause and recognition but also the lure of free beer and pizza … oh, did I leave out girls?

Coinciding with Richie's musical rebirth was an urban folk movement, led by The Kingston Trio along with The Limeliters, The Brothers Four, and Peter, Paul, and Mary. The coffeehouse scene was flourishing, with Chicago, Los Angeles, Denver, San Francisco, San Diego, and New York City's Greenwich Village serving as the epicenters of this revival. The Kingston Trio changed the world for us back then just like The

Beatles did for rockers years later. When something fresh and exciting comes along, everyone hits the pause button on their musical direction. There was no question in Richie's mind that's where he needed to be. While on spring break, his trio ventured to the Village and played the legendary Café Wha? The scene was just as Richie had imagined: musicians everywhere and patrons looking to be entertained and moved. Something deep inside clicked for Richie, and he could clearly see the future. All roads pointed to New York City.

Armed with an acoustic guitar, tape recorder, suitcase, and a book called *How to Live in New York City on $5 a Day*, The Monks moved to the Big Apple. It was there that Richie met Peter Tork (The Monkees) and banjo player Charlie Chin, who later recorded with Buffalo Springfield and Stephen Stills. Richie says today that God obviously had a plan in mind. "How can you look at the infinite mind of God with a finite mind when He sees the whole picture? The fact that I met Stephen Stills in a little club in a city of eight million people and we later formed a band together seems a bit beyond coincidental to me."

In time, The Monks disbanded. Richie then appeared in a failed off-Broadway play, recorded a one-off record deal, and toured with the Au Go-Go Singers, a nine-member Greenwich Village folk group. He was struggling and at one point, sleeping on a discarded mattress in a small apartment with four other people.

During this time, Richie had brief brushes with Stephen Stills, Neil Young, and a Harvard dropout named Gram Parsons. Parsons put The Byrds' *Mr. Tambourine Man* on the turntable and altered the course of Richie's life. "That album was totally cutting edge and made me realize how much I wanted to make music," Richie said.

Fortunately, Parsons' influence was limited to music. Richie recalled visiting his apartment one night when Parsons went to the freezer and pulled out a tray of sugar ice cubes laced with LSD and dropped it in Richie's hands. "We're going to take these and get high," Parsons announced. Richie's heart began racing, and his hands were shaking. Pot was one thing, but hallucinogens were asking for trouble. He told Gram he couldn't do it. He was relieved by Parson's answer—"Well, smoke this [marijuana] and make sure we don't jump out the window."

It took courage for Richie to say no to Gram, knowing the rest of the gang might not accept him. To me this was a foreshadowing of how God's guiding hand was on Richie, and the Holy Spirit was watching out for him.

But these were crazy times, and if Richie and I held a three-day seminar, I don't think we could describe what the music scene was like then. It sparkled, it danced to a whole new refrain, there was freedom, beautiful hippie chicks, drugs, new chord progressions, harmonies, and to be a part of it was completely intoxicating.

Richie's thoughts kept drifting back to Stephen Stills, who was gifted and as driven as anyone he'd ever known. Richie couldn't picture Stephen giving up until he had achieved his goals, which was the kind of person Richie wanted by his side. He had to find him.

In the '60s, it wasn't easy to stay in touch. It usually consisted of writing a letter or calling a friend of a friend to find someone's whereabouts. Imagine tracking down a migrating troubadour. Richie wrote Stephen's dad in El Salvador, but the letter was sent back for insufficient postage. He wrote again, adding a few more stamps. A few weeks later, Stills was on the phone from Los Angeles, summoning Richie to join his new band.

When Richie arrived in Los Angeles in August 1965, he parked his Martin guitar and suitcase in Stills' small Hollywood apartment and crashed in an outer room. When he discovered he and Stephen were the only members in Stills' new band, he threatened to leave. He calmed down, and they spent countless hours in that tiny apartment forging a new sound, melding their harmonies, and crafting the foundation that would be the basis of what was ahead. "Our lack of cash forced us to spend most of our time in Stephen's apartment, and the only way to make it tolerable was to play music. From early in the morning until late at night, we devoted ourselves to learning songs," Richie said. Many of them ended up on Buffalo Springfield's first album and have become modern-day classics.

Richie's remembrances of his early career remind me of Guns N' Roses. Slash grew up with my youngest son and spent countless hours in my home studio, sitting in the dark playing his guitar late into the night when the room was not in use. Guns N' Roses paid their dues like all bands did in those days, which meant not eating well and living in substandard conditions. Slash said the day the band left Geffen Records' office with a mega deal under their belts, the only thing they knew to do was to go back to the one-room place they were living in Hollywood. They sat on the floor amongst their equipment, looking at each other and staring off in space for a while, not quite able to take it all in. They were not used to having money, but finally one of them broke the elongated silence and said, "Maybe we should go get some pizza?" Theirs is a great story but it's one of many, especially during an era when bands and artists made their bones the hard way—they worked for it. Actually, they did more than that—they starved for it, practiced for it, gave a piece of themselves for it, and lived for it for days, months, and years. Guys sleeping in the same bed had nothing to do with sexual preference—it had to do with crashing on something other than the floor.

But it would be a while before Richie and Stephen tasted success, going through a succession of groups and configurations looking for the right combination. They networked the Sunset Strip club scene but came up short. Finally they decided to look elsewhere for collaborators. Neil Young was foremost on Stills' mind. They had first crossed paths earlier that year in Thunder Bay, Ontario. Young was playing with The Squires, and Stills was on tour with The Company. Their brief meeting left them with a strong desire to work together.

One day, Young and fellow Canadian and bass player Bruce Palmer were cruising Sunset Boulevard in a black '53 Pontiac hearse with Ontario plates. There was no mistaking the car. Richie and Stephen were heading in the opposite direction with Barry Friedman (aka Frazier

Mohawk), when they saw it, made a U-turn, and after shouting, hand waving, and much excitement, the four musicians got together and decided to form a band. Drummer Dewey Martin, who had played with The Standells, Patsy Cline, and The Dillards, was later added to the roster. (I loved this band then and I love this episode now—just reading this paragraph makes me smile.) That's how things were in Los Angeles back then—no one thought things through too much. It had more to do with feelings and common dreams stoked up by the vibe of the times and those streets—Hollywood Boulevard, the Sunset Strip, Santa Monica Boulevard, Melrose Avenue, La Cienega, and the ones that ran through the canyons: Laurel, Benedict, and Topanga.

Taking their name from an Ohio-based steamroller manufacturer—The Buffalo-Springfield Roller Co.—they steamrolled into the LA music scene in a short amount of time.

Buffalo Springfield not only created a new sound, but they also burned up the street and rose above the crowd with their free-form musical madness. It was classical, country, rock, soul, and jazz all wrapped up into one. Listening to their first album today is like looking at a great master's painting and discovering something new every time. This band never made it as high on the charts as some of the others of that era, but they had their moment as the number-one band in many of our hearts. You'd have to tie me down and stuff old cabbage in my mouth to keep me from singing along whenever "Nowadays Clancy Can't Even Sing" plays on the radio or my iPod.

As the band's prospects were starting to grow, the same could be said for their dating options. One night at the Whisky, Richie met his future wife, Nancy Jennings, a tall and stunning looker. "Nancy and a friend were in front of the stage, and my heart was thumping. I remember wanting to know who this girl was and looking down at her and singing 'Sit Down, I Think I Love You.' I finally got to meet her, and here we are forty-eight years later."

While Richie romanced Nancy, every wannabe band manager and

record-label talent scout in the industry was trying to woo Buffalo Springfield. The buzz surrounding this relatively unknown group was astounding. They fielded offers from all the majors, eventually signing with Ahmet Ertegun, the legendary head of Atlantic Records, and its sister label, Atco. All this a mere six weeks after they formed.

Everything moved fast and furious in the beginning, but in their two-year life span they never became as big as they'd hoped. While history has been kind to the band, their fast start eventually drifted into the slow lane, says Richie. "I don't think we ever sounded better than we did during those first few weeks at the Whisky. We had first-rate material, and our sets featured songs that would be on our first album. The songs were powerful, unique, and fresh. We had become a tight-knit team, where the whole became greater than the separate parts. Sadly, the dynamic would change, but at that moment in our short history, we were producing original music with a power that few other bands could match."

When their first album, *Buffalo Springfield*, was released in October 1966, it failed to reach everyone's stratospheric hopes. Their first single, "Nowadays Clancy Can't Even Sing," was met with indifference as was their follow-up, "Burned." They felt they were much better than their sales or airplay indicated, but their reputation didn't extend much beyond Los Angeles. There's an old saying in the music industry about true artistry and commerciality not always being a good mix. Many felt they were ahead of their time. *Ouch.* That comment really irks artists when they are told this!

It is said that desperation is as powerful an inspirer as genius, and Buffalo Springfield found that out with Stephen Stills' "For What It's Worth." Perhaps no other song best summed up the '60s than this protest song about the November 1966 Sunset Strip riots. It became an anthem for the times, symbolizing worldwide turbulence, particularly the Vietnam War. Today it's one of a handful of songs that musicologists, social critics, and historians point to as defining the decade, *and* it's ranked number sixty-three on *Rolling Stone*'s list of The 500 Greatest Hits of All Time. The irony in all of this is, "For What It's Worth" struck Richie as a pleasant little song, but not much more. Luckily, Ertegun disagreed. He recognized the song's potential, had them record it on December 5, 1966, and moved heaven and earth to have it placed on their debut album. This was easier said than done given that 250,000 copies of the original version of *Buffalo Springfield* had already been delivered to stores a few weeks prior. Recalling them was a monumental task.

Pulling back thousands of pressed copies of a record for any reason is a nightmare for a record company and a harrowing experience. I lived through the granddaddy of all recalls with The Beatles' *Yesterday and Today*—aka the "Butcher" cover. (Pulling back that objectionable product was so serious that a company-wide Capitol memorandum was sent out stating that any employee caught taking a copy out of the building would be immediately terminated regardless of their tenure or importance to the company—no discussion and no exceptions!)

Ertegun's gamble paid off, and the song shot to the Top 10 in early 1967. However, the record was a slow mover, becoming popular in widely scattered markets and regions of the country at different times, failing to take the country by storm. This scenario drives record companies crazy. If a new record gets heavy airplay and sales at the same time, it shoots up the charts, becomes a hit, and bigger sales follow. But when sales and airplay are spread out over several markets at different times, its total sales on any given week keep the record from showing up strong on the national surveys. A record that has sold twice as many copies as another record could potentially earn only half the chart position because of scattered airplay. Richie says the group's 1967 tour underscored this point. The band was playing high schools, colleges, ballrooms, clubs, and other odd venues. They were often packaged at festivals with other groups like The Beach Boys, Strawberry Alarm Clock, Chad and Jeremy, The Turtles, Paul Revere and The Raiders, and Jefferson Airplane.

As with any band, there were problems. Stills decking Palmer during a performance in New York. Neil Young suffering epileptic episodes during live performances. They were unhappy with their managers, received poor financial compensation, and were not getting along with their producers. Young left a couple of times, and Palmer was busted for pot possession (twice on the same day!) and deported to Canada for a few months. They were falling apart. "It's hard to get momentum going when somebody is leaving the band every month or so. Buffalo Springfield was together for about two years, and in that time nine people were in and out of the band. It was always one step forward and three steps back."

Their breakup was a slow process, drawn out over a year. The band continued to make music while suffering through misunderstandings and mistakes. Even decades later, Richie still wonders how everything went sideways for such a phenomenal lineup of talent.

One thing that remained steady was Richie's relationship with Nancy. They were married in March 1967 and remained inseparable. They were young, in love, and experiencing all the wonderful things a honeymoon period brings.

Things looked up when Buffalo Springfield was invited to the Monterey International Pop Festival in June 1967, a landmark event. I was there on behalf of Capitol Records. Capitol was becoming aware that even though we had the biggest acts in several categories signed to our label, there was a buzz about a whole new music and we were on the verge of being left behind. I was too busy with Beatle matters to attend Woodstock and too consumed with other Capitol artist projects to accept John and Yoko's Montreal bed-in invitation, but if I had to choose between those three incredible events, it would be an easy decision to pick Monterey. It was a mind-boggling, historical, and beautiful event. Not one arrest, not one beating, no big mess, no misunderstood motives or naysaying pundits. Monterey was truly peace and love, flower power, an odd mixture of lost and found innocence and the coming out party of a generation that had the gift of just going with the flow… if just for those three days. Monterey was … Monterey! I wore a white button-down shirt, black knit tie, wingtip shoes, and dress slacks to the event. I came home with my shirt unbuttoned down to my naval, sleeves rolled up, barefoot, flowers in my hair, and wearing someone else's jeans.

In what should have been Buffalo Springfield's finest hour, the band couldn't get its act together. Neil Young pulled another no-show and was replaced by David Crosby, while Bruce Palmer, who recently returned from Canada, was rusty. Richie came down with tonsillitis. Sadly, the group, known for its tight, high-energy performances, was lackluster and rough around the edges.

Miraculously, the group pulled together for *Buffalo Springfield Again*, considered by many to be their finest work. The album was released in November 1967 and featured several rock classics, such as "Mr. Soul," "Rock and Roll Woman," "Broken Arrow," and "Bluebird"—all staples of FM radio in the late '60s and early '70s. Richie contributed heavily to the album with "Sad Memory," "Good Time Boy," and "A Child's Claim to Fame," the latter song venting his frustration about the group's interpersonal dynamics and dysfunction.

Last Time Around in 1968 was their swan song at Atco. The songs were mostly a Furay-Messina affair. Upon its completion, the group disbanded, save for a May 5 concert in Long Beach. Richie recalls dealing with a mixture of excitement and disappointment during the show, as did their fans, who showed up in large numbers. This resulted in a fiery performance and one of their best in a long time. It was a fitting end to a band that experienced high highs along with searing frustration.

Buffalo Springfield, while brilliant, suffered from a lack of direction and continuity and never felt they had a strong producer guiding them. It was only after the band broke up that they became mythical and legendary.

Richie had an exit strategy and knew the direction he was headed and with whom. This time around, he was not going to be just a member—he was going to lead the charge along with Messina and Rusty Young, a pedal steel guitar player from Colorado. Because Buffalo Springfield was so dysfunctional, Richie selected musicians who not only played the same kind of music but also were personally compatible. For that reason, he took a pass on Gregg Allman and Gram Parsons—who insisted Richie dump Messina because he "would never amount to anything." Richie, Jim, and Rusty eventually picked future Eagle Randy Meisner (bass and vocals) and George Grantham (drums and vocals) to complete their new band—Poco. They continued the synthesis of country and southern California rock while never losing their rock edge.

Poco was "discovered" at the Troubadour in West Hollywood during a two-week stand in October 1968, opening for the Nitty Gritty Dirt Band. When *Los Angeles Times* music critic Robert Hilburn wrote that Poco was going to be "the next big thing" (shades of Buffalo Springfield or as Richie describes it, "the kiss of death"), record offers came rolling in. Poco signed an astounding nine-album deal with Epic Records and in May 1969, released its debut album, *Pickin' Up the Pieces*, a not-so-subtle reference to the wreckage of Buffalo Springfield. Critics wrote their work was reminiscent of The Beatles and The Byrds, hailing this seminal work as a triumph. *Rolling Stone* called *Pickin' Up the Pieces* a "perfect album."

Richie believes the song "Pickin' Up the Pieces" foreshadowed his emerging spirituality. "There's a line about 'we're all going home,' and I often wondered what that meant. I wasn't a Christian back then. It could have meant going back to the farm or to the ranch, but I think it meant going *home*. When we check out of this life, there's going to be a home for us somewhere, and for the believer it's heaven. For the nonbeliever it's not going to be heaven. There were lines in my songs that I wrote before I consciously gave my heart to Christ … snippets of spirituality, so to speak."

Much like Buffalo Springfield, Poco realized they were entering into a nightmare with beautiful music. Before *Pickin' Up the Pieces* was in the can, Meisner left after a dispute. He was replaced by Timothy B. Schmit.

(Meisner later became a cofounding member of the Eagles. When he left them in 1977, Schmit once again filled his slot).

After Poco delivered the final mix, Columbia president Clive Davis invited band members to his New York office to listen to "his" mix of their single "Pickin' Up the Pieces."

"Clive, that's great, but where's the steel guitar?" Richie asked. "That's what really makes us different from other bands. That's our deal."

"You can't have a hit record with a steel guitar on it," Davis said dismissively. Whether Davis was right or wrong, he got his way. Davis was irritated by Meisner's departure because of the expense for extra studio time to fill his parts and redesigning the album cover. Pogo creator Walt Kelley's threatening legal action against the group for the similarity in their name also didn't help matters. Richie thinks Davis "checked out on the group" and put little effort into promoting the group and their debut album.

Poco also missed out on a crucial concert when their manager turned down an invitation to perform at an upstate New York festival in favor of another gig. The festival turned out to be Woodstock, which drew close to four hundred thousand people, further defined a generation, made its performers near mythical, and launched several careers. Poco wasn't one of them.

Pickin' peaked at number sixty-two on the *Billboard* charts. The musical style, while highly original, got lost in the AM-FM mix. Were they too country for rock or too rock for country? Either way, they failed to generate airplay, the lifeblood of any group during that era. Richie expected a rocket ride to stardom with all the stellar reviews, but record sales putted along on fumes.

However, the group developed a reputation as an exciting live act and toured nonstop. No longer playing to intimate gatherings at the Troubadour, Poco played to thousands, opening for Jimi Hendrix, Janis Joplin, Santana, The Who, and Rod Stewart. In between gigs, they recorded their second studio album, *Poco* (1970), but it stalled on the charts, peaking at number fifty-eight. The third time proved to be the charm for Poco with *Deliverin'*, a live album which broke into the Top 40. However, it came at a great cost with the sudden departure of Jimmy Messina, who felt Richie exerted too much control. Jimmy left and joined forces with Kenny Loggins.

Richie grew increasingly more frustrated and strengthened his resolve to succeed by pushing himself and the band harder. Because of sluggish record sales, Poco was forced to go on the road for months at a time to earn money. Ah, the road…

Richie began stepping out on his marriage with a secretary at CBS. For Nancy, it was a slap in the face. She had just given birth to their first daughter, Timmie Sue. "When you're on the road for so long, you don't know what's real and what isn't. It was very hard at that time because I was so driven to be a rock and roll star. I had seen Stephen Stills and Neil Young go off to great success. I saw Jimmy Messina and Randy Meisner do the same. I kept asking, 'What about me? I'm just as talented as those guys. What about me?' I was so consumed and driven to succeed that I had no grasp on reality. As far as I was concerned, Nancy had it good. I provided a nice home. We drove nice cars. We dined at nice restaurants, and she wore nice clothes. I felt I gave her all these things, but what she really wanted was me … but I was on the road living a double life."

The road is a mistress. It represents liberty, it resembles a voyage, it becomes a narcotic, and in time it can be your downfall. No one can really understand those who we call "road warriors" unless they have been there and done the endless miles and restless stopovers. In the beginning, the road and places are exciting, invigorating, and give you a sense of freedom. Everything, everyone, and everywhere is new and feels like an adventure. You become yourself, so you think, for the first time. No one back home, who is a part of your real life, is around to observe your moves or motives. People follow you, fondling your ego, and you become this incredible free-flowing being. Reality fades into fantasy, and a new separate reality becomes real. You get off the tour bus or step out of the limo, and there is a soft spotlight on your ruggedness and wonderfulness. Even your own applause becomes deafening. Then one day it becomes routine, and you have to try new things and leave principled ways to keep the excitement meter pegging at ten.

Home and hearth become so far in the distance that you find you can exit and enter alternate lives each time you get on the next airplane and get off at the next town. The warmth of your God-given mate is replaced by the sizzling allure of strangers—people you don't have to be accountable to. Like the stage and the concert, you give, you get, and then leave for the next town. All this time you are so lost in your sensual gluttony that you think you are the one using them. In time the walls of the hotels, lobbies, bars, backstage dressing rooms, unfamiliar places, and phony people start closing in. They become what you wanted them to be—meaningless, and then you begin feeling alone and trapped. You can't go upstairs and tuck in the kids because you are in a hotel far away. You can't fall into the arms of someone you love and someone who honestly loves you in return. One day it gets so claustrophobic and cold that you feel like you are going to fall apart. You keep getting further away from home, to the point where you don't know if you will ever find your way back. Then you start doing strange things. Ah, the road…

When the tour finished, Richie went home to face the music. He suggested a trial separation to give them time to think. For Nancy, there was nothing to think about—she wanted out and a divorce. Nancy and Timmie moved back in with her mother. Within days, Nancy, along with an attorney friend, made plans to divvy up their belongings. Richie was startled that she was so quick to move on with her life. Confused and upset, he went back on tour, taking his mistress with him. A few weeks later while in Texas, Richie was wracked with guilt. "That's when the scales fell from my eyes. In a moment I realized I was making the worst mistake of my life. I was terrified and felt sick inside. I had no explanation for the way this feeling came over me, but I know now that it was the Holy Spirit stepping into my life," Richie says.

I love the deep meaning behind this simple comment. It's obvious Richie was not a believer at this point, yet seeds had been planted over the years and were fermenting in his soul. Being "racked with guilt" was a feeling he now knows was the Holy Spirit speaking to him. But because of where he was spiritually, he was unaware that God was tapping on his heart, asking to be let in. Richie was the center of his own little universe, and he found himself tottering between condemnation and conviction.

It can be hard to make sense of the way God enters your life at your weakest moment, especially when He is not an important part of your life. So Richie's head wasn't aware that it was the Holy Spirit talking to him, but his heart sensed he was being drawn into a lifetime walk with the Lord. These are the times when we are most open to hearing His voice and begin to realize He is a patient God. He knows the absolute perfect time to set us down for a serious talk. When we ignore the invitation for too long, He sometimes finds it necessary to knock us down to our knees. Either way, He is going to have a conversation with us. So now, when Richie looks back from the standpoint of a committed Christian, he can understand what was happening. The Holy Spirit was jumping in there just in time—before it was too late. God was speaking to Richie, trying to get him to listen up. What appeared confusing and chaotic was a divine moment. But with all this holy stuff coming down, Richie, although moved emotionally, was not ready to move spiritually into God's waiting arms.

The reason for that experience in Texas is now clear, and Richie learned that you can't ignore God and get away with it. Our God is a gentle and loving God, but He is also very smart, knows how to get our attention, and is willing to go to extremes to save us from ourselves.

After Richie came to his senses, he and Nancy agreed to reconcile. The process of wooing his wife back was humbling. After many tears, long talks, and some firm ground rules—mainly that Nancy would be the only woman at his side on the road—they began rebuilding their marriage.

Poco also made changes—Messina was replaced by singer/guitarist Paul Cotton, formerly of Illinois Speed Press. They cut *From the Inside* (1971), but it failed to produce any hits. The same lineup recorded *A Good Feelin' to Know* (1972), and Richie was convinced a commercial breakthrough was imminent. "We were on tour to support the album and kept listening for airplay on the title song—our first single from the album. Instead we heard 'Take It Easy' by a new group called the Eagles. My heart sank because I knew then—the stardom the Eagles would soon be experiencing would never be ours."

Richie's disappointment was profound, and in a desire to end things gracefully, he agreed to make one final Poco album, 1973's *Crazy Eyes.* In typical Poco fashion, the work was released to critical praise and lackluster sales. It was proof enough for him that Poco had run its course. Richie did have an exit strategy in place, thanks to David Geffen, head of Asylum Records. Geffen assembled what he felt would be country rock's first supergroup, teaming Richie with veteran musicians J. D. Souther and Chris Hillman. They later called themselves Southern-Hillman-Furay, or SHF.

"You'll be as big as Crosby, Stills, and Nash," Geffen said. That's all Richie needed to hear, and he bit.

Hillman brought in two other members of his former band, Manassas, as role players—pianist Paul Harris and pedal steel guitarist Al Perkins, formerly with The Flying Burrito Brothers. Jim Gordon, one of the finest session drummers of his time (The Beach Boys, John Lennon, Derek and the Dominos), rounded out the septet. Richie was fine with everyone except Perkins. He didn't have a problem with Perkins' musicianship or personality; it had to do with Perkins' guitar. It sported a fish sticker with the words "Jesus is LORD." "At the time, I was blind to everything other than my personal quest for success. I was convinced Al's Christian faith would drag us down. He could have been a member of any other religion; he could have been an alcoholic or drug addict, a womanizer, anything other than what he was, and I wouldn't have objected. I was hung up on appearances, and because Al was an outspoken Christian, I feared he might turn off music fans."

Hearing these words coming from someone like Richie, who is now totally sold out to the Lord, is delightful in its irony. You could say he ended up where he thought he never would go. We didn't wear Dockers and penny loafers in those days, because it wasn't cool and nobody would want to hang with us if we did. Just ahead of that non-coolness would be to spout Scripture or be found with a Bible in your guitar case. Besides, if you had a sold-out Christian in the band, that meant you would have to stop having fun on the road, or worse yet, be "told on" when you got home. You also lowered the number of potential people to party with by a large percentage, especially if you were in a trio.

Richie sensed trouble when SHF entered rehearsals. He felt everyone was overly polite, afraid to speak up, and unable to connect on a deeper level. The affection or creative spark wasn't there as it was with Poco, which led to serious soul searching on Richie's part. He entered a period of lingering doubts about his personal life, and he felt unfulfilled and questioned where his professional life was going. Something was churning in his guts, telling him it was time to pull off the road he'd been on, because the signs ahead were contradicting where he thought he was going.

The pathway into the world of success, even though fraught with struggle, always has that beckoning glitter that lights the way and keeps you going. You not only get a glimpse of all the wonder, wealth, and worldliness that lies ahead but you can also smell the intoxicating perfume of sweet success that wafts up from its bowels. What you don't know is that God has planted His goodness in your soul from day one, and it breaks His heart to see you deceived and headed for the trash heap that the rottenness of sin eventually dumps you into. Of course, we all know garbage dumps burn their trash once the pile gets stinky and too big. (Play the song "God Is an All-Consuming Fire" here). Richie was unaware of the profound battle he was about to face. The devil likes having talented people like Richie around because their misguided actions are often his best advertisements. People emulate those they admire, and the devil was not going to make it easy for a big someone like Mr. Furay to leave the party without a fight.

Surprisingly, Richie reached out to Al Perkins during this period. One evening he invited Al and his wife, Debbie, to join Nancy and him for dinner. Al asked if he could bring some tapes, and Richie said fine, thinking they were of the musical variety. Following a pleasant meal, Al's tape was a sermon from Pastor Chuck Smith from Calvary Chapel in Costa Mesa, California. Richie hadn't been to a church service in decades, and the sixty-minute tape meant he was in for a long evening. Realizing there wasn't much he could do, Richie sat back and listened, taking in a sermon Smith titled "The More Sure Word."

Richie remembers the sermon almost word for word. "Chuck talked about the many biblical prophecies regarding the Messiah, prophecies made hundreds of years before Jesus was born. He pointed out the overwhelming odds against a single individual fulfilling these prophecies. Accomplishing just eight of them would be equivalent to a blindfolded man having one chance to find a particular silver dollar in Texas if the entire state were covered with identical-sized coins piled two feet deep. Yet, the Bible lists more than three hundred prophecies that Jesus fulfilled. I was frustrated with Al, but beneath the surface I was moved by what Pastor Chuck had to say about Jesus. A seed had been planted."

The devil is a crafty deceiver, but if anyone thinks they can outsmart God by living for that snarly jerk, I don't ever want to fly on the same airplane with them. God can be so patient, and I marvel at His perfect timing. Al Perkins entering Richie's life at this time was no coincidence. It's hard to conceive that God had no idea that this pairing would lead to Richie becoming a pastor someday. God is so unfathomable that once you sense His presence and invite Him, His Son, and His Spirit into your life, you move from being confused by what He can do to blinking in astonishment at His ways. He is the greatest economist of all time, and there is not one wasted moment in our lives once we hand our tangled messes over to Him. Al was an instrumentalist and Richie was a wordsmith in the band, but God decided to use Al that night to be the host DJ who played the lyrics of the song Richie needed to hear.

Smith's sermon also had a profound effect on Nancy, who committed to Christ shortly after that evening. In Nancy's case, it was the result of her reading a book Al's wife gave her called "Satan Is Alive and Well on Planet Earth" by Hal Lindsey. Curiously, she kept the news to herself and didn't share it with Richie. He'd find out the reason why soon enough.

When the band finished rehearsals in Colorado, the Furays rented a house in the San Fernando Valley, where Souther-Hillman-Furay entered the studio and Nancy entered into a new life of faith. During the sessions, tensions rose quickly between the group and drummer Jim Gordon, who may have been experiencing the onset of schizophrenia (he stabbed his mother to death in June 1983 and was sentenced to life in prison). He was replaced by Ron Grinel.

Other departures were forthcoming. Nancy told Richie their marriage was over. Richie did everything to break her resolve, but nothing could change her mind. What made matters worse was that SHF was about to embark on a long tour in support of their self-titled debut.

Richie operated under a black cloud but was about to get a silver lining. The seed that Al Perkins had planted in Richie finally sprouted. His salvation was completed when, one night after a dinner with the Perkinses, Richie accepted Jesus Christ as his Lord and Savior. He recalls, "There were no fireworks going off when I joined them in prayer, and no big emotional trip. The feeling was more a readiness to learn firsthand what Al, Debbie, and Nancy had already discovered. In retrospect, I believe I was born again, but afterward, I couldn't comprehend what had taken place."

Okay, here I go into a no-man's-land in discussing my musings on the subject of knowing when a person becomes saved. Because I am not looking for agreement, I can take the pressure off the discussion and just pass on my street view of the occurrence. First, I believe the Apostles' Creed sets the standard for salvation. I also believe God made us all different while, at the same time, giving us uniqueness. He provides us with many individual ways to enter into His resting place, His kingdom, His heart, and His glory. If He only provided one manner, one time, and one place for this to happen, then it is plausible, for example, that we would all have to go on the third Thursday of even-numbered months to a Wal-Mart parking lot in Des Moines or some neutral place in order to do the deed. This is not saying Jesus is not the one and only way—it is suggesting He is more interesting than just having one way to go about *the* One Way. We often envy those who claim to have had a Damascus Road experience. How cool it would be to be knocked to the ground, struck speechless, tanned by a burning bush, or feel like we have been exported to heaven for the event. (Hearing bells and feeling giddy are also nice touches.)

If you worry about whether you are saved or not, then I believe that means that you are. If you weren't, you wouldn't care about it or be worried in the first place. For me there was definitely no one moment. It was a gradual process, a compilation of moments, teachings, events, and seeds being planted over an extended time. Some of this stuff came about when I was an active stench in the nostrils of heaven. I love how God brings little gems from those days to mind that let me see how He has always had my best interests at heart.

It came to a point where I began thinking more about Him and less about me. I could see how things ran better when I let go and gave Him control. I became more receptive, and He became more audible and conceivable in my life. I wanted what He wanted more than what I wanted. Before I drift away in a halo of pure white light, I admit that I don't always stay with the program. The thing I like now is that instead of being under condemnation when I get busted for these wrong actions, I come under conviction instead. Conviction has a positive slant to it when sorting out a situation—it gives hope. Condemnation is, well … very condemning and offers no hope. If someone stops me on the street and asks if I am a Christian, my answer is sure and immediate. Yes, *I am*! He is the I AM and *I am* His! Once I couldn't even spell Christian, and now I are one.

While Richie may have been on fire for the Lord, the same couldn't be said for Nancy's feelings toward her husband. Thinking his salvation would bring them closer, he called to tell her the "good news," but his words were met with silence. Richie says today that even though they had moved past his infidelity and their first separation, he had committed a much bigger error: he took Nancy for granted. Nancy wanted a husband, a loving, caring, and nurturing partner, but Richie was still in brass ring mode. Through his actions, he had been sending a message that she was not as important as his career. Her feelings for him over time had paled.

Richie only had his newfound faith to get him through this dark period. He tossed out his stash of drugs and pills. He stopped drinking and became a devoted Bible reader. After the tour, which Richie describes as "lifeless," he was ready to come home. However, Nancy wouldn't budge, which led to a seven-month separation. Richie was virtually homeless and stayed for extended stretches with Al and Debbie Perkins and a few Christian pals. For days he'd walk around in a fog. Without fellowship, he says he didn't know what he would have done.

One day after a visit to a Christian bookstore, a violent thunderstorm broke out as he was heading north on the 605 Freeway in Los Angeles. It was raining hard and he was alone. As the heavens opened up, Richie began crying so hard he couldn't see.

"My chest was convulsing with heartache, I pulled onto the shoulder of the road, and once my heart stopped racing, I called out to the Lord, begging Him to reunite me with my family. In the midst of my torment, a voice—a still, small voice that would become louder as I grew in faith—resounded within me. 'That's how much I want you to want me,' it said. There was so much meaning in that statement that it took me a moment to process it. God was telling me to refocus my priorities. Once I came to grips with that, I knew I would be ready for a reconciliation with my wife and daughter."

When Richie talked about his ride down this stretch of lonely highway, I cried. There was a depth of pain flowing from his heart that touched a familiar place in my soul. He knew how badly he blew it, and knowing he wasn't the same person anymore that caused this tragic outcome made it so difficult … if only he could back up and have another chance. He was facing being separated from the most precious people in his life, and he had no one else to blame. That's when Richie realized he needed to focus on godly restoration in the most rigorous way he knew how. Richie's heart had been shattered, and its every beat hurt within his miserable chest.

Richie knew he was going to have to humble himself—he needed to strip to the waist, put his head down, his eyes up, his knees to the floor, his nose to the grindstone, his ears to the ground, his face into the wind, his hands on the plow, and his shoulder to the wheel. It was hard working from that position, but that's the point—he had found himself in a tough position, and it wasn't going to be easy.

While Richie allowed God to work on him, He was also healing Nancy, who came to believe if she left Richie before he became a Christian, she wouldn't be violating God's prohibition of divorce. Richie's acceptance of Christ presented her with a spiritual and moral dilemma she wasn't prepared to deal with.

Despite his personal turmoil, professionally Richie was flourishing. Souther-Hillman-Furray's 1974 self-titled debut was certified gold thanks to the single "Fallin' in Love," which charted in the Top 30. The album charted faster than any of Richie's other releases, and that meant another tour to support the record. After one of the last shows of the tour, in St. Petersburg, Florida, Richie says he had a transcendental experience, and the Lord not only spoke to him, but showed him who He was. "I went to sleep in the hotel and awoke in the middle of the night. It's hard to describe the bright, shining light I saw glowing in front of me, but it was the brightest light I'd ever seen—I knew it was the Lord. Almost anyone seeing this might have panicked, but for some reason I experienced nothing but the deepest sense of calm. I sat in bed and looked at the light and don't know if it lasted ten seconds or ten minutes. What I can say for certain is that I didn't hear a voice and I didn't see a figure. I just sensed the Lord's presence. He was in the room, and I felt an assurance that my life was going to get back on track and I was going to get my wife and family back."

That's what it's like to hear from God. Christians sometimes have a problem with semantics and use wrong words to describe this experience. It can sound lofty to the skeptic and even appear we have an inside position with God. When I sense God is talking to me, it is more of a feeling than an audible thing. There is awareness, a prodding, or a motivation to do something specific pertaining to an issue that is troubling my heart. I always walk away a better man after He sits me down to talk things over … man to man.

One day during the seven-month separation, Richie was deep in prayer and heard another voice. It told him to go to Nancy in Colorado—immediately. When he showed up on her doorstep hours later, Richie was grateful he listened. Nancy announced she was pregnant but didn't want another one of his children. She was scheduled to have an abortion, and Richie's arrival had disrupted her plans. Richie talked her out of the abortion, and it was canceled. "Today we have a beautiful daughter Katie, who has five kids of her own. Had I not listened to the Lord, I shudder to think of the outcome … and I'd love to say I have these moments all the time, but I really don't. That was a moment when I heard God's voice and He told me to act quickly."

Still not fully reconciled, Richie returned to California. However, a short time later, Nancy agreed to come back. Their resolve was tested time and again. During a subsequent counseling session, Nancy raged: "I don't love him, I never loved him, and I'll never love him again." Richie said each statement hit him like a hammer; however, he knew all things were possible through God. After the blowout session, Nancy packed her belongings and headed back to Colorado alone, but Richie held steadfast to the belief that he needed to put his family back together.

Souther-Hillman-Furay owed Asylum another record, and Richie remembers their second album, the appropriately titled *Trouble in Paradise*, as a blur. "I have no recollection of helping J. D. or Chris. I can barely recall their songs. I was there physically, but not emotionally. That's the only time in my career I may have compromised the professionalism I've always prided myself on."

The three principals agreed *Trouble in Paradise* would be their last and wouldn't support the album with another tour. That was a blessing in disguise, as Nancy, who was well along in her pregnancy with Katie, asked Richie to move back in with her after the album was finished. Reconciliation didn't come quickly—there was still hesitation and doubt. For weeks, Richie walked on eggshells as Nancy vacillated back and forth on whether or not she wanted the marriage to work. Richie had a lightbulb moment when he suggested Nancy ask Jesus to restore the love they once shared. Richie says that was a key moment. "The Lord was giving me on-the-job, or in this case, on-the-'Job' training, teaching me about my role as a husband. He wanted me to take the initiative in leading my wife in our marriage, just as Jesus does with His bride, the church. Husbands are to love their wives with a self-sacrificing love."

Even after Katie was born, Nancy was planning on leaving Richie, who says, "The Lord eventually prevailed and she never did." Nancy's love for Richie eventually returned. It has continued to grow and deepen ever since. His first album after Souther-Hillman-Furay, *I've Got a Reason* (Asylum, 1976) was his first Christian effort, and many of the songs were colored by his marital tribulations and rock-solid faith.

Working on a handshake deal, Richie assured David Geffen that the album would be Christian influenced, but not preachy. Richie was among the first major born-again performers to speak openly about his convictions in secular settings rather than retreating to the friendlier confines of a Christian record company. He wanted to make music for everyone, hoping his audience would find his songs easy to embrace and enjoyable. The Richie Furay Band played tunes from Buffalo Springfield, Poco, and Souther-Hillman-Furay as well as his solo material. Always the pioneer, Richie says, "I saw no need to abandon my earlier work. They formed my musical foundation, and none of them contradicted my Christian beliefs."

In 1982, Richie left the music industry and became senior pastor of a Calvary Chapel church in the Denver area. It was a move that even shocked him. "Looking back, I can see the Lord never takes anything away that He doesn't replace with something that's far greater. I had thought music was what it was all about for me, but I was quickly learning that for life to have real meaning, Jesus has to be the foundation; everything else must be built on Him!"

And building is what God had in mind for Richie. In 2000, after eighteen years of holding services in a Boulder gymnasium, Richie moved his growing congregation into a permanent location in Broomfield, Colorado. His accomplishments as a musician, husband, father, grandfather, pastor, and servant of the Lord are astonishing. He reminds me of the apostle Paul, who went through a great many changes before teaming up with the Lord. Like Paul, who was knocked to the ground and then got up and did great things for the Lord, Richie also spent time on the ground, on his knees, and then built something from the ground up and has witnessed to many people over the years. Paul moved from place to place while Richie planted roots, but both made a powerful commitment to walk in God's footsteps from that day on.

God has bestowed upon Richie many blessings, and He keeps adding. In addition to highly publicized reunions with Buffalo Springfield and Poco, in 1997 Richie was enshrined in the Rock and Roll Music Hall of Fame in Cleveland, Ohio—his birth state—for his contribution to Buffalo Springfield. He has the statue to prove it, but as always, his priorities are straight. "It's awesome. I've lived my dreams, and it's beyond anything

I could have asked for. To have my name written there with Elvis Presley and Ricky Nelson … it's touching to know the music I made had an impact on people. But let me tell you, there's nothing more important than my name being written in the Lamb's Book of Life."

Richie used to play music and give performances for encores. Now he prays words and gives praise for the biggest encore of all—eternity with God.

MARK FARNER

Grand Funk Railroad

Grand Funk Railroad, known affectionately as "The American Band," earned eleven consecutive RIAA Gold/Platinum Record Awards from 1969 to 1975. They surpassed The Beatles in record sales in 1970 and were the only group outside of the Fab Four at the time to sell out New York's Shea Stadium. The Beatles did it in seven weeks—Grand Funk did it in seventy-two hours.

TWELVE

CLOSER TO HOME

MARK FARNER | Grand Funk Railroad

Look up the definition of *resilient*, and chances are you'll see Mark Farner's smiling face. From losing his father when he was nine years old and getting kicked out of high school at seventeen, to barely surviving near-fatal car and airplane accidents and hypothermia, Mark has seen his share of tragedy. While stumbling through overnight success, sudden wealth, derailed relationships, angry mobs, lost fortunes, betrayal, million-dollar lawsuits, death threats, and an epic battle with the IRS, he amassed quite a decadent rock and roll resume.

To be fair, I should give Mark's complete resume: founding member of Grand Funk Railroad, philanthropist, health-food pioneer, craftsman, horseman, supporter of veteran causes, and a tenor with a legendary golden throat.

The legend began in the working-class auto industry town of Flint, Michigan, on September 29, 1948. Mark recalls a fond upbringing and a special time in America. "Flint was where everybody had a decent home, a couple of cars, and a garage. It was a place where a man and woman could raise a family. The auto industry provided all that. It was a time when patriotism ran high and 'Made in the USA' meant something."

Shortly after his birth, Mark's parents, Delton and Betty Farner, moved to Mark's maternal great grandparents' fruit farm on the outskirts of Flint. His grandparents and great-grandmother lived nearby, and other relatives were a stone's throw away. The orchard yielded apples, pears, peaches, plums, raspberries, and yellow Queen Anne cherries. Kearsley Creek ran through the property, and the farm bordered a large forest where Mark and his cousins played war games and built tree forts. Later he learned to hunt pheasants and rabbits in those same woods.

Betty Farner was doting and protective (she came from an abused household according to Mark) while Delton, a World War II veteran, was fun loving, easygoing and a jokester. "My dad worked swing shifts, so when I saw my dad, it was quality time. He loved on us and was always kidding around. I remember one time my sister and I came home and Dad met us with a serious look on his face. He says, 'You kids go to your room right now!' We were freaking out because holy mackerel, he was mad. We turned the corner to our bedrooms, and there was a bow and arrow on my bed and a storybook on my sister's bed. When we turned around, my dad had this huge smile on his face. He was that kind of guy."

Sundays were set aside for family gatherings, and Mark recalls hearty picnics where mouthwatering Southern fried chicken and Sloppy Joes were served. Dessert was beautiful music, which included bluegrass, country, gospel, and blues, performed by his relatives. "My mom sang better than anyone I knew and taught me how to sing harmony. My dad played guitar, and various relatives played the banjo, fiddle, and saxophone while everybody sang along."

The harmony and happiness of Mark's idyllic childhood was shattered on January 5, 1958, when Mark was nine. Delton and coworker Vernon Smith were driving home from a local union hall and were broadsided at a railroad crossing by a train, killing them instantly. When Mark heard the news, he thought it was another one of his father's pranks. When he saw his mother's face, he knew otherwise. "I don't know exactly what happened or the circumstances of the crash, but it changed my mother's life. She had to identify his body at the morgue. He was decapitated, and she identified him by a birthmark on his leg. It was one of the biggest funerals the city of Flint had ever seen. My dad was known for his big heart. He always felt he was lucky to have survived World War II. I remember him crying when he told a story about not being able to get to his buddies in time. His heart was to help people, and there was an outpouring of support when he died. My mom was overwhelmed, and when she stood up to leave the funeral she passed out. She was a virgin when they married and Dad was her soul mate. It was that way right to the end. She never did recover. When she lost him, she lost her stability."

Mark was also inconsolable. After the initial shock of his father's death, Mark realized he wasn't coming back. "I remember hearing lots of sobbing from my mom and my aunts and uncles in the house. There were many things going through my nine-year-old mind and so much confusion and hurt. I knew a little about the Lord from my Great Grandmother Root, who had taken my sister Diane and me to a Free Methodist church in Davison. One night at home in the middle of all of this crying, Billy Graham was on television and looked into the camera and said, 'If anyone out there is hurting, get down on your knees in front of the television set,' I was there praying with him. What he said not only registered but gave me great comfort and strength. I received Christ in my heart at that time."

Mark's mother was unable to find the same comfort in faith but found solace in alcohol, astrology, and Ouija boards. She transferred the load of responsibilities to her son. "I know my mother, and when she began talking to me about this I knew it was serious. When I looked into her eyes, I felt she was talking to the spirit man in me. In that conversation she snapped me out of whining and feeling sorry for myself—and she made me get off the pity pot. I had limitations to what I could do, but I knew my mother needed me to stand tall and so I did."

Mark manned up and grew up real quick. He looked for father figures in other men and forgot about his relationship with the heavenly Father. "Being young and having no one to teach me the Bible or the ways of salvation, I walked away from the Lord. He didn't leave me. I left Him."

There's something very poetic and beautifully mature in Mark's feelings toward God during this time. Many people, including pastors and long-time Christians, have a tendency to blame God when bad "stuff" happens, and then they accuse Him of being the One who checked out on them. Mark had a knowing at an early age that stayed with him as the years of good and bad played out. He knew his mistakes were his alone, and that day on the floor with Billy Graham became a bonding moment. Leaving God during hard times is a fairly common phenomenon, but somehow Mark knew where he stood in the equation—that God never gives up on us, and that it would all come to a head someday regardless of current circumstances. God never left Mark—and as mad as he was, he did "man up" by confessing he was the one leaving.

An overactive kid, Mark's energy levels were off the charts. He felt best when working or sweating, and he channeled his energy into football in eighth grade. Despite his size, Mark was aggressive and agile and was a starting defensive linebacker. Like all natural-born entertainers, Mark lived for the applause. "I remember the first game of the season when me and another teammate made a tackle together and heard our names over the loudspeaker. We said to each other, 'Did you hear that? This is great, man—they called my name!' 'Yeah, they called mine too!'"

This is just a wild guess, but I wonder if this was a pivotal moment, a seed-planting event, that drove our young hero from a local football field up to a stage door with his name on it and the thrill of hearing his voice soaring above the roar of stadium-sized crowds.

Gridiron glory came with a price. Mark developed water on the knee and broke his finger in a scrimmage game. Sensing his frustration, Mark's mother rented him a Kay guitar along with six prepaid lessons for his fifteenth birthday. Like all great musicians, Mark took obsession to a whole new level, spending hours with his guitar, even sleeping with it. "I think music is in all of us, and it's just a matter of unlocking the key and getting there. I recently picked up slide guitar, and I'd never played one in my life. But now, I can play slide and it feels so good. I'm playing and singing with it thinking, *How did that happen?* I'm in the learning phase, and it sounds good. It just happened."

Musicianship is a gift. The package gets opened when someone hands a gifted person an instrument that can be used to express his or her God-given talent. There's something about their touch—they possess a unique phrasing and nuance that dances among the notes and chords. These chosen few are often surprised by how quickly they learn to play and how little coaching they needed to become accomplished. That is why many great artists are self-taught—it's as if they already had it in them, and all they had to do was dig it out and polish it off. When it does surface it becomes their lover, and they can't wait to experience its complexity and wonder. It's probably why Mark slept with his guitar—they were one the minute they touched. It's a transcendent thing because it is a blessing, and how we use our gifts in life is very much a spiritual matter. I love a simple Scripture in my Living Bible: "You can't ignore God and get away with it" (Galatians 6:7). That's the reason many famous entertainers go awry later on—they don't thank God for their gift, and they misuse it and abuse it, until one day it turns on them. They believe they're the ones who created their talent and this delusion eventually caves in on them, burying them in their ego madness.

Mark was almost sidelined for good when a friend's '65 Chevy, cruising at 120 miles per hour, swerved to avoid another car that pulled out in front his lead-footed friend. Their car went down into a ditch, jumped a culvert, and went airborne. When the vehicle finally landed, it was headed for a row of unforgiving oak trees.

"Oh God, please—Jesus save us," Mark screamed, diving for the floorboard, waiting for the inevitable impact. Except it never came. Although the car did go airborne a second time, it landed on a pair of boulders. The undercarriage was severely damaged, but Mark and his friend didn't have a scratch. Today he believes God intervened supernaturally. "We should have been dead, and I knew something supernatural had occurred. We couldn't figure out how that car had been transported from one side of that oak tree to the other, absolutely unharmed. It all took place in the blink of an eye."

Outside of Wonder Woman or Superman jumping in at that particular split-second moment, I can find no other explanation than that it had to do with angels. I believe God orders His angels about to make sure His plans for His children go according to His purpose. I will leave this as is for now, but it's not the only time these phenomena appear in this book—so identical in form that it becomes easy to consider the possibility of their divine existence. Mark had two fathers who loved him and watched over him, and only one of them was gone.

The times were a-changing, and so was Mark. The Beatles helped his internal and external transformation after they appeared on *The Ed Sullivan Show* in 1964. He stopped applying VO5 to his hair, lost his duck tail, and wore his hair dry and long. This didn't go unnoticed by a football coach, who singled him out for discipline when he saw Mark hanging out with his "new long-haired friends." This irritated his coach, and he shoved Mark against a brick wall. "There was a brass picture frame of the superintendent of schools on the wall, and my head bounced off that frame. I put my hand back and felt that it was warm and wet. It was blood, and Coach was standing there with this smirk on his face. I tagged him in the eye. At the time I had rings on my fingers; it unzipped his eyelid right at the eyebrow, and it fell down over the top of his eye. He dropped to his knees, blood on his face. He got up, went crazy, and started throwing haymakers. If he had connected, he could have killed me. I was about to drill him again when some teachers grabbed him and my buddies grabbed me. I was expelled. I took an attorney with me to appear before the school board, and the coach, who was also an algebra teacher, said if the school let me back in, he was going to resign from his job. They took one look at me and my long sideburns and I guess you could say … I got laid off from high school."

Mark tried to finish high school at night, but that conflicted with his budding musical career, which by the mid-60s was well under way. For those who aren't old enough to remember, Michigan produced some of the best music of that decade. Besides the Motown scene in Detroit, the state minted the careers of Bob Seger, Mitch Ryder, Alice Cooper, Iggy Pop, MC5, Ted Nugent, Meat Loaf, Glenn Frey, and ? (Question Mark) & The Mysterians. Mark had already played in a few bands when he became a member of Flint, Michigan's popular Terry Knight and The Pack. Knight and the Pack reached number forty-six on the national charts with "I (Who Have Nothing)" in late 1966.

That was the same year I met Terry Knight. We partied in New York City with our mutual pal, Robin Leach (*Lifestyles of the Rich and Famous*), who like us, was making his bones in the music industry. At the time I thought "I (Who Have Nothing)" was a super cool record. Music exec David Spero recently sent me a copy of the song, and I couldn't believe how corny and goofy sounding the production feels today.

By early 1969, Mark had played in close to a dozen different groups, but nothing ever clicked. Power trios such as Cream, The Jimi Hendrix Experience, and Blue Cheer, which mainly consisted of guitar, bass, and drums, were the rage in the late '60s. Mark formed alliances with drummer Don Brewer and high school classmate Mel Schacher. Naming themselves after the Michigan landmark the Grand Trunk and Western Railway, they chose Grand Funk Railroad. Like a locomotive, it didn't take long before the group picked up steam.

During rehearsals at a tiny union hall in Flint, Grand Funk immediately sensed they had something special. As with most bands that experience phenomenal success, the group dynamic is always greater than the sum of its parts. They felt Grand Funk could be America's answer to the United Kingdom's legendary Cream. They soon became the epitome of a three-piece band that could nail your ears to the wall. Who knew that in time the nails that Mark would be driving home were the ones he remembers from a hill, a cross, and a kind man who brought us grace, mercy, unconditional love, and the hope of a blessed eternity.

Despite the fact that GFR was new and paying their dues, they were determined not to play small bars and record on local record labels. Don Brewer suggested they reach out to Terry Knight, who told the band he had landed a job as an A&R man at Capitol Records.

I smell something funny in the caboose shed at Grand Funk. I had known Terry for a few years by the time GFR came to Capitol Records in 1969, and I was an executive at the label when they had their first million-selling album. Between 1965 and 1970, I was involved in some way with every act on the label, either in marketing, promotion, artist relations, or subsidiary label responsibilities, and I spent time in the A&R producer's eleventh-floor offices almost every day. I never saw Terry sitting in an office. I knew all the producers and was never told he was on staff. Grand Funk was signed to Knight's Good Knight Production Co., and that contradicted Terry's assertion to the band that he worked at Capitol. Staff A&R men at Capitol Records were not allowed to sign bands to their private production companies—they wooed them and then they signed them to the record company that gave them their eleventh-floor office, a prestigious title, and a salary. It's that simple. Being a producer and having a production company was a cool thing in those days, but being on staff as a producer at one of the three biggest labels in the world was a powerful thing.

Despite Knight's (supposed) newly acquired power, Mark was resistant to accept him in the role he proposed to the band. He knew his character was questionable and that Terry had been fired from a Detroit radio station over a payola scandal. But Knight was irrepressible, persuasive, and somehow always managed to land on his feet.

"He's a chameleon man," Mark cautioned. "A turd, a con man. I don't trust him."

Brewer acknowledged Mark's assessment of Knight, but said it was their ticket out of Flint and one true shot at stardom. They forged ahead, knowing they'd have to keep an eye on him. When Knight came to Flint to hear Grand Funk and sign them to a contract, he sucker punched them with this one stipulation:

"The only thing I demand of you is to do what I say," Knight said. "I'll discuss any decision with you as long as you want, but only afterward."

Even though Mark was suspicious, he accepted Don Brewer's opinion on the matter with skepticism. There is a caustic Faustian reality about this scenario—young, naïve artists trading out quick money and fame, becoming owned by someone, and in the end, living a life of long-time heartache.

The May 1, 1969, management contract was a three-year deal with Knight's option to renew if the group grossed more than $200,000 in their third year. However, Grand Funk Railroad's recording contract was with Knight's Good Knight Production Co., so they were not directly signed to Capitol Records. Knight would deliver their product to Capitol and then in turn pay the group out of the proceeds of his deal with Capitol. The three young, naïve musicians agreed that Knight would receive 25 percent for production and management off the top, in addition to a booking commission.

In those days, a production company that brought an artist to a record company could typically receive somewhere in the area of twelve points (percent) from the label based on net sales, and then make a separate deal with their artist. Following general industry standards at the time, it's possible Good Knight Productions gave the band six of the twelve points. So let's do the math. Imagine Capitol Records cut a million-dollar advance check to Good Knight Productions, who took its 25 percent ($250,000) right off the top for its production and management fee. That left $750,000 to be divided equally between the band and Good Knight Productions, based on their 50 percent share of points (six of the twelve points). So an additional $375,000 was added to the production company's $250,000, while band members split the remaining $375,000 three ways, which meant each member's share would be $125,000.

But we are not done yet, and here is the real kicker to the Grand Funk deal: before Mark and the others would receive their share, Knight could deduct the arbitrary fees mentioned above. I am not sure how the additional "booking commission" works in this scenario, but that ambiguous term scares me to the point of quivering. Good Knight Production's ability to deduct other abstract fees automatically put them in the position of having an even bigger piece of the pie. Now this is already a financial house of horrors for the band, but the fact that Good Knight Productions would also be keeping track of the band's finances *plus* storing their money in Good Knight Production's bank account, moves me from quivering to blood-sweating convulsions. Simple math: out of the $1 million, each band member would receive *maybe* $100,000 apiece. Terry Knight could receive $700,000 or more.

Oh Lord, won't you buy him some Mercedes Benzes!

Unfortunately, I've seen this scenario many times throughout my tenure in the music industry—this sort of contract was a legal license to take advantage of artists. Basically it meant someone with this control could look at every dollar that came in, decide how much they want, and then give the band what's left, if there is any. Plus, if they happened to be a little dishonest, and all the money is in their bank—well, they could simply steal it if the mood hits them.

According to Mark, here's where Knight really cleaned up: he told Mark, Don, and Mel that for just 10 percent they could get their songs published through Storybook Music, Knight's publishing company. What Knight failed to disclose—and Mark had to eventually learn the hard way—was that Knight would also receive 50 percent of his publishing royalties in perpetuity. According to Mark, Knight punctuated each contract presentation with, "Hey, we're brothers!"

Mark, Don, Mel, and Terry celebrated the signing of the contract with a six-pack of beer and dreams of rock and roll stardom, which was right around the corner.

After a few test gigs in Buffalo, Detroit, and Toronto, Knight landed Grand Funk a coveted spot at the Atlanta Pop Festival for the Fourth of July weekend in 1969. The promoters promised Grand Funk a noon slot on opening day, if they played for free.

The two-day festival, which took place a month before the watershed Woodstock in New York, drew more than one hundred thousand people. The bill included Led Zeppelin, Janis Joplin, Creedence Clearwater Revival, Joe Cocker, Chicago, and a dozen other acts. According to Mark, the band almost didn't make it to the gig on time after an 800-mile trek. "A friend of ours lent us his van, and we rented a U-Haul trailer. A wheel fell off the trailer, sparks were flying, and the trailer began fishtailing. By a miracle, we were able to get it under control. Luckily at the next exit we found a trailer rental and had it fixed. We arrived with broken gear and amps—our roadies soldered wires right up until stage time. Not only was our stuff working, but it was pumping! The crowd loved us and gave us a standing ovation at the end of our set. We were instantly transformed into rock stars."

As Mark relays this story, I can see God's fingertips all over it. It's surreal when events like this happen. One minute you are on the side of the road feeling like you're not going to make it, and the next day you are a rock star. It's almost impossible to comprehend when the pendulum starts swinging in that direction, but when God's invisible hands are on our time clock, it is no wonder we get lost with our heads in the clouds, or shall we say … the heavenlies. I try to imagine what it would be like if we could see God's plans for us from beginning to end but then I get a reality check, drop to my knees, and thank God for not consulting or revealing what He has in mind. Of course, when we are operating on our own and not including God, we think events are the results of our personal genius. But God's hand was conducting this scenario all along—and Grand Funk Railroad had left the station and was up to speed.

From the Atlanta Pop Festival, Grand Funk Railroad never looked back. They were the first and only American group to earn eleven consecutive RIAA Gold Record Awards, six of which earned platinum status. They were the biggest-selling recording group of 1970, surpassing The Beatles record sales, and the only group outside the Fab Four at the time to sell out New York's Shea Stadium. The Beatles did it in seven weeks—Grand Funk did it in seventy-two hours. They were not only "An American Band," they were *the* American band from 1969 to 1975.

In time, they also became the American dysfunctional band. Grueling tours, lost fortunes, blatant rip-offs, ego clashes, substance abuse, sexcapades, and bitter lawsuits slowly rotted the group from the inside out. The band of brothers was killing themselves in a myriad of ways with the volume turned up to ten. This was truly sex, drugs, and rock and roll gone triply wrong.

Mark says despite all the trappings of stardom, he made sure to say his prayers every night before going to bed. "My mom taught us how to pray. You know, 'Now I lay me down to sleep'? I used to do that in case there was a God, in case there was a hell. I prayed to God for us to find success. I prayed for us to be a good band and that I'd be able to say things that were on my heart. So one night I put a P.S. on the end of my prayer and said, 'God, would you please give me a song that will reach and touch the hearts of people that you want to touch?' That song was 'I'm Your Captain,' and it came to me in the middle of the night. I sang it for the guys and they went, 'Wow, that's a hit!' They were right."

Not only was "I'm Your Captain" a divinely inspired hit, it became the unofficial theme for Vietnam veterans coming back to America, which makes Mark very proud. Some things he was not so proud of though. "I considered myself a Christian all those years, because I prayed every night and He kept answering my prayers. But I was still drinking, smoking dope, running around with women, doing things that rock stars are noted for doing."

One sin almost cost him his life. It came as a result of caving into peer pressure from his rock idol, Jimi Hendrix, backstage at a July 1970 music festival in Randall's Island, New York. "Jimi's right-hand man, a guy everyone knew as 'Rabbit,' came to my dressing room and said, 'Jimi wants to see you, man.' So I go, we hug and exchange 'How ya doings?' and niceties. Then I look over Jimi's shoulder and see these guys in the corner doing lines of something, and they invite me to do it with them. I said, 'Oh no, I don't do that man.' Rabbit kept after me while Jimi's snorting these huge snowdrifts of lines. Rabbit takes out a knife, sticks the tip in it, and brings it up to my nose, and I say, 'Okay, I'll do just a little whiff.' I did and I was so out of it that later on I fell off the top of an equipment truck to the ground. I was scraped up by a couple of assistants and taken by limo to the hotel, where I threw up all night and experienced cold sweats. I was sick, sick, sick. Let me tell you—that was the cure. Had I taken any more than that, I probably would have died."

Almost two months to the day Farner snorted Hendrix's "special blend," the legendary guitarist was dead.

By the end of 1971, Grand Funk had sold more than twenty million albums and toured nonstop for the better part of three years. The Railroad's gravy train was chugging along at a frenetic pace. Grand Funk grossed close to $5 million, but a majority of the cash went directly into Knight's pockets. The group finally wised up and took another look at the contract they signed in '69. They discovered after three years with Knight, their personal fortunes were estimated at less than $200,000 each (for the first two years of the contract, they were given a $350-a-week allowance). Not only had Knight taken his generous cut as manager, producer, promoter, booker, and publicist, he had invested their money in tax shelters, oil wells, real estate, and urban renewal schemes. "We had just finished a tour in Europe where we cleared about $1.5 million. Terry said we'd take a big tax hit, so we should let him deposit it in a Swiss bank account. As always, we went along with the suggestion because we were all 'brothers.' Later at a deposition, he was asked about the money in the Swiss account and he said, 'What money?' We never saw that money again."

Litigation and lawsuits ensued with Knight, but the Grand Funk express rolled on without him. The band signed a new three-year, six-record contract with Capitol in June 1972 and rallied big time. They produced several AM-oriented songs, including "Rock and Roll Soul,"

"Loco Motion," "Some Kind of Wonderful," "Bad Time," and the group's signature anthem, "We're An American Band." Mark also wrote several Christian-inspired tunes, such as "I Can Feel Them in the Morning" and "So You Won't Have to Die," in which Marks sings, "Jesus is the solution." He recalls, "It was a time to say it, man, and it made people wonder what we were all about. We were doing blood drives for the Red Cross and raising money for The Phoenix House, a drug rehabilitation center. A lot of the soldiers were coming back from Vietnam hooked on heroin, and we led the way for people to hope and believe. It's just simple humanity. When you have somebody who's giving back and offering up hope like we were, it does inspire."

So here's Mark with one foot in the devil's den and the other on God's back porch. But that day on his knees as a child with Billy Graham was not something that would ever go away, no matter how far back its place in the ticket line had been relegated. These leanings that Mark was having toward kind works and service kept surfacing, and it is obvious that God was working in his life and in a way softening him up for what eventually happened down the line.

After their February 1974 out-of-court settlement with Terry Knight, Grand Funk began seeing some real cash. Mark had no problem spending it, buying thousands of acres of land in Michigan and Canada, airplanes, expensive cars, trucks, boats, horses, three-wheelers, motorcycles, snowmobiles, guns, farming equipment, and a recording studio. He even bought a bank. "I'd come off the road, go on spending sprees, and buy two of everything in sight. That was a learning process for me because I found out you can't buy joy or happiness. It can't be purchased."

Mark's lifestyle wasn't conducive to a happy home or his first marriage to Cheri Chestnut. They were both unfaithful, and their union only lasted a few years.

To take the edge off his chaotic life, Mark smoked tons of weed and was high almost every waking moment for two decades straight. "I would put a joint out at night, pick it up in the morning, and smoke the roach before I pulled the covers off. No doubt about it—I was addicted. I know now my thinking processes were severely hindered by it."

I had to laugh when Mark described his little scenario with the wonder weed that we all loved so much. We poor souls had been convinced by our drug dealers that it wasn't really habit forming, so why not have a smoke as often as we felt like it and relax? I find this amusing because his routine was identical to my daily/nightly ritual at that time. One of the phrases for smoking weed was "turning on." The act of turning on basically meant that not only were we removing ourselves from meaningful communication with the world, but we were also "turning on" the do not disturb sign to God. It was also called "chilling out," but spiritually that meant putting ourselves out in the cold—away from God's all-consuming fire. When we were doing the New Age thing, we were told that by getting high we were getting closer to God. Once again semantics threw us a curve—by getting stoned we had no need for God, and the only "*closer*-ness" was being a *closer* of the door that He was knocking on.

While Mark fired up, the sales from Grand Funk's last three albums, *Born to Die,* the Frank Zappa–produced *Good Singin', Good Playin',* and *Hits*—all released in 1976—flamed out. Tensions had been brewing for several years as the hits, the misses, financial mismanagement, and continual pressure of working nonstop on the road and in the studio (contractually delivering two albums a year) caused artistic stagnation and eventual burnout. There were also the diverging styles of Mark's and Don Brewer's songwriting direction. Mark wrote songs that weren't afraid to tackle tough social and political issues, while Brewer's hedonistic-based numbers stood in stark contrast. It came to a head when Brewer derailed the Railroad in October 1976 during a rehearsal. He arrived late and announced he "had to do something more stable with his life."

"Are you calling it quits?" Mark asked. Brewer affirmed it with a nod of the head. After twelve gold albums, ten platinum records, nineteen charted singles, two number-one singles, and twenty-five million albums sold, "The American Band" had lowered its flag to two-thirds mast.

Mark bounced back with his first self-titled solo album in 1977 and his second, *No Frills*, in 1978. That same year he married Lesia Dennis, who was sixteen at the time. In the span of a year, Lesia went from a comfortable home to helping take care of a 1,600-acre farm and having a baby boy—Jason, who was born September 27, 1979. Innocent teen, married to a rock star, and motherhood—all in the span of about a year and a half. Then six months after she gave birth to Jason, she became pregnant with their second son, Joseph. She was also taking care of a third kid—her twenty-nine-year-old husband. Mark admits today that he was slack in helping care for Jason, boozing it with the locals, smoking pot with his buddies, and coming and going as he pleased. When he was on tour, Lesia was left to fend for herself. Their affections for each other began to dwindle and by 1983, it had deteriorated so badly that Lesia finally left. Mark said it felt like a mule kick in the gut. "We were living in the house where I sawed all the lumber in the backyard with a six-cylinder Hercules. We built this house together. We took a piece of paper from a notebook and drew the design of our dream house. I came home one day, found a note that said she'd left, and it flattened me. A week went by, and I knew she wasn't coming back."

Mark was sitting at the dining table, consuming a six-pack of beer and smoking a joint while watching his two sons playing in the living room. What was he going to do? It didn't help when the boys kept asking, "Where's Mommy?" He looked over at a stained glass window in the corner of the room, and a ray of light hit him square in the face. According to Mark, the corner of the room opened up and revealed to him a vision. "This quick flash went off, and I saw myself on my knees as a nine-year-old boy in front of that television set, praying along with Billy Graham to heal my heart because my father had just died. I knew then that I needed to find God again."

I believe God purposely gave Mark that dramatic childhood incident to serve as an anchor and a precursor to a solid moment of salvation He had established in the future. Mark realized his Father had been with him then, now, and always. Poetically, Mark was renewing his vows. Almost everyone in this book has shared a similar revelation, and while each encounter is unique, it is easy to see a sweet sameness about each one. My moment was entirely different from Mark's, but when I contemplate what happened with him, I am taken back to mine. One thing is for sure—it places everything past, present, and future in a new and proper order.

Good to his word, Mark went church hopping in search of a place that would help him put his life back in order. Knowing that he could be taken advantage of in his emotionally weakened state, Mark tested the churches he visited. "I'd walk in with my long hair, head band, Hawaiian shirt, faded blue jeans, and sneakers. If the pastor and congregation got past that, then I might listen. If I heard hellfire and brimstone, I got the hell out of there because that's not what I needed. I needed to hear about God's love."

His first visit was to a small church where the pastor beat on the pulpit and hollered at the congregation. Mark noticed many of them had sad faces and looked beaten. "God ain't here," Mark said as he extricated himself from the pew and left early.

In September 1983, after weeks of searching, Mark attended an Assemblies of God in Onaway, Michigan. He was greeted by hugs from several of the congregants, mainly little old ladies who could read Mark's countenance. "God placed me there that day to hear the message from this eighty-year-old pastor, who spoke on 'Marriage According to God's Law.' The message was about how people walk out on the commitment of marriage too easily, without realizing that matrimony is holy to the Lord. His words were like six live rounds to my heart, and God doesn't use blanks. I felt this pastor was singling me out and knew my whole story. When he gave the altar call at the end of his sermon to get saved, I didn't just walk, man. I ran!"

You can study God, but in order to graduate into His fullness you not only have to have been blessed by Him but also suffered for Him. Only when a person has experienced extreme highs and disastrous lows, and been battered by the painful velocity and whiplash of traveling between the two, can one begin to understand God's character. Think about His plan for Jesus. Jesus had to come down here and go through everything we would be going through—He had to taste and feel the same stuff so He could relate to us. It wasn't like God was going to protect Jesus by home schooling Him, and then if He passed a written test He wouldn't have to get His feet dirty or His hands scarred.

After the service, Mark asked the pastor if he could pray with him to bring Lesia back to him.

"You pray, I'll agree," the pastor replied.

God not only answered Mark's prayer by bringing Lesia back, but as Mark later learned, she accepted Christ on the same day in a town fifty miles away from her husband.

That's how God does it. He puts pieces together—broken pieces, faded pieces—and when He touches these discarded pieces, they are put back in place and sparkle once again. Burnt stones and torn pages, building new paths, leading to more wonderful stories.

I am a street guy. I boil things down to street-level terms so I can understand. I even do that with God. I need something basic to hang on to when things get complicated. My first pass at simplifying my relationship with the Holy Trinity and the Bible was to create a catchphrase that I could always return to when my spiritual walk began teetering.

Either I believe or I don't.

It's that plain for me. I narrowed my entire life down to those two choices. After a while it became obvious which one works. Mark stopped believing at one point in his life and everything fell apart—but when he and Lesia came back together as believers, a new life began. To quote an old friend, Billy Preston, from my Capitol/Apple days, "That's the way God planned it."

Mark put down his guitar for a while and picked up a Bible, soaking in God's every word. He also rededicated himself as a husband and father, taking a long hiatus from the music business to become the man he'd always wanted to be. But those musical fires couldn't be smothered forever. After attending a Mylon LeFevre concert, Mark was inspired to evangelize by mixing old Grand Funk songs with his newfound faith.

In 1988, he and Leisa formed a ministry called Common Ground. In true Farner fashion, he took the Word to the people who needed it most. His new band, the Godrockers, performed in bars, nightclubs, and churches—anywhere he could touch people's hearts. And touch them he did. His first appearance was at a biker bar near St. Petersburg, Florida. Mark corrects me when I tell him I heard he helped save fifty souls that day. "We didn't save fifty people, because Jesus says that, 'No man comes to me except by my Father.' God sent me to draw them, but I do not ever want to take the credit for bringing somebody to the Lord. It's always God that brings them, and it was our privilege to help others get both feet in."

Mark knows that when we set out to witness to people about God's wondrous plan, we are seed planters at best … just doing our job. Hopefully we can also water and prepare them for the Master Gardener, but it is always God that harvests and polishes the fruit that grows out of the soiled soil of our souls.

That same year, Mark sang the John Beland composition "Isn't It Amazing," which earned him a Dove Award nomination and reached number two on the Contemporary Christian charts.

John Beland and I have shared decades of history in the music business and I could write an entire book about our travels, but something that happened during our association is "amazing." I must gently explain that over these years, John and I had probably done about every rebellious thing we could dream up. We were recording in Austin, Texas, at Willie Nelson's Perdenales studio not long after Mark had his big hit with John's song. I was a new Christian at this point, and let's just say John was still having a good time back then. So, we're in the studio and John shared with me that because of Mark's hit recording of his song, people were tracking him down in order to thank him for bringing them to the Lord through his song! John had written it as a love song and had no idea how God was going to use it, him, and Mark to open people's hearts to the Lord.

It wasn't all anointing and grace once Mark became a Christian. Mark's faith was tested several times. The first was an epic IRS battle. Back in '76, Mark, Don Brewer, and Mel Schacher had invested together in a coal venture as a tax shelter. The IRS decided in 1990 that the investment was not legitimate and levied a $250,000 assessed tax to each member. Don and Mel settled with the government, but Mark stood his ground. The battle went on for years, at times straining his marriage to Lesia, but never their faith. "At times you have to laugh at the *Infernal* Revenue Service's logic. They were going to take all of my possessions in the house and arbitrarily decided I could keep $2,500 of my tools so that I could still make a living. I told them, 'That's not even half a guitar, dude!' Providentially, that IRS thing helped me to wake up."

Another financial hit and hammer blow came in the form of Mark's Grand Funk band mates, when they reunited in 1996. The mid-90s were in full classic rock renaissance mode, and promoters were prodding Mark, Don, and Mel to put the Railroad back on the track. A fourteen-city "test" tour was booked, the group rehearsed, and the chemistry was still there. An anthology box set was discussed and the idea of recording new material. The vibes were good and the tour was extended into 1998. That's when, according to Mark, the guillotine came down. "We were in a hotel room one night after a gig, friends again after all those years being apart. Don Brewer came to me and said, 'Everybody needs to sign their ownership of the trademark into the corporation so we can protect ourselves.' I said, 'Yeah, sure, that sounds good.' He then said, 'I've got the papers upstairs. Let me go get them.' Well, I should have had a clue he was up to something, but I didn't put two and two together until it was too late. Don had been to law school and I never finished high school. So I signed my one-third ownership of the trademark into the corporation, not realizing that two thirds—Don and Mel—could vote me out of the corporation, which they did. I never considered they'd do something like that. Unfortunately, I found out the hard way."

Still, Mark says he forgives Mel and Don, and for that matter, Terry Knight, who was killed in 2004 when defending his daughter from a knife-wielding boyfriend. "I tried to contact Terry a couple of times before his death. I wanted to tell him I forgave him. I wanted to do it for the sake of my heart. He was a crook and screwed us out of millions and took half of my publishing. But it was too late and when you don't forgive someone, they hold a certain power over you. It controls you. I don't want to give anyone power over me, so it's easier to forgive and move on. God rewards those who diligently seek love, and the Holy Spirit showed me I had to let this go or it could eat me alive. The power is mine to do with it what I will, and so I chose to forgive."

Another big test of faith came on July 4, 2010, when Mark's twenty-one-year-old son Jesse sustained a near-fatal fracture to the C5 vertebra in his neck. He was paralyzed. Emotionally, Mark and Lesia were a wreck, but they remained strong, bolstered by prayer and well wishes. Mark was crestfallen when Jesse asked him to "pull the plug" if his condition didn't improve. Mark was angry with Jesse's request, telling his son he was disappointed in his attitude, considering that so many people were pulling and praying for him around the clock. The power of prayer is awesome—in less than two weeks, Jesse was singing a different tune. His nurse had fallen in love with him, and a new zest for life was evident. "I walked into the room and there was this glow on Jesse's face. He was bitten hard by the love bug. I knew that look, and I asked him, 'So dude, you still want me to pull the plug?' Jesse replied, 'Dad, I'm the luckiest man in the world.' That showed me prayer works, and now my faith is stronger than ever."

Mark had his own physical handicaps to overcome. In October 2012, he had a surgical procedure to help deal with a bundle branch block in his heart. He believes he died on the operating table. “I left my body twice, and they brought me back with the paddles. I’m telling you, I was in heaven with Jesus. I really was. It was for a brief second, but it was something special. Heaven was wonderful and I got a taste of it. I feel like I am cheating now because I know what it is going to be like and others don’t. I do know God brought me back for a reason.”

With a newly fitted pacemaker, Mark is ready to rock again. In 2014, he was a guest on the Happy Together tour featuring The Turtles and Flo & Eddie. His voice remains untouched by time, and he is as energetic as ever. Mark only knows one speed—warp speed—but now it’s fueled by God. While the discussion of mortality scares most individuals, Mark, who is in his late ’60s, acknowledges that he is getting “closer to home.” Or as he puts it, “I look forward to what follows when I leave the bone suit.”

The word that defines Mark’s journey best would be *extreme*. He had an extremely beautiful childhood with a father that every child would love to have. His father’s death was not only exceptionally tragic but also extremely brutal. From there the successes and betrayals were beyond the norm and, let’s face it, Grand Funk Railroad became famous because they made extremely big, loud, and monumental music. His conversion, his trials, his near death, *and* his renewed-life experiences were of the caliber of Rocky meets The Little Engine That Could—Martin Scorsese directing, of course. He manned up and did it big, this child of a good God.

Like David, Mark stood tall when he was still small—and as he traveled his ragged path into the world, Goliath still lurked around every corner and behind every tree. Mark was our last interview and ironically, his story is the perfect consensus of all the stories. It is a modern-day Bible story full of parables, drama, and redemption. You can just feel his heart pumping like a power trio in the background, and as we read between the lines and look behind the stories, above and through it all we see Jesus.

Isn't He amazing?

FINAL CHORD

We probably did our best work when we were young and didn't know any better. I don't think any of us realized during the early years, the foundations we were laying, the importance of the relationships we were developing, or just how meaningful our passions were at that time. We told our stories and made music because we loved it—we would have done it anyway and would still be doing it regardless of if we ever made a dime. Some did get *real* good and as abilities and acceptance blossomed, many were thrust into adventures never imagined. Yes, there were some train wrecks and as philosophers have said, "It is the journey and not the destination" that is our reward. I would like to deftly offer that the origins of the journey are equally delectable.

The point fermenting herein is that like bourbon and backbeats we have mellowed over time and locked into a little lighter and more secure groove, discovering that the memories and people of our beginnings are some of our greatest treasures. From whence we came has granted us revelation, and now in these "later years," we remember who we once were and the innocence of what we were all about when setting out on that journey. Fences have been mended and walls torn down, allowing us to see how special it all was. We see those days, those people, and those places for what they were and the purity of it all. We hadn't become complicated yet and could pretty much take each other at face value. When the only thing we had when we were young was our love of music, we didn't have to worry about people taking anything from us other than an occasional good idea.

The dear people in this book were unknowing embryonic spokes in a melodic wheel of spinning rhythmic fantasies that actually created whole new genres of music. I am amazed, not so much by how much music these people have made, but by how loud and long the echoes have reverberated through the hearts and souls of so many in the succeeding decades. Today these artists sometimes carry their Strats and Yamahas in their hearts instead of anvil cases. In *Rock and a Heart Place*, they blessed us by picking these pages to step out on the stage of life, beautifully unplugged, and bestow what they have learned over the years. For this we are grateful.

So it is God's wondrous peace and love we send to surround each and every one who gave of their time and their goodness, to share their souls and soul mates, to bare their years and tears, and to tell of their travels and testimonies with Marshall Terrill and me. We all started our journeys with songs and stories that somewhere along the way turned into personal hymns and impassioned witness. We found our true Father in places we thought He would never visit, and though it was tough for a while, He led us safely out and we feel good about that now. There will always be special things we will miss about those days—especially those who have left us before the tag ending … but we'll see them again at the biggest music festival, the greatest worship service of all time, singing together in His eternal choir.

God bless us all,

K

Ken Mansfield

"Some come to dance and some come to play.
Some merely come to pass time of day. Some come to laugh,
their voices do ring. But as for me I come for to sing!"
—Bob Gibson, Troubadour 11/16/31 – 9/28/96

APPLAUSE

An author's life can be very lonely at times, but once again I have been blessed with an enduring band of steadfast word mates who have traveled with me for years, turning the pages of my books. So I give thanks to these great friends and even greater critics … Bucky Rosenbaum, Gabe Wicks, Dave Schroeder, Joel Miller, Brian Mitchell, and my gifted coauthor on this long and writing road, Marshall Terrill. While everyone generously gave encouragement, friendship, and insight, Marshall also included reams of biographical materials, long hours of exhaustive research, and his inspired words to work with as we put our hearts into this book.

Double kudos to Brian Mitchell, who believed in this project from the beginning and made it his personal quest to find the perfect rock-solid publisher place for our efforts—BroadStreet Publishing and its visionary leader, Carlton Garborg.

Cheers and standing ovations to the great artists who shared their stories with us.

To my wife, Connie, the heart in my rocky place … deepest thanks for hanging in there during the years this project invaded our lives. And yes, my love, the book is finished, so we can talk again!

As always, a tithe from the proceeds of this book will go to Nancy Alcorn's incredible Mercy Ministries for young women (www.mercyministries.org).

Peace and His love,

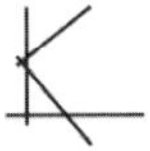

ABOUT THE AUTHORS

Ken Mansfield's legendary career in the music industry began as a member of the Town Criers, a successful southern California folk group in the early 1960s. From there he moved to executive tenures as US manager of The Beatles at Apple Records, director at Capitol Records, vice president at MGM Records, and president at Barnaby/CBS Records. As a record producer, he was instrumental in launching country music's "Outlaw" movement in the 1970s, producing Waylon Jennings' number-one 1975 landmark recording, *Are You Ready for the Country*, and Jessi Colter's number-one hit "I'm Not Lisa." Ken also produced the Gaither Vocal Band's 1991 GRAMMY® and Dove Award–winning *Homecoming* album, which also launched another historical movement, the resurgence of Southern gospel music via the *Gaither Homecoming* series of recordings, videos, and concerts.

Ken is now an ordained minister, a sought-after speaker, and the author of four other books: *The Beatles, The Bible and Bodega Bay*; *The White Book*; *Between Wyomings*; and *Stumbling on Open Ground.* He and his wife Connie currently reside in Florida.

Contact Ken at kmansfield.com.

Marshall Terrill is a veteran film, sports, and music writer and the author of nearly twenty books, including best-selling biographies of Steve McQueen, Elvis Presley, and Pete Maravich. Three of his books are in development to be made into movies. Terrill resides in Tempe, Arizona, with his wife, Zoe. For more information on his books, visit www.marshallterrill.com.

OTHER BOOKS BY KEN MANSFIELD

THE BEATLES, THE BIBLE AND BODEGA BAY presents two portraits: the young man in London on top of the Apple building (and on top of the world!) watching The Beatles perform for the last time, and the older man on a remote Sonoma County beach on his knees, looking out to sea and into the heart of his Creator. *Considered one of the top three best Beatles books of all time according to the rock editor's list on Amazon.com, and the only book outside of The Beatles Anthology that was approved by The Beatles and their management.*

THE WHITE BOOK invites readers to know the characters of The Beatles and the musicians of their time—the bands that moved an industry and a culture to a whole new rhythm. This engaging and unusual account spans some of the most fertile and intense decades in music history. *"There is something quite Lennonesque about Ken Mansfield's soul searching—his tales are astonishingly clear and vivid."* —Barnes&Noble.com

BETWEEN WYOMINGS (My God and an iPod on the Open Road) is a modern-day Ecclesiastes tale, where with his wife, Connie, and a van named Moses, Ken metaphorically recreates the travels that took him into the homes and careers of entertainment legends. Readers are called to reflect on the highways of their own lives, the turns and detours that press them into the heart of a Creator who has been there all along. *"Mansfield's prayerful musings are quite extraordinary."* —Publishers Weekly

STUMBLING ON OPEN GROUND is a story of trial and faith like those found in the books of Esther and Job. It's a private dialogue between Ken, his wife, Connie, and the God who transformed them in the middle of a heartbreaking disease. *"Ken is jarringly honest about everything—life, success, fame, disillusionment, faith, cancer.... This book might make you a little uncomfortable, but that's probably why you should read it."* —Bernie Leadon, founding member of The Eagles

To contact or order autographed books directly from Ken, go to

www.kmansfield.com

For bookings: Ambassador Agency, Outreach Events, or Premier Speakers Bureau